Praise for Jumping the Curve

"A thoughtful, unique, and action-oriented perspective on dealing with the many challenges that businesses face."
— JEFFREY PFEFFER, professor of business, Stanford University, and author of *Managing with Power*

"A must read. Captures the guiding principles that drive business success: an orientation toward creative vigilance, an understanding of the need for unified consistency, and most importantly, a realization that customers define satisfaction."
— PAUL J. ORFALEA, founder and chairperson, Kinko's Copy Centers

"Stringent advice on what *not* to do. . . . The book's focus is clearly successful business strategy, but it has application to education, nonprofit, and government circles."
— COLLEGE AND UNIVERSITY PERSONNEL ASSOCIATION JOURNAL

"A great guidebook for those who have discovered that the world has changed overnight."
— PAUL SAFFO, director, Institute for the Future

"This book does the best job yet of providing a historical framework when explaining the societal changes affecting businesses today. Recommended for all business collections."
— LIBRARY JOURNAL

"*Jumping the Curve* provides the roadmap to negotiate the obstacles to entrepreneurial success in the global village."
— ROBERT C. MACAULEY, founder and chairman, AmeriCares

"A coherent, practical framework and specific, innovative strategies for responding to and managing inevitable change."
— NAPRA TRADE JOURNAL

JUMPING *the* CURVE

Nicholas Imparato *and* *Oren Harari*

Foreword by Tom Peters

JUMPING *the* CURVE

INNOVATION
AND
STRATEGIC CHOICE
IN AN AGE
OF TRANSITION

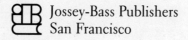
Jossey-Bass Publishers
San Francisco

Substantial discounts on bulk quantities of Jossey-Bass books are available to corporations, professional associations, and other organizations. For details and discount information, contact the special sales department at Jossey-Bass Inc., Publishers. (415) 433-1740; Fax (415) 433-0499.

For international orders, please contact your local Simon & Schuster International office.

 Manufactured in the United States of America on Lyons Falls Pathfinder Tradebook. This paper is acid-free and 100 percent totally chlorine-free.

Library of Congress Cataloging-in-Publication Data

Imparato, Nicholas, date
    Jumping the curve : innovation and strategic choice in an age of transition / Nicholas Imparato, Oren Harari ; foreword by Tom Peters. — 1st ed.
      p.   cm. — (Jossey-Bass management series)
    Includes bibliographical references and index.
    ISBN 1-55542-705-7
        0-7879-0183-3 (paperback)
    1. Strategic planning. 2. Organizational change
3. Organizational behavior. 4. Corporate culture. I. Harari, Oren. II. Title. III. Series.
HD30.28.I45 1994
658.4′012—dc20

94-25578

FIRST EDITION
HB Printing 10 9 8 7 6 5 4 3 2
PB Printing 10 9 8 7 6 5 4 3 2 1

CONTENTS

To
Mary Jo and Dorothy

F O R E W O R D

Nick Imparato and Oren Harari have written a marvelous book.
It is a joy (carefully chosen word) to read.

The coauthors have been bloodied by extensive exposure
to the real world. They know of what they speak. And yet,
though pragmatists in the end, they lead us back through history, insisting (wisely, I think) that we ground ourselves in the
bases of the enormous changes that are buffeting us. Personally,
I felt better than I'd felt in a long time precisely because Nick
and Oren built their scaffolding so carefully.

But this is not a book about the past as much as it works to
place us in a continuum of yesterday to tomorrow. It *is* a book
about today, and tomorrow. It is practical to the core. And it
soars to the heavens. To do both is an extraordinary act—and
the authors have pulled it off.

At the center of Nick's and Oren's argument is the need to
innovate—now and forever more. Amen.

I look back at my own work, and sometimes innovation is
on the front burner, sometimes it's not. Or at least I haven't
always seen the future as clearly as I should have.

These days—individual or corporation—it's innovate or
else. And when you've patted dry today's grand, glorious, and
bold innovation—well, then, do it all over again.

Read this book slowly. Read it quickly. Read it more than once. Allow it to do its mischief to you. That is, allow it to get under your skin and cause itches and rashes of the sort that may just save your individual (or corporate) hide.

Enjoy! (I did.)

Palo Alto, California   Tom Peters
June 1994

PREFACE

A primary lesson of history is that periodically, and often at the most inconvenient times, society needs to make a sharp break with old habits and deliberately learn new ways of behaving. The world is faced with such a moment today. We need to look at the world anew. The demand is not only on our presence of mind and talent but also on our courage and intellectual honesty.

In this spirit, amid dramatic changes in technology, value systems, and global commerce, businesspeople have begun to sense that they must alter the way they lead their companies. Memories of past success, however, have too often handicapped substantial progress, frequently hindering even an understanding of the scope of corporate renewal that is needed. The pressures to lower costs, improve quality, and shorten cycle times have frequently been treated as inconvenient adjustments to a "normal" way of doing business—bumps in the road, necessary deviations from "the plan."

An alternative view is that the adjustment needed goes to the very core of what business is about. A wave of social and economic change that started in the middle of this century is not subsiding; it is accelerating and spreading. Business is in the middle of something big. The turbulence in the marketplace is not just about commerce and business; it is one aspect of a more profound upheaval. Our organizations need to change because our civilization is changing, and nothing short of radical transformation in management will suffice.

Today, managers often feel overwhelmed by a sense of disarray and anxiety. They have learned that piecemeal solutions for accommodating fundamental change do not work. There must be a fresh framework that helps managers move from confusion to clarity, and from half-measures to integrated solutions.

As a basis for that framework, we look to the familiar S-curve that describes the natural life cycle of an organization. A new business starts out on the bottom of the curve, struggling with early development, then expands over time, as represented in the steep upward ride of the curve. Finally, success tapers off: the line turns horizontal again at the top. This is a critical juncture. Persisting on the same curve—that is, depending on a pattern of behaviors and attitudes that was once successful but is now losing effectiveness—characterizes poor performance. Leaders need to recognize, even anticipate, the moment that requires moving on, and that demands jettisoning an original pattern that was based on an earlier set of market conditions, product technology, or management style. If they don't do so, they doom the organization to stagnation and failure. Aspirations, fortunes, and careers wither away.

What is so dramatic today is the sight of huge numbers of companies across an array of industries approaching the top of the S-curve at the same time. In effect, an entire cohort of businesses rooted in the assumptions of the industrial age is simultaneously faced with the same challenge. From a manager's perspective, this is the real meaning of what advisors and policymakers call an "economic restructuring." In these circumstances there is almost a universal demand for leaders to invent new S-curves for their organizations, each curve based on a different set of assumptions or business opportunities that will enable the organization to rise to new levels of success. The leap from here to there—from a familiar curve to a new one, from one business theory or methodology to another—can be intimidating. Our purpose in this book is to persuade managers that the need to jump the curve is the fundamental challenge in their careers. We will explain in detail, in terms of basic leadership and business decisions, what it takes to jump the curve and come out stronger on the other side.

HOW THIS BOOK CAME TO BE

The rate at which managers are inundated with diverse recommendations and options is accelerating and appears more striking each day. Complexity mushrooms, yet managers need coherent solutions to problems that arise daily. They tell us that despite their readings and attendance in valuable seminars, they still are looking for a connection between a larger perspective and specific recommendations for what to do on Monday morning. Our book satisfies this need. It is designed to help individuals create and manage sustained change by connecting the "big think" to the problems and options they face on a day-to-day basis. The goal is to provide a set of recommended actions that allow managers to react swiftly to the market changes that are taking place—and to shape those changes in a way that is propelled by a broader perspective on the role of business and leadership in the vortex of epochal change.

The book is a balance between interpretive synthesis and original research. We have combined survey studies, consulting experiences, interviews with practicing managers, and a thorough review of the research literature, all conducted from 1989 through 1993. We relied on proprietary assessments of the impact of environmental factors (such as the emergence of time as a competitive weapon and higher customer expectations) on managerial and corporate performance; small discussion groups on culture, financial performance, and methods of improving operational processes; and survey studies using published questionnaires and inventories regarding values and work life. More than two thousand managers from private and public organizations—computer companies, banks, police departments, universities, hospitals, and retailers—participated in a series of investigations that evolved over the five-year period. We conducted more than one hundred interviews with CEOs and their equivalents—from Africa, Asia, Australia, Europe, and Latin America—as a function of various university programs and consulting engagements. More detailed references and commentary regarding a specific research methodology or project component are provided in the text or endnotes as appropriate.

In reporting our findings, we occasionally have not used names or individual statistics; our decision in some cases to forgo these details reflected our intention to protect the anonymity of the organizations that requested it. Unless otherwise noted, all quotations in text and all epigraphs from executives are from personal interviews and conversations.

Finally, both authors brought their unique experiences and talents to the project; the finished product represents a genuine collaboration.

WHO SHOULD READ THIS BOOK?

First, we have written this book for the executives and managers who sense that dramatic change is necessary for business and management and who seek practical advice on how to recast their own roles and how to position their organizations for future success. *Jumping the Curve* also provides leaders with one source that integrates a whole spectrum of issues—from reconfiguration of processes to personal responsibility, from customer responsiveness to performance and profit models, from technology applications to justice in the workplace. Reading the book will expedite the process of looking beyond the rigors of one's own position in order to recognize challenges that are companywide.

In addition, we wrote this book for readers who do not ordinarily consider themselves businesspeople but who wish to understand better the interactions among business, technology, and socioeconomic developments.

OVERVIEW OF
THE CONTENTS

We proceed in two steps, as reflected in the two main parts of the book. In Part One we present the question: given the scale of change that is taking place in the business environment, is it reasonable to assume that the way managers conducted work three or five years ago is the way they should be conducting it today? Is it even rational to think that as institutions falter, ideologies are overturned, and markets break apart and recombine, managers can continue to do the same things they used to do and still be effective? The reality is that individuals and organizations have to adapt to a new set of circumstances. A sense of history helps by generating some confidence and optimism about how we can handle the current tumult. Previous generations have met changes this large before; there is every reason to believe we can rise to the occasion as well.

In Chapter One we explain how the changes that are occurring now are similar in several ways to the changes that came at the dawn of the Modern Age. In effect, what we are experiencing today in terms of sociotechnical change has not been seen since the demise of the Medieval Age. In both instances, changes in technology, trade patterns, and commercial structures combined with a pervading sense of both danger and opportunity to create a new epoch.

Chapter Two traces the roots of the current sea change in business to the middle of this century. Dramatic events in politics, economics, and commerce spurred the development of a new world; new business dynamics, including an increased emphasis on innovation, customization, and customer satisfaction replaced mass production economics. The challenge for organizations around the world became how to deal with and capitalize on the turmoil they were helping to create.

Chapter Three argues that a reluctance to identify with the new era limits options and performance. Through research results and examples, we document that managers become much more effective once they have let go of conventional managerialist mind-sets and grasped the new responsibilities of postmodern leadership. We identify the critical determinant of management success during this age of transition—accuracy of role perception—and discuss thirteen factors that embody this concept. We then introduce four organizing principles that demonstrate ways to integrate the diverse functions of the organization—principles that we propose leaders will need to use to jump the curve and move wholeheartedly into the new era.

Part Two discloses what jumping the curve looks and feels like for a wide range of companies that are leading the way. We elaborate on each organizing principle within a pair of chapters. The first chapter in each pair demonstrates the pragmatic and business rationale for the organizing principle itself; the second offers both a broad strategy for setting that principle in motion and a set of specific initiatives that provide concrete courses of action.

Chapter Four illustrates how changes in markets, developments in technology, and increased competition from across the globe call for innovative activities that go beyond conventional notions of product research and development. We review efforts of companies ranging from printer Quad/Graphics to medical device manufacturer Nellcor to insurance broker Sedgwick James, and make a case for the first organizing principle—*look a customer ahead*—on the basis of profit and market share, as well as on a broad model of discontinuous change. Chapter Five highlights the traps and pitfalls—such as accepting a corporate culture of mediocrity and searching for the quick fix—that undercut meaningful innovation today. For the leader intent on avoiding such problems, we provide concrete recommendations, including ways to prepare for obsolescence and to create a vigilant organization.

In Chapter Six we describe the genesis of the second organizing principle—*build the company around the software and build the software around the customer.* The search for a new metaphor to replace mechanistic ideas about work yields the view of the organization as brain. This approach generates processes that depend on knowledge and information flow, which allow leaders to better exploit new opportunities and improve business methods immediately. Emphasizing intelligence rather than mass and size prioritizes different skill sets and processes and establishes different criteria by which to evaluate competitors. In Chapter Seven we discuss how companies from Mrs. Fields' Cookies to advertisers Young & Rubicam have used expert systems, groupware, mass customization, and paperless management to leverage knowledge, spur collaboration between and within organizations, and increase marketing power.

Chapter Eight asks how a leader operating in an unsettled, ambiguous environment can harness a vast diversity of information, ideas, technologies, and people to achieve a unity of purpose within the organization. Our third organizing principle—*ensure that those who live the values and ideals of the organization are the most rewarded and the most satisfied*—points to the answer. In Chapter Nine, we discuss how leaders can use this organizing principle to help create organizational coherence, credibility in leadership, and integrity in the organization. In both chapters, we offer snapshots of the organizing principle in action in organizations from hospitals to software suppliers.

In Chapter Ten we argue that, by virtue of our rights-happy society, one of the major problems in business today is the absence of responsibility. We discuss the implications of responsibility for business success, especially as it pertains to service guarantees, and we contrast the pseudo-guarantees that now proliferate in the marketplace with genuine guarantees that reflect a deep, abiding sense of responsibility to the customer. Adopting our fourth organizing principle—*make customers the final arbiters by offering an unconditional guarantee of complete satisfaction*—fundamentally changes the conventional meaning of such terms as *customer satisfaction, quality,* and *guarantee.* The way organizations are run also changes, because the organizing principle demands that activities, processes, and decisions must be evaluated on their ability to deliver on the guarantee.

In Chapter Eleven we discuss common misconceptions and fears about putting together an unconditional guarantee and demonstrate this organizing principle in action—for instance, in the genuine guarantees offered by such companies as Delta Dental Plan and First Image. We outline an approach that allows organizations to use unconditional guarantees as strategic tools.

Finally, in the Epilogue, we review additional implications of the current transition for organizational purpose and the character of managerial life, ranging from discussions of intellectual homelessness to considerations of the meaning of success. We conclude by raising possibilities for a more optimistic future.

THE CHALLENGE UPON US

Too many times in organizational change, when all is said and done, more is said than done. World society cannot let that be the final judgment of corporate reinvention today. The stakes are too high. At the same time, there is no way to turn the tide, to reverse the social and technological developments of the recent past. Yet despite the imposing nature of these challenges, the means to be successful are available to us. We are out at sea, having pushed away from one shore yet still a distance from the other side. Like sailors who can't see their destination but can still see the shore they have just left, we are pulled by memories of the security and familiarity we once experienced. In the face of this reluctance, success rests in going forward.

ACKNOWLEDGMENTS

One of the main benefits of being at the University of San Francisco is the opportunity to work closely with high-caliber MBA students. We are fortunate that outstanding students were attracted to our work and helped us immeasurably in gathering the research. In particular, we thank Harald Becker, Micheline

Kirsebom, Bjorn Lovaas, Sally Morton, Roberto Schaechter, Richard Searle, Kathleen Smith, and Liv Venbakken. We are truly indebted to Lip Chin Ho, Tanya Kufner, and Antonia Malvino for contributions and moral support well beyond the call of duty. Our work could not have advanced without their dedication.

We would also like to acknowledge our colleagues Gene Benton, Randall Fields, Lewis Gann, Elisabeth Gleason, Herbert Harari, Chuck House, Amal Johnson, Lou Kearn, Louis Kolenda, Ray Larkin, Don Morford, Paul Quinn, Jeanne Speckman, and Tom White, who separately reviewed early drafts of portions of the book and gave us invaluable advice.

We also wish to acknowledge the support of other colleagues and friends: Steve Alter, Rex Bennett, Gasper Caravello, Pat Carroll, George Conrades, Mark Dowling, Debbi Fields, Suzanne LeGaye, Bill Maier, Linda Mukai, Robert Solomon, and Gary Williams, Dean of the McLaren School of Business, University of San Francisco. We appreciate all the special efforts they made on our behalf as our work progressed. We are especially grateful to our colleague Tom Peters for writing the foreword; we would like to thank him and all our friends at the Tom Peters Group for their encouragement.

Many people at and associated with Jossey-Bass helped make this book a reality. We want to first thank Barbara Hill for helping us get organized and always being available to answer questions and help out. Thanks also to Sarah Miller and Alice Rowan of the production department, and Lisa Shannon, Laura Simonds, Inez Templeton, and Terri Welch of the marketing department. To two people in particular, we wish to offer our most heartfelt appreciation. Sarah Polster, our editor, read a rough draft of our proposal and immediately "got" what we were trying to do. Her insightful, supportive commentary quickly convinced us that we had found ourselves a terrific partner. Her calm, astute, professional demeanor throughout the taxing process of writing, rewriting, and revising was vital in getting us through it. Finally, developmental editor Janet Hunter warrants all the positive adjectives we can muster. She coaxed deadlines out of us, shaped the manuscript through repeated iterations, and was always there for us—professionally and personally. Our debt to her cannot be overstated.

Foremost, we are indebted to our parents and other members of our families, especially Mary Jo and Dorothy, and Lauren, Sarah, Ilana, and Ariel. Their love and support deserve our deepest gratitude.

June 1994   Nicholas Imparato
San Francisco, California   Oren Harari

THE AUTHORS

Nicholas Imparato is professor of marketing and management at the McLaren School of Business of the University of San Francisco. He has been a visiting scholar at Stanford University, a visiting scholar at the Center for Ethics and Social Policy, Berkeley, and an associate professor in the Department of Computer Sciences at Boston College. During a series of special leaves from the University of San Francisco, he held senior management and executive positions, including senior vice president and Ford Liaison at First Nationwide Bank and chief operating officer of Coit Services, a diversified multinational organization with operations in radio broadcasting, interior home care, and commercial real estate.

Imparato has been a member of the boards of directors of both privately and publicly held companies. He is currently a member of the development committee of the Board of Trustees of the University of San Francisco and the Board of Advisors of Park City Group. He is a prominent speaker and consultant with companies and management groups around the world, particularly in the areas of global change, transformational leadership, intelligent organizations, and marketing strategies focused on innovation. He has worked with enterprises as diverse as AT&T, Beijing Electrical Products Office, Dole Packaged Foods, Fujitsu,

IBM, ICC (Ingenieria en Comunicación y Computación, S.A.C.V.), Lawrence Livermore Laboratory, Merchants Home Delivery, Mrs. Fields Cookies, Silicon Graphics, and Wells Fargo Bank. Imparato's numerous honors include the University Distinguished Teacher Award and the Teaching Excellence Award in Executive Education, given as part of the People's Republic of China Program at the University of San Francisco.

Oren Harari is a senior consultant and renowned speaker with The Tom Peters Group and has spoken about competitive advantage, transformational leadership, and organizational change to numerous audiences around the world. In that capacity and independently he has worked with such major organizations as All Nippon Airways, ARCO, AT&T, Dayton Hudson, Dole Packaged Foods, Fidelity Investments, ICI Australia, Merck, Swedish National Board for Industrial and Technical Development, 3M, Voluntary Hospitals of America, and Unisys Latin American and Caribbean Group.

Harari is professor of management at the McLaren School of Business of the University of San Francisco, where he has received both the University Distinguished Teacher Award and the Annual School of Business Research Award. He is also an associate with the Owner Managed Business Institute in Santa Barbara, an international educational and consulting organization for privately held and family businesses. He received his Ph.D. from the University of California, Berkeley, and has spent the last fifteen years studying organizations and leaders who not only respond immediately to the marketplace but who lead and transform it with their innovations. He believes that in the chaotic competitiveness of today's world markets, bold— often radical—management approaches are the key to success.

Harari writes a national monthly column, "The Cutting Edge," for *Management Review*. For five years, he also wrote a biweekly national column, "On Management," for the *Gavin Report*. He has written for many other professional publications, such as *Harvard Business Review* and *California Management Review*. He has co-authored, with David Beaty, an international management book entitled *Lessons from South Africa: A New Perspective on Productivity and Public Policy.*

Both authors can be reached at the University of San Francisco.

PART ONE

Straddling
Two Worlds

The Familiar and the Unknown

C H A P T E R

1

We've Been Here Before: Historic Parallels to Our Tumultuous Age

First came Chaos.
—Hesiod

Nothing stops an organization faster than people who believe that the way they worked yesterday is the best way to work tomorrow. To succeed, not only do your people have to change the way they act, they've got to change the way they think about the past.
—Jon Madonna, CEO
KPMG Peat Marwick

Every generation believes it lives in a time of accelerated change. Yet *change* is a far too mild and misleading word to account for the relentless social tumult and market chaos that managers face today. Businesspeople also stress the challenge to their organizations. One executive is convinced that "when the rate of change inside an organization is slower than the rate of change outside an organization, the end is in sight." Xerox chairman Paul Allaire describes most dramatically what is needed: "We have to change our culture, our organization, the way we manage, our systems, our processes and how we behave as individuals."[1]

THE CHALLENGE

The chaos we see around us—the breakdown of institutions such as government and family, the sense of urgency and feelings of stress shared around the world, the go-stop-go-stop patterns exposed in so many organizations, the confusion of the marketplace experienced by producer and buyer alike—is all evidence of a deep, underlying, and abiding change in the fundamentals of our lives. Whatever we choose to call these upheavals, the basic and common truth is that they are signs of a new order breaking out from the old, a global society moving slowly and fitfully into a new epoch. More than just economies are changing. Civilization itself is being transformed.

Understanding that we are at a moment of epochal transformation focuses the point of view presented in this book. The transformation is not like the transitions and changes we in business are accustomed to discussing. This alteration is not on the surface of things; it goes to the core of what our lives and institutions are about. The combination of turbulence we are experiencing today—in values, commerce, economic order, technology, politics, and social structures—requires business to rethink its core assumptions—its mission and procedures, "from the way we build factories to the way we answer the phone," as Anthony Evans, Raychem's director of business development, told us.

Today's leaders are called upon to confront the basic reality of this transformation. Our contention is that without doing so, all efforts to create meaningful and productive work environments will fail. The tried-and-true traditional ways of running our enterprises don't work very well any more. Just pressing the pedal harder or grabbing expert formulas can't produce the needed results, either. Somehow, even the lessons drawn from the many books, magazine articles, videotapes, and training packages on how to be a terrific manager don't tell us how to make the quantum leaps that appear to be necessary even to keep up, much less stay ahead. Ignorance of the changing worldview and the altered socioeconomic dynamics that come with it limits our options, restricts our opportunities, and confines our actions to patterns of response that are either irrelevant or only fleetingly successful.

WARNING SIGNS

The public statements of our country's leaders mirror the private queries and doubts expressed more broadly by the people. In the pronouncements of policymakers and in the discussions of business leaders, questions are raised about our response to crime in the streets and suites, our responsibilities to the disadvantaged, the proper uses of economic power, and the meaning of work and money. There is concern about a broad range of issues from education to immigration, and a thoughtfulness about the assumptions and values that solutions should reflect. There are difficult questions; there seem to be no easy answers.

The national mood also reveals a tension between renewal and collapse, between reconstruction and exhaustion. There is talk about revitalizing our society and systems with diversity, pluralism, technology, and New Age encouragements for the heart. Organizations renew their commitments to basic values. At the same time, appeals to bigotry and racial tensions increase, and special interests and ethnic factions tribalize our society. In the United States, our infrastructure is showing signs of failure, with roads and bridges that are unsafe and a health care system that consumes 14 percent of our gross national product yet permits one baby of every one hundred born to die within the year. Our businesses face difficulties in unfamiliar arenas and competition from unexpected sources. We find ourselves struggling to keep up with counterintuitive new management practices, with explosions in science and technology, with debt and credit crunches, and with wildly fluctuating industry trends.

The strain is visible everywhere. The homeless are ubiquitous. Average individual wages fell about 14 percent between 1970 and 1992 after adjustment for inflation. Household income is up only marginally and then primarily because more women and mothers are working. Concern over the quality of life is expressed almost daily. Whether it is the news that nearly four thousand students drop out of school every day or that nearly one-third of Americans feel that their tap water is unsafe to drink, the message is the same: life in the land of plenty is not as good as it should be.

Americans are not alone in their disorientation. Corruption and scandal have shaken governments and social institutions around the globe. In early 1990, Italians were horrified when they found that no one had stopped to help a young child who was wandering along a freeway after her father had been killed in an accident. In Japan, young entrepreneurs can make available a rent-a-family for the equivalent of about $1,000 a day. Professional actors with some training in psychology visit lonely parents, playing the part of their grown children when a busy schedule makes a visit from the real sons or daughters too difficult. The list of problems across Europe and Asia includes experiences that are almost impossible to fathom, as when French officials knowingly distributed blood infected with the virus that causes autoimmune deficiency syndrome (AIDS).[2]

Corporations reflect the turmoil in their continuing announcements of downsizings and restructurings. In the United States, profit margins have been squeezed by interest payments as a percentage of output that more than doubled from the 1960s to the beginning of the 1990s. In Europe, Renault broke with tradition in the early 1990s and let go thousands of employees, despite its status as a government-owned company. Its interest in privatization shook a French—indeed, a European— symbol of state gospel, namely, belief in the stability of government-run companies.

The contraction in resources, begun in some industries in the mid seventies, has endured and spread. Although organizations have been eliminating jobs, too frequently they have retained the functions that went along with them—so those who remain have heavier workloads that they are expected to complete at a quicker pace with higher quality. Despite all the talk about leisure and time-saving technology, many employees are working far more than forty hours a week. We postpone vacations, and when we finally do take one, we call the office or our voice mail daily and receive fax messages during what is supposed to be our time for rest and relaxation. Our spouses often are working, and family life may suffer as we both try to juggle the uncompromising demands of separate professional lives. Ironically, even those families whose combined income approaches six figures find that after mortgage payments, real estate and income taxes, car payments, and child and elder care obligations, they are still living from check to check, month to month. In the end, psychologists and physicians talk of a sleep deprived, hyperactive society that is frenetic in daily life.

We experience the symptoms of disequilibrium daily. And while on an aggregate basis society as a whole may be moving forward slowly and inexorably, as individuals we often experience the changes as explosive, seemingly random and unpredictable, sometimes overwhelming. For the businessperson, the disorientation is particularly pervasive. Some examples of the comments we have heard from managers in the course of our research sound familiar:

- "The plain truth is, I'm scared. They expect me to know what to do and I don't. No one does. Every decision I make has the potential for career wipeout."

- "I'm always given more demands and fewer resources. Can you imagine the pressure? Can you imagine all the balls I'm juggling? So I try to get more organized, but all my planning and budgeting isn't doing the job. Nothing I learned in business school seems to apply."

- "I know what we're supposed to do—all that stuff about innovation and entrepreneurship. But try failing around here. Try not meeting your numbers every quarter. Try questioning your boss. Try doing something really different. You're harpooned before you know it."

- "This business is exploding. Everything's changing. Technology, information, competition, markets, you name it. I don't know how I can possibly keep up with it all. I can't even keep up with what my people are doing."

- "The stress on my family is incalculable. I haven't had dinner with my kids during the week once in the past two months."

- "One of my golfing buddies was laid off six months ago. Good creative marketing man—can't find work. He envies me, but I keep on telling him that ever since our reorganization, I've got P & L [profit and loss] responsibility for a new business unit, which simply means that if I don't create new ventures constantly, I'm history too. The pressure is unbelievable."

The stress felt by many of these people is driven by factors that go beyond the peculiarities of their own companies and industries. There are major trends, new realities, that seem to confound our ability to cope. As managers, we have been taught for a century about the value of mass marketing; yet we are now seeing markets fragmented into increasingly slender segments. We have been taught about the importance of internal order, the boxes of budgets, planning documents, and organizational charts deemed important by corporate staffs; yet there is little evidence that these efforts are any more helpful than less bureaucratic techniques that have a rebellious cast to them. We have been taught about the advantage of work groups with homogeneous values and backgrounds; yet the workplace reality is greater diversity, posing issues in coordination, quality assurance, morale, and, most of all, customer satisfaction. We have been taught about the importance of mutual employer-employee loyalty; yet, a wave of restructurings and international alliances has diminished our faith in reaction to job loss and public disregard.

Some managers are determined to grit their teeth and tough it out by grimly doing more of the same—that is, more of what got them in trouble in the first place. In one firm, the CEO's response to declining earnings and market share was to change the quarterly financial reviews to a process he felt afforded him more "control." Accordingly, he insisted that the company close the books every month and held his vice presidents accountable for knowing the status of each of literally thousands of line items. Unsurprisingly, earnings and market share continued to decline as, for two weeks of every month, managers were obsessed in absorbing and justifying "the numbers." This was personal survival in its purest form, though it had little to do with nurturing a business. In another organization, executives responded to a decline in market share and product profitability by demanding unreasonable price sacrifices from partners in the distribution channel while at the same time withdrawing critical support services. In a pathetic example of self-deception they convinced themselves that making the demands was a harder choice than focusing on the design problems of a product that was clearly behind competitor innovations.

Managers complain that while they are drowning in data, they don't have enough information. Headlines appear unpredictable, events out of control. There is less surprise in each surprise and less awe in each awe-inspiring event. The spate of newspaper headlines and corporate bulletins tends to numb our appreciation for what is happening or weakens our ability to act. Accordingly, there is the chance that managers will react by throwing up their hands in despair. If this sense of impotence goes unchecked, the psychology of the organization becomes something akin to learned helplessness, the belief that since there is nothing we can do to affect the environment around us, why bother to try?

At some point we may wonder how we are ever going to get through it: the next year, the ongoing reorganization, the house payments, the school tuition. Our nation's contemplative moment is an admission that the old ways need to be reexamined, that we might be running harder but that we aren't moving. Meanwhile, deep down, we know or at least sense that we are leaving something behind and heading toward something new. This sentiment was verbalized by Tony Frank, retired postmaster general, when he was chairman and CEO of First Nationwide Bank: "We're smart enough to know that the way the world has been is coming apart," he said. "We're not smart enough to know how it's going to be put back together again."

NEW DAWNS

Every beginning is in part an ending of something else. The challenge of a new epoch is not only a matter of moving forward with new processes or goals but also a matter of letting go, of terminating familiar ways of responding. At the same time we come to expect uncertainty as a constant companion, we see the need to dispatch old and familiar patterns and routines. The moment, as a long, collective goodbye, demands much of us.

Obviously, the immensity of the event contributes to the difficulty in dealing with it. Yet epochal transformations of the kind about which we now speak have occurred before—and the impact hasn't been limited to any single sphere of human activity, such as work or religion or education. Each transformation affected everything people did, thought, and dreamed about. The impact was not confined to a few generations. Nearly all events that followed were influenced by a historic cataclysm. And the repercussions were not limited to any particular geography; every spot on the globe was eventually affected. In short, the impact of each transformation was universal: in manner, in time, in place.

Consider the following problem: suppose you were asked to divide the history of Western civilization into two or three or four major epochs, huge swaths of time that had some common theme. When we have done this exercise with managers over the past ten years, they have offered a variety of analyses. A frequent interpretation is to define three periods: the agricultural age, the industrial age, and the information age. Managers in the computer business have marked epochs by the "discovery" of writing, the invention of printing, and the development of the personal computer. Some use the birth of Christ and the industrial revolution to define the major periods. Others have divided epochs according to technological innovations from different disciplines: the discovery of fire, and the invention of the plow, the automobile, electricity, or atomic weapons. A few have defined history as "before America" and after 1776. Rarely is there any consensus around one particular analysis offered by a member of a group, though there is usually a sound, historical basis for each point of view. In short, we can identify many breakpoints, each reflecting to some degree our own values, historical sensitivities, and professional experiences.

On the other hand, professional historians and philosophers generally agree on when the epochal changes have occurred. They traditionally maintain that these dramatic transformations have occurred only twice in the entire history of Western civilization, thereby breaking history into three periods.[3] The first period is called the Classical Age, the second is called the Middle Ages, and the third is called the Modern Age. As shown in Figure 1.1, the first age goes from early civilization to the years 313–476, a time that marks the fall of the Roman Empire. The second age stretches from that point until medieval life declines and gives way to the rudiments of modern social

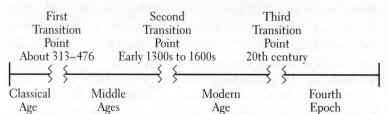

Figure 1.1. Epochal Time Line.

structures. This process spanned different years in different parts of Europe, but began in Italy during the 1300s and continued through the scientific revolution of the 1600s. The third period that began then continued until sometime in this century.[4] None of these changes, therefore, was abrupt or sudden; each dovetailed with a wide array of human activities. Graham Greene once remarked that there is always a moment in time "when a door opens and lets the future in."[5] Nietzsche, more directly, called these moments of epochal transformation "new dawns."[6] Today we are in a period of similar transformation, a source of both turbulence and renewal.

The Pace of Change

We should be mindful that the current transformation will occur more quickly than did previous transitions. The Middle Ages lasted one thousand years and the Modern Age has endured half of that. Events today will compress into an even tighter time line. As historian Arthur Schlesinger has noted: "A boy who saw the Wright brothers fly for a few seconds at Kitty Hawk could have watched Apollo II land on the moon in 1969."[7]

The most dramatic driver, of course, is the revolution in communication and information technologies. Thousands of years elapsed between the discovery of writing and the invention of the printing press, about a hundred years transpired between the electric telegraph and the crystal radio, and about a decade marked the time between the invention of the transistor and the advent of communication satellites. Since then, the pace has continued to accelerate. Jack Reilly, retired senior strategist for IBM-USA, whose career with the company spanned three decades, made the same point in an interview with us. "The biggest news about change over the next forty years is going to be how fast change speeds up for all businesses. One element in the formula for success is going to be understanding the truly fundamental change that's taking place, and how increasingly fast that is going to happen."

Most important, we also need to remember that as a new epoch emerges from the modern period, so too did the modern world arise from the civilizations that came before. Business leaders can benefit by examining moments of epochal transition in the past to see what parallels exist in today's world. By using events at the beginning of the Modern Age as a "distant mirror," in historian Barbara Tuchman's words,[8] we can get some perspective on the more fundamental aspects of the changes we think are occurring today. Not least significant, our optimism will be enhanced because one lesson of a glance backward is that we, as a society, have endured epochal transformations before and have come through the pain and disorder the better for it. Realizing that our predecessors have endured the scale of social turmoil and commercial chaos that we are experiencing now should help us deal with the challenges we face—indeed, even help us capitalize on them—as we hurtle toward the unknown.

Before the Modern Age

The ebbing of the first great epoch was underway by the year 313, represented in the collapse of Greco-Roman civilization (the time of Sparta, Alexander the Great, Homer, and Socrates; of Cicero and Virgil; of Ptolemy, and Caesar and Cleopatra). At that time, the emperor Constantine hastened events by converting to Christianity and by issuing a proclamation that granted religious freedom to everyone throughout the empire. Both actions reduced the dominance of the pagan tradition and by the year 400, Christianity had become the official state religion.

During the fifth century, the Roman empire also had to defend itself from German invaders. As troops on the frontiers were recalled to help in the continuing defense of Italy, the Germanic peoples along the Danube and the Rhine pushed through the border areas and established their own kingdoms around the empire. In 476 the Germans pillaged Rome yet another time and removed its last emperor. The German emphasis on agriculture disturbed urban growth and accelerated economic decline.

By the end of the fifth century, the high mark of the classical legacy had passed and Rome had become a place of "want and wretchedness."[9] According to Edward Gibbon, the decline was due to "immoderate greatness." He argued in *The Decline and Fall of the Roman Empire* that "prosperity ripened the principle of decay" and that "the causes of destruction multiplied with the extent of conquest." Both observations are familiar to critics of contemporary society. Comparisons are made to the excessive materialism of our times. Various experts compare that age and the present on the basis of social decadence and political corruption. Further, consider the self-destructive outcomes of what historian Paul Kennedy describes as the cause of the decline of the British Empire, and, more currently, American power: "global overstretch."[10] Military protection of widely spread interests creates resource demands that a nation cannot long endure before it jeopardizes its own economic well-being and social stability.

As the first epoch merged into the second over the next several centuries, the order of the Roman empire was gradually replaced with the disorder of a continent in the midst of political disintegration.[11] Then, much as today, people felt disoriented and confused, occasionally even terrified.

The significance of the transformation is that the medieval mind, representing a new perspective and outlook, slowly replaced the worldview of the ancients. Whereas the classical mind had enjoyed a tolerant polytheism, medieval mentalities, building on their Judaic roots, would offer a monotheistic vision of One Supreme Being, One Truth.[12] The conception of life as a trial, a testing, and redemptive opportunity in the face of Original Sin, promoted humility, often fear, in the service of God as the path to salvation. Consequently, human rationality became subordinated to God's will as humankind tried to synthesize secularism and spirituality. Observation and empiricism became less important than dogma and biblical scripture. Although science did exist, the natural world, for all its splendor and promise, was secondary in the medieval mind to the peace of the eternal kingdom. Whereas the Greeks had left their legacy in art, philosophy, and science, and the Romans in law, administration, and military technique, the medieval mind centered on reaching out beyond human existence—thus, the Gothic cathedrals, religious processions, and monastic retreat from a "busy" world. This period, sometimes referred to as the "age of faith," which developed after the collapse of Rome, offered a way of looking at the world that lasted for a thousand years, from approximately the fourth and fifth centuries to the 1600s.

The length of time required for the medieval world to replace classical civilization suggests the complexity of the transition process. There is a lesson in this for us today. Interactions and unpredictable impacts occur among social customs, political events, and intellectual developments. Ambiguity arises as worldly experience interweaves remnants of the era that is passing with the first glimmers of the one that is being created. Ultimately, the result is a transformation in attitudes that is vivid and striking.

Transitions continued during the medieval period. A number of innovations, such as the stirrup, the heavy plow, and the windmill, affected everyday life in a variety of ways. Agricultural production rose, the size of the population grew, contacts among population centers increased. Writing before 1375, Petrarch, Dante, and Boccaccio set the Italian Renaissance in motion.[13]

Nonetheless, the emergence of the modern era in the fifteenth century is still the watershed event. This was the time that brought about the unequivocal collapse of one order and the rise of another that has endured to our time. Civilization took a dramatic new course and established a path to the future that was clearly different from what had gone before. The beginning of the modern era, in short, was the last time man crossed over the bar to a new world.

AS NEW WORLDS STIR

Our ability to see similarities between what happened in the past and what is happening now strengthens our view that the modern era is deconstructing in front of us. We can identify a number of points of correspondence between the beginning of the modern era and current times:

1. Major, revolutionary developments in communication and information technology

2. On a grand scale, a pervading sense of vulnerability and, at the same time, a feeling of being on the threshold of tremendous opportunity

3. A far-reaching change in trade patterns

4. An environment of expanding horizons, spurred by exploration and scientific discovery

5. A series of commercial revolutions that have yet to play out all their ramifications

"The past," wrote the popular historians Will and Ariel Durant, "is the present unrolled for understanding; the present is the future rolled up for action."[14] In this spirit we now take a closer look at the analogies we have made in order to get a better feel for the context of our own tumultuous time. It would be unwise, of course, to overstate the similarities in each case. We are not so concerned about specific lessons to be drawn from each set of corresponding events, although they do exist, as we are about the pattern of evidence that brings home in startling relief the most important reality businesspeople have to face: the very environment in which they want to operate is undergoing a change that penetrates so widely and so deeply that the conduct of business, like all human endeavor, will be affected in unavoidable, often unimaginable and dramatic ways. What follows, as we examine each point of similarity in more detail, are the observations that make this insight credible.

From Printing Press to Telecommunications

The invention of the printing press was a major event in the early modern period. Printing spread rapidly after the completion of the Gutenberg Bible in 1455.[15] Once the preserve of clergy and noblemen, books became available to the growing populations of European urban centers. Printing presses reached Goa, the capital of India at the time, in 1557 and, according to historian Fernand Braudel, "reached Japan during the Christian century, 1549–1648."[16] As the invention of writing had done, printing allowed access to information on an unprecedented scale. Diffusion of ideas was no longer hindered by the constraints of handwritten manuscripts. The printed book was easier to transport than rolls of manuscript that might be as long as fifty feet. Before publishing began to drive down the prices of books, they had been so expensive that they were often chained to a stand or shelf in the library. By 1500 the printing press had produced in Europe around six million books (some estimates are as high as twenty million) relative to a population of about seventy million, covering a variety of topics, including medicine, history, classical literature, law, and astrology.

In looking back at the arrival of printing, we see how this new technology challenged routine ways of thinking and behaving, often in completely unpredictable ways. During the second half of the fifteenth century, printing served the growing demand for books among "merchants, substantial artisans, lawyers, government officials, doctors and teachers who worked in towns . . . in order to conduct their businesses and civil affairs."[17] But its consequences went further than that. By helping to usher in the early elements of a capitalist economy, printing revolutionized the structure of everyday life. A whole system of social relations and intellectual perspective was challenged.

Today, similar social and economic upheavals are being fostered by electronic commerce. Personal computers, laptops, fax machines, cellular telephones, and personal digital assistants all arouse, even more than mainframe computers, the feeling that there is a contemporary analog to the impact of the printing press.[18] Some have argued that the Information Age actually began, not with the development of the transistor or with the prototype computers used in World War II, but when IBM made it acceptable for everyone at work to have a personal computer (PC) on his or her desk.[19] Yet the hardware, the boxes, cables, and wires are not the primary source of value: software is the heart of the revolution that is taking place. This attitude was captured in a controversial remark by Larry Ellison, founder of Oracle, a major supplier of database products. He noted, "In the year

2000, we'll understand that there was no IBM PC. . . . What there was, was a Microsoft PC for which IBM supplied the first compatible hardware."[20] Software now exists for virtually every human and commercial endeavor. With it, anyone can have access to the information that society has developed, or in a business sense, the information that middle or senior management elites formerly monopolized.

Basic processes are affected. Lag times and "information float"—the time between the development of information and when it can be used—effectively become anachronistic concepts. During courtroom proceedings, attorneys use their laptops to tap into case-precedent databases and, while a witness testifies, call up the witness's deposition to check for discrepancies with oral testimony. Inventory and sales application software have turned our thinking about the value of time itself upside down and have focused on competitive strategies where speed is the crucial variable. Just as Gutenberg took us from a paperless society to one dependent on paper, the computer, in the name of efficiency and timeliness, takes us from paper dependency to a different and higher form of paperless environment, one where electrons instead of ink and linen provide the medium for our enterprise. This environment, where information on anything can be available instantaneously, unsettles the foundations of our previous ideas while it raises questions about lines of authority, the value of hierarchy, the nature of relationships, the role of management, and the proper use of information. The long reach of history may show that the single greatest contribution of information technology is that it caused us to rethink—everything.

Organizational life today is replete with evidence of the turbulence and uncertainty associated with the new technology-rich environment. As information is absorbed by different parts of the organization at different rates, disjunctions often emerge. Customer data may be used by ambitious salespeople before the implications of this information are fully understood by people in finance, purchasing, or product development. Even within the same group or team, differences of opinion can develop regarding how data should be used, how it should be organized, and at what level it should be analyzed and recomposed. Conflict, ironically, can be heightened as a more diverse set of view-points becomes available to inform decision making.

The destabilization represented by information technology recalls the way printing instigated challenge and dissent. It made the Bible more readily available in the vernacular as well as in Latin, the official language of the Roman Catholic church. These local Bibles became a counterpoint to the papal authority of Rome and contributed to the development of nationalist churches. Besides abetting the Reformation, printing also promoted the scientific revolution. By facilitating documentation and reference, printing enhanced the ability of scientists to compare their observations with the assertions of authority. The standardization of print also made learning to read and the sharing of information easier, and thus democratized the learning process.[21]

Braudel observed that printing "enlarged and invigorated everything."[22] The same can be said of computers, yet the computer goes much further than printing as a revolutionary innovation. Literacy, for example, never surpassed 25 percent in northern Italy or Burgundy—culture centers after the Renaissance—until centuries after Gutenberg, when resources (pulp paper) and institutions (public education) were developed extensively to support it.[23] By contrast, the impact of computers has been almost universal, with applications as diverse as helping the deaf hear and allowing architects to test models of bridges and high-rise buildings. Now we not only expect that each person will have dozens of computers, in cars, appliances, home offices, telephones, and so on, but that these computers will talk to each other as well as counsel us, warn us, amuse us, feed us (and our lawns), and plan for us. Just by the sheer amount of data they have to process, insurance companies, banks, and government agencies make people participants in the computer revolution whether they choose to be or not.

The combined impact on the structure of the economy is profound. Technology renders borders, distance, and geography increasingly less relevant. Harvard's Michael Jensen describes the operations of the *Journal of Financial Economics* as follows: "[The journal] is now edited by seven faculty members with offices at three universities in different states, and the main editorial administrative office is located in yet another state. The publisher is located in Amsterdam, the printing is done in India, and mailing and billing are executed in Switzerland. This 'networked organization' would have been extremely inefficient two decades ago without fax machines, high-speed modems, electronic mail, and overnight delivery services."[24]

Essentially, the makeup of the work force and the nature of work are being changed. Machines often replace human labor, a process that has been underway for a century. Computer-aided manufacturing reduces the labor factor in the production of automobiles and steel, electronic security systems replace human guards, and executive information systems reduce dependence on middle managers whose prior task was to gather information. This process of automation is at the heart of the much talked about "economic restructuring." The problem it poses for job creation, given the irrelevance now of a whole set of historically useful skills and talents, is stunning.

Automating work is only part of the issue. According to Shoshana Zuboff, tasks will increasingly become "informated," as the information contained in the product/process will change what people are expected to do at work.[25] If the information is already collected and organized, the next task is to do something with it. Hence, we now see increasing demands on creativity, education, and learning. With this shift, the knowledge economy has put a greater emphasis on products that are more intellect based than dependent on physical labor. Software and semiconductors become more important than steel and bricks. In these ways, the information explosion puts a greater emphasis on human capital.

As significant as the printing press and computer are as agents of epochal change, other activities also contribute to a sense of historic transition. Among these is a sense of impending chaos, and the feeling that traditional sources of security are weakened. These attitudes were ubiquitous at the close of the medieval age.

Vulnerabilities: No Place to Hide

Europe's population increased significantly during the second half of the Middle Ages. By the year 1300, however, its capacity for food production was no longer sufficient. A combination of imprudent farming techniques and an unfavorable change in weather patterns produced the most devastating famine of the Middle Ages in 1315–1317. Malnutrition, epidemics, and inadequate health measures reinforced the sense of peril. Fragile villages lived on the edge of extreme deprivation and endured "the constant, threatening presence of death"; the margin between survival and disaster had "narrowed dangerously."[26]

In these miserable conditions, even a small event could create a catastrophe. But catastrophe came in the form of the most violent episode of the entire epoch: bubonic plague, the Black Death. Entire communities were wiped out. Nearly one-third of Europe's population died. In England the toll was closer to half. Population levels were still below the pre-plague estimates more than 150 years later.

The psychological and social consequences were equally dramatic. The failure of prayer to neutralize the disease fostered skepticism among the suffering population. Flagellants sought divine intervention; mysticism increased; sorcerers and mind readers proliferated. Promiscuity and debauchery were common, as people lived "a day of pleasure" in the face of their own mortality. The death of a sizable portion of the clergy undermined the influence of the church, a process abetted by the election of competing popes at about the same time.[27] Because the number of farm laborers declined, their wages increased and the end of serfdom, although not the hardship of peasant life, was accelerated. Artisans and skilled craftsmen raised prices when the demand for their manufactured items exceeded the supply. Many feudal landowners lost power and influence. Economic contraction and dislocation accompanied the view that "the world saw itself as being dealt terrible blows by unseen arrows."[28]

Meanwhile, the murderous destruction of the Hundred Years' War sapped the energies of France and England. The carnage and waste were exacerbated with new techniques in warfare. At Crecy, the English overcame French knights with the longbow. The Swiss showed how to organize pikemen, sometimes six thousand in a phalanx, to move quickly back and forth across a battlefield while holding formation.[29] Small, portable cannons and individual firearms subsequently proved even more lethal. The outcome of this train of events was that infantry, large contingents of foot soldiers who were commoners, replaced mounted nobility and cavalry. Additionally, artillery, using gunpowder to project large cannonballs weighing hundreds of pounds, wreaked havoc on medieval fortifications. "The royal siege train became so respected," says one authority writing about the final battles of the Hundred Years' War, "that many fortified places surrendered the moment the big guns were placed in battery." Turks used artillery cannons to conquer Constantinople in 1453, a city with "the most formidable defensive walls in all Europe." They renamed it Istanbul and threatened "the West."[30] The reliability of traditional defenses was obliterated with the advent of a new warfare.

Political, religious, and commercial institutions faltered. Chaos was in the air. The sense of vulnerability was endemic. At the same moment, a process of renewal had begun. The stage was being set for the creation of the Modern Age. The humanist spirit in Italy and the first intimations of the Renaissance appeared. Dante advanced the use of vernacular language. When scholars retreated west to escape the terrors of the Black Plague in Byzantium, they brought their knowledge of the classics. By the late 1400s, economic decline had ceased and Europe was about to enter a period of prosperity and expansion. The transition from an expectation of adversity to a sense of hope was encouraged by exploration, the emergence of nation states, and the rise of capitalism.

The remarkable achievements of our own times have been well chronicled, yet, like life at the beginning of the modern era, our age is also marked by a sense of pervasive vulnerability. There is an analog to the disease and deprivation of the medieval age. One threat appears vividly in the implications of the extraordinary population growth of recent years—about a quarter of a million people per day. Most of this growth, about 90 percent, has been occurring in the developing world. If current projections hold, at the end of the next century, Nigeria's population will exceed 500 million, nearly the equivalent of all the people in Africa in 1982.[31]

Services, institutions, and policies are buckling under the pressure. More than half a billion people worldwide are malnourished. The drive to increase food production, however, has

had high costs, including the erosion of soil nutrients, defor-
estation, depleted ocean fisheries, and degradation of water resources. Education and health services race to keep up but fail.
The number of people living in "absolute poverty"—a phrase
coined by Robert McNamara to refer to those literally living on
the margin of life—continues to rise. The world economy struggles to provide jobs and income to the huge and growing labor
pool. Some observers suggest that taken together, the data bring
into question the continued habitability of the planet.[32]

The feeling of vulnerability, expressed as environmental
concerns, is borderless. The depletion of the rain forests in Brazil
and Thailand diminishes the planet's ability to restore the oxygen basic to life all around the globe. Chernobyl waste pollutes
the air in Poland and Scandinavia. Without even knowing about
some particular ecological event, let alone having responsibility
for it, we share in the consequences. Increasingly, these consequences reach into every corner of our lives: the food we eat, the
water we drink, the medicines we use. International health organizations warn us about the spread of disease—from tubercu-
losis, malaria, and cholera, to little-known but lethal "emerging
viruses"[33]—that today can be facilitated by the ease of worldwide
transportation. Before the end of the century, the AIDS virus is
expected to have infected 40 million people. The sources of
menace seem to be everywhere.

Fears of nuclear weaponry and genetic experiments gone
awry are another dimension of the same issue. Reports of drive-
by shootings, carjackings, and the havoc of random crime augment our fears. Neighborhood streets, parks, and even our own
homes are no longer secure. Terrorism adds to our feeling of vulnerability. School buses, restaurants, airport lounges, and hospitals have all been terrorists' targets. In such an environment, the
battlefield is not defined on some map but by where you are. The
boundaries of safety have been altered, made permeable by the
fusion of desperation, aggression, and technology.

Anxiety has been accentuated by the fragmentation of
nation-states, a familiar political device. In the past, establishing
nationhood provided peoples with distinct and recognizable
structures to be a part of, and provided outsiders with easily understood references for identifying others' loyalties. This form of

political organization became widespread during the modern period.[34] Today, ethnic tribalization and political separatism (in Bosnia and Iraq, for example) reinforce a sense of disorder. At the other extreme, even supranational arrangements can be threatening as national sovereignty is compromised by the policies of regional and international organizations. Economic gains from transnational compacts are achieved as the influence of the nation-state disintegrates. The failure of countries to deal adequately with ethnic cleansings, ecological disasters, and mass migrations yields a disquiet for everyone about the absence of security, once promised in the notion of nationhood.

Although business has to contend with this environment in much the same way as every other component of society, the feeling of "no place to hide" develops in other ways as well for the commercial enterprise. Business grows more anxious as it learns how easily disaster can strike. Reports of just one negative incident can have dramatic and immediate impact on an organization's image, culture, and operating procedures. An incident no longer has to be a catastrophe like the Bhopal disaster to get instant play. In 1993, the Denny's restaurant chain found itself in the middle of a firestorm of criticism after five black Secret Service agents were refused service. Denny's moved quickly to correct the problem, with the full knowledge that in today's environment one mistake, so subject to instant media attention, can sink a company. The margin for error appears to have shrunk dangerously.

Fear is caused in organizations by many factors. Job loss and "downsizing" are a common threat. The abundance of information creates another tier of anxiety; information overload often paralyzes managers. Everyone knows that organizations can no longer tolerate functions working at cross purposes, insulation from customer complaints, or poor coordination in responding to customer needs. Yet new technological tools, organizational restructurings, and redesign of processes generate a feeling of uncertainty that can further immobilize employees' ability to react to new situations.

Some years ago a senior vice president of Banc One, an organization generally regarded as an industry leader, attended an executive retreat we helped to facilitate. The majority of the other participants were executives from various segments of the information technology sector. At the time, the Banc One executive felt smug about being in the banking business, especially after hearing story after story about American manufacturing firms wilting under the Asian challenge. Shortly after he returned to Ohio, a touring group of Japanese managers visited his comfortable midwestern office. As a matter of protocol he met with them and was shocked at the depth and sophistication of their questions about Banc One, including its technologies, marketing strategies, and performance ratios. They had clearly done their homework; they even knew the ages of the children of several executives. Although an assault on his bank was not a necessary outcome of their interest, their unexpected and detailed familiarity made him uncomfortable nonetheless. He recognized, as have executives at General Motors, IBM, and other giants, that even large domestic markets are not immune from the competition of skilled and ambitious European or Asian companies. Nor is the threat one-sided. IBM, as one example, has four software manufacturing units in Asia. In recent years, the company has earned about one-third of its operating profits in Asia at the expense of local competitors from India to Japan.

If history is philosophy by example, a lesson of the waning of the Middle Ages is that collapse is often interlaced with opportunity, that in moments of darkness can come the birth of something far grander than what had existed before. In the economic dislocations at the end of the Middle Ages, there were people alert and willing to adapt successfully. Some landlords abandoned the centuries-old manorial system and rented land to peasants. Some began to raise sheep to capitalize on the demand for wool and to escape dependence on labor-intensive agriculture products. Quick-thinking peasants bought land. Guilds of local craftsmen grew more powerful in urban areas. "The texture of society" was modified as "clerks became merchants, former workmen became employers and contractors."[35]

In similar ways, the stresses of today's world have presented numerous openings for adaptation and advantage. As we shall see, creative activity can develop even in the conflicts and tensions that leave us feeling at risk.

Trade Patterns

Columbus and others helped to usher in the modern era by loosening the centrality of the Mediterranean Sea for European commerce. Briefly, there was a shift in patterns of economic hegemony or influence. The Italian city-states—Genoa, Venice, and Florence—had been major centers of trade. Goods traveled west from India and Asia across caravan routes in Persia, Afghanistan, and the Middle East. Traders carried to Italy spices, gems, and other products first encountered by Europeans during the Crusades. Treasures from sub-Saharan Africa also worked their way north to Egypt and then across the Mediterranean to the Italian peninsula and, eventually, to the population centers of northern and central Europe.

Columbus and other explorers shifted the focus of trade from the Mediterranean to the Atlantic. After the verification of sea routes to Asia and the Americas, a coastline on the Atlantic Ocean became a key factor in national economic success. First, Spain and Portugal grew to preeminence, even having Pope Alexander VI divide new-world authorities between them in 1493. Subsequently, the French and the Dutch acquired ascendance. Finally, the British built the most expansive empire the world had seen. Although the Italian peninsula still remained valuable (as indicated by centuries of conflict among Austrian, French, and Spanish rulers), the Mediterranean, the inland ocean, lost significance. An indisputable transformation had occurred.

The parallel today is that attention and excitement in trade and commerce have inexorably moved from the Atlantic to the Pacific. In 1960 America's trade with Asia equaled about half its trade with Western Europe. As of 1992, the U.S.trade with Pacific Rim nations exceeded trade with Atlantic nations by $60 billion. U.S. trade with Japan was greater than the aggregate of trade with the United Kingdom, France, Italy, and Germany.

Since 1960 the Pacific Rim has tripled its share of world gross national product (GNP) and has replaced the Atlantic as the world's number one trading region. By the early 1990s, it accounted for 22 percent of world trade. While the European community's trade grew about 6 percent during the 1980s, the rate of trade for the Pacific Rim grew about 9 percent. The vibrancy of the Pacific market creates new competitors as well. Japan and the Four Asian Tigers (Taiwan, Hong Kong, Singapore, and South Korea) observe the economic assertions of other countries in the area—for example, Malaysia and Thailand—with mixed emotions. Some have predicted a "Chinese Century," as savings, investment, and wealth grow at an extraordinary rate throughout China and East Asia.[36] If the statistic that less than one person in ten on the planet has access to a car is extrapolated to Asian markets, one appreciates the huge shift in economic vitality that is possible.

What we are seeing today, however, is more than a one-dimensional parallel in trade patterns. Not only has the Pacific risen in economic vitality; just as noteworthy is the pattern of change worldwide that has been initiated. Indeed, the globalization of trade is, for many observers, the signal event of our time. In one sense, this is not a new phenomenon. Thomas Jefferson remarked more than two hundred years ago that "merchants have no country. The mere spot they stand on does not constitute so strong an attachment as that from which they draw their gains."[37] His observation is even more salient today.

What is new is the huge increase in the number of nations and people who are participants. Previously, a relatively small percentage of the world's population was involved in the global market economy. Most people lived in places that were more or less disconnected from the market system that had been developing since the sixteenth century. One index of growth is that by the beginning of 1992 the aggregate capitalization of thirty stock markets in developing nations exceeded $500 billion.[38] Thus, capitalism today is experiencing a universalizing trend, accelerated by international agreements from the United Nations to GATT (General Agreement on Trade and Tariffs) to NAFTA (North American Free Trade Agreement).[39] On the basis of either market diversification or the numbers of people alone, the result will be revolutionary in its impact on how business anywhere will be conducted.

Although Asia is clearly the more dominant economic force now, the economies of Mexico and South America are also beginning to exert themselves more aggressively in the rhythm of free trade and open market policies. Latin America, in fact, is the fastest growing regional market for U.S. goods. As one example, the demand for telecommunications services in Latin America has actually been growing 60 percent to 70 percent faster than the Asian market; American Telephone & Telegraph (AT&T) predicts a growth factor of "200–300 percent in the next decade."[40] Foreign investment projects are increasing throughout the area, as is the support of international lending organizations in Argentina and other countries working toward trade liberalization.

An important aspect of the current switch to the global model is psychological; it is less about organizations than it is about attitudes. How many American executives believe, let alone anticipate, that in a few years their businesses will be less American and a lot more Mexican? A lot more Taiwanese? A lot more Indian? If the North American Free Trade Agreement expands to include other nations (as Chile has requested), the autonomy identified with nationalism will be further diffused. Sadly, many businesspeople who speak of a globalized economy often miss the point that nationalism, and all it implies for the protection of "home" industries, one-sided alliances, a narrow base of potential customers and partners, and an insular view of culture, is an approach to political organization that is slowly decreasing in relevance.

Expanding Horizons: Explorations and Scientific Inquiry

Exploration and the scientific revolution combined to expand how the Europeans thought about the world at the dawn of the Modern Age. Columbus's efforts followed a line of Portuguese and Spanish endeavors to move down the African coastline and around the continent to the treasure lode of the East. Obviously, these achievements were not accomplished by a few individual adventurers acting alone. They were enterprises that also involved the coordination of royal treasuries and scientific counsel. They were enabled by innovations in ships' rigging and the development of the magnetic compass and the quadrant. A world new to the Europeans revealed treasures of ore, plants, wildlife, and artifacts of the indigenous population. New products such as potatoes, corn, tobacco, and chocolate became available.

The scientific revolution represented more than technological tools used for navigation. The whole enterprise, sometimes marked with the beginning of the Renaissance and sometimes with the publication in 1543 of Copernicus's treatise
concerning the rotation of the earth around the sun, constituted
a radical shift in the intellectual assumptions that had been the
foundation of Greek and scholastic thinking. The scientific
worldview that emerged was more secular, less religious, and
more quantitative.[41] The drive to control nature through discovery of basic laws of the universe had begun.

One vivid analog to the Columbus venture is seen in the exploration of space. A signature of our times is the successful reach
toward the stars. Besides the excitement of this "last frontier,"
other activities and ventures promote the feeling that we are at
the threshold of another historic age of discovery, that we are wit-
nesses and participants in a burst of creativity such as the world
has not seen since the modern era emerged. Advances in oceano-
graphic studies and materials science (polymers, ceramics) fan
our enthusiasm for pushing the borders of what we already know.
Molecular computers, using biologically based circuits, and tiny
microprocessors that can restore sight for victims of some kinds
of blindness, interweave the discoveries of electronics and cell bi-
ology. The promise of genetic engineering for agriculture (producing disease-resistant crops), for bioremediation (developing
microorganisms for removing environmental wastes), and for
medical applications (prevention of disease with genetic therapy)
increases our excitement.[42] In fact, it is feasible that most people
working after the turn of the century will be working in industries
that don't exist now. Indeed, as John C. Malone, chief executive
of Tele-Communication, Inc., has noted: "The overwhelming
majority of revenues we get by the end of the decade will be from
services and products that have not yet been invented."[43]

As with the discoverers of an earlier period, today's researchers hold forth the promise of life immensely improved by
their quest of worlds now unknown or unimagined. Prior to the
scientific developments at the dawn of the modern era, life in
Europe was much like it had been for a thousand years. The medieval fabric that held a society together was ripped apart by
human curiosity and the desire for progress. Clearly, the discov-

eries of our day, as the national debates on the use of atomic energy or extraordinary life-sustaining medical procedures demonstrate, can be expected to be equally destabilizing. The technologies of birth control and fertilization, for instance, ask the most fundamental question of all: what is a human life?

Ultimately, discovery leverages the value of society. Early in the process, innovations are often used to do what has always been done, only quicker or cheaper. Later they are used to invent whole new ways of doing what has been done before, even to invent totally new activities. The enlargement of the computer's role in society—from data processing to reengineering to "virtual reality"—shows what happens. Outcomes can be profound even if not planned. The automobile begat highways, which begat suburbs. Nowhere more than in the realm of discovery can we appreciate the complex and unpredictable results of our efforts. Each historic moment of great scientific and technological breakthroughs—the 1600s or the industrial revolution—leaves an immediate impact and a legacy for future generations that can't be planned or foreseen. Contemporary unease is heightened by an instinctive awareness of that unpredictable inheritance; a new arc of civilization and organizational life is being created by people who are not sure what it is they are creating.

Commercial Revolutions

The combination of all the destabilizing forces described thus far caused a commercial revolution at the dawn of the modern era. Capitalism, building on centuries of prior efforts, began to develop vigorously at the end of the fifteenth century. Later, in 1776, Adam Smith set down the free market tenets of the capitalist philosophy and lowered the boom on mercantilism.

Our purpose here is not to describe how the capitalist political economy changed medieval life, but to point out that the kind of change that took place once before holds lessons about the flexibility that is necessary now. Commercial activities of all kinds grew. Subsistence farming was replaced by farming for profit. Mining, textile manufacture, and shipbuilding all developed rapidly. Building activities expanded and contributed to the urbanization process. In short, there was an explosion of enterprise in many directions simultaneously.

Corporations became organizations that had a separate existence from the people involved with them; a company became an "artificial being." These organizations separated the roles of manager and owner/investor and limited the liability of the investor. Money became as important as land, and organized money exchanges (bourses) were established throughout Europe. As the economy became monetized, great concentrations of wealth developed. Eventually, banking was redefined by the Bank of England through its role in the management of government finances. Different kinds of organizations and institutions came forward to participate profitably in the emerging environment.

In addition, a price revolution, triggered in great part by the flood of New World bullion, dramatically increased the costs of just about everything during the sixteenth century.[44] Although there is some disagreement among historians as to how much hardship was caused by the price increases, there is considerable agreement that pain, confusion, and discontent were widespread, especially in the period from 1543 to 1551.[45] From the early 1540s on, people were aware that they were experiencing something different from what their parents had experienced. From their perspective, they were living through a period of price volatility that at the very least had not been a common experience for a century or more. The real incomes of unskilled laborers and small farmers failed to keep pace with the rise in prices and, generally, wages rose less than the prices of agricultural products. The brunt of the pain was suffered by the poor, the peasants, the elderly, clerks, and others on fixed incomes. The nobility accused the middle-class merchants of greed; and "middle-class writers attributed the deplorable situation to the commercial activities of the nobility."[46] Social turmoil ensued. Peasant revolts were commonplace throughout most of the sixteenth century. Civil unrest always threatened as governments found it increasingly difficult to keep pace with their growing expenses. By the first half of the seventeenth century, complaints about economic decline and exorbitant prices were frequent in government proceedings and treatises on political economy. It was clear that the economic landscape was changing.

As capitalism changed before (from mercantilism to laissez faire economics), it is altering now. Economic models offered by the Germans and the Japanese, characterized by a stronger collaboration across diverse constituencies (public and private sectors, labor and management, managers and investors), increasingly interact with American ideas of a more individualistic and entrepreneurial bent. It is not unreasonable to expect that the various styles of capitalism in the global environment will influence one another and create further change.

Additionally, there is a broader range of value-related concerns. A growing number of executives, for example, are coming to realize that the "cost versus environmentalism" dilemma is often as flimsy as the so-called "cost versus quality" dilemma used to be. The consequence is greater attention to developing a "sustainable economy," emphasizing how to manage the expenditure and replenishment of renewable resources (for example, water), how to systematically substitute alternatives for nonrenewable resources (for example, solar energy for oil) and how to develop techniques for the control and removal of pollutants and waste (for example, biodegradable products).[47]

Finally, recent levels of worldwide inflation parallel the inflationary stresses in the sixteenth century. The delinking of currencies from the gold standard and the arrival of floating exchange rates have been credited with propelling much of the inflation seen since the mid 1970s. As one illustration, prices in the United States nearly tripled between 1965 and 1982.[48] The economist George P. Brockway noted that Joseph A. Schumpeter had been working for the nine years before he died in 1952 on the *History of Economic Analysis*. In a subject index that ran for thirty pages in his exhaustive research of all great and near-great economists, there is no listing for the subject "inflation."[49] Yet no one doing business today would think of assessing an opportunity without "factoring in" the cost of inflation, or more precisely, how the risk of inflation could be accounted for or "matched" elsewhere. Other economists say that "inflation anxiety," which didn't exist before, is now an assumed variable in personal and business planning.

Inflation, of course, has occurred before in the modern era (and throughout history). Its added significance now is that the rise in energy costs during the 1970s exposed the weakness of the production and distribution systems that had been the trademark of the post–World War II economy among industrialized nations. The general increase in price levels caused doubts about the fundamentals of the global economic structure that had been developing since the middle of the century. Inflation had occurred simultaneously with a slowdown in the world economy—creating stagflation, a situation in which, in blatant contradiction to standard economic theories, both problems threaten at the same time.[50] Also, the social disharmony and mistrust of the rules that marked earlier inflationary times were apparent in the 1970s and 1980s on a global scale.[51] As many learned, inflation damages the values that hold a society together. Speculation, consumption, and self-indulgence push aside trust, diligence, and hard work. People become inordinately concerned with how much they make and less concerned with what they do. They become more interested in "making a living than making a life."[52] Jealousies and feelings of entitlement encumber productive relationships. As John Maynard Keynes once said, "There is no subtler, no surer means of overturning the existing basis of society than to debauch the currency."[53] The social divisiveness and suspicions that are aroused cut into the cohesion that civic life, both domestic and international, needs. All this is part of the turbulence we experience.

Summing up, the tensions and crises of current times are part of a broader picture that reveals a world in the middle of historic transformation. This perspective is not just another exclamation about the "new millenium." It holds that there are similarities between the beginnings of earlier eras and the events that are occurring today. The comparison, if reasonably drawn, suggests that the beginning of a new and fourth epoch has arrived. Taken together, the advances at the end of the Medieval Age that came from the new humanist outlook, the scientific revolution, global exploration, and the rise of capitalism brought epochal change. One way of life—and one worldview—passed on and was replaced by another. In similar fashion, events today reveal transformations in the modern world's way of thinking and behaving. At the minimum, it appears that the need for adaptability, optimism, judgment, and a more inclusive attitude is heightened. This demand is not a gimmicky response, quick to grab the latest fashion. Rather, it is born of a thoughtfulness about another time, another and earlier passage of civilization. The conflict between passing and emerging worlds reflects both the chaos that business dreads and the opportunity it relishes.

C H A P T E R

2

Turning Point: The World Has Never Been So Awake

We believe that full economic collaboration between all nations, great and small, is essential to the improvement of living conditions all over the world, and to the establishment of freedom from fear and freedom from want.
—Harry S Truman

There are three kinds of people who are anachronisms in business today: those who still think the world is flat, those who don't believe in gravity and those who think you can depend on mass markets.
—Amal Johnson
President, Baan, USA

Comparing the beginning of the modern era and its end begs a question. When did the latest epochal transformation—the transition we are still in—begin? When, finally, could we say that the new, postmodern era, though incompletely developed, began to take on a recognizable shape? These are legitimate questions because our answers illuminate our perceptions about how we think today's moment might turn out. In the most straightforward terms, we look at where we have been to learn where we need to go and how to get there. Such inquiry and reflection are necessary if we are to keep a sense of perspective about the new behaviors that are required, and at the very least, to avoid feeling victimized by the swirl of events in our companies and industries. If managers understand the connection between what they do and the momentum of social and economic trends that influences their options, they will find the world less chaotic, and events will look less random. Understanding how and why business is in its current situation sheds light on what the appropriate responses should be and hints at the decisions, actions, and attitudes that will be effective tomorrow.

As noted earlier, our purpose thus far has not been to show an exact point-to-point correspondence between events at the beginning of the modern era and current times. That, even if possible, would be a difficult task of historical analysis and not germane to our objective. It is the general pattern that matters most—the collage of personalities and events that creates the impression that holds our attention and influences the way we think. As dramatic as events were, the change that took place more than five hundred years ago was more than the sum of discrete events. The periodization and the declaration of one or more events as key turning points are less significant than the grand picture: illusions shattered, technology celebrated, provincialism endangered, orthodoxy challenged, and the conduct of life reshaped.

In a book entitled *The New World Order*, written in 1940 at the outset of World War II, H. G. Wells wrote that the "world has never been so awake."[1] With typical prescience he was clear about the possibility of disappointment. "Little may come of it, much may come of it. We do not know." He was also doubtful that any individual or group would be singled out as "father or founder" of a new order. The maker, instead, would be "man, that being who is in some measure in every one of us." By the same token there would be no "day of days," as Wells put it, when the new world order would suddenly come into being. No single event. No individual momentous action. Instead it would be a collective achievement, a function of innumerable personalities and activities.

This sentiment makes a lot of sense to us. If progress is to continue, it will be built on the successes of the past and an understanding of how the past operates today. To paraphrase Isaac Newton, in social development as well as science, today's achievements are built on the shoulders of giants.

Just the same, a longer perspective says there is also a moment when things begin to move more quickly and in a more discernible direction so that the parade of events merges into one impression. If nothing else, there is an instant of recognition for something that was previously less certain or more obscure.

It is likely that the new stage of civilization we are experiencing today has been developing throughout most of this century. The most common view is that the new age began with the first world war, with the "fall of eagles," such as the Romanov and Hapsburg dynasties. Internationally, European domination of the globe was weakened as stirrings of colonial revolt grew in Africa and Asia and a burden of debt lay heavily across Europe. The horrors of the experience undermined the beliefs that had held European society together, particularly ideas about the goodness of humanity and the meaning of life. For many non-Europeans, the conflict appeared to be a European civil war that had depleted its authority and influence. Optimistically, Mohandas Gandhi in India, W.E.B. DuBois, a leading spokesman for African-Americans, and Dr. Sun Yat-sen in China championed a world integrated on the basis of mutual respect, not economic exploitation and racism.

Turn-of-the-century science added to the sense of turmoil. Sigmund Freud's interpretation of dreams unsettled images of who we were. European physicists pursued quantum mechanics and questions about certainty, and by 1919 Albert Einstein obtained experimental verification of his theory of relativity. These events began a revolution that challenged our understanding of the basic laws of nature and, like the Copernican revolution before, caused us to look at the entire universe in a way that was contrary to common sense. At about the same time, electricity, the motor car and airplane, jazz, abstract art, and sexual liberation began to revolutionize social structures and customs. Culture was being remade.

There is much evidence, therefore, that in the early part of the twentieth century a new world was being created. Patterns of everyday life, economic relationships, and political organizations were being transformed. All of these were bound to stimulate a new perspective, much as previous cultural and commercial changes had ushered in other epochs.

Increasingly, however, historians group together the events that occurred between August 1914—the beginning of World War I—and August 1945—Hiroshima and the end of World War II—as elements of the same convulsive process. Not until the end of the Second World War did the democracies of the West take realistic steps to ensure their victory over totalitarian regimes. Only then did the British, managing the largest and most potent empire, surrender to historical inevitability and leave India and Africa, essentially ending the imperialist period. It was not until the end of World War II that the role of women, in transition since the turn of the century, became clearly different from what it had been. It was not until the middle of the century that the possibilities of nuclear energy and other life-changing technologies began to be understood by nonexperts. Finally, it was not until after the Second World War that global politics and economics became the foundation of government policies around the world.

GENESIS OF THE NEW ERA

It seems to us that the moment in history when a confluence of events lets us finally grasp, clearly and unequivocally, the arrival of postmodern life is 1942. If the new epoch were to be called the Atomic Age, then certainly Enrico Fermi's report on splitting the atom, on initiating a nuclear chain reaction, was a major event. If the new era were to be called the Space Age, then the launch of V2 rockets by German scientists was a landmark. If the new epoch were to be called the Information Age, then the development of the first automatic, electronic computer (ENIAC) was clearly a milestone. If the new era were to be called the Age of Aviation, then successful testing of the commercial jet engine was a hinge event. If a challenge to the way we thought about world economic systems marked the dawn of the new order, then the publication of Joseph Schumpeter's *Capitalism, Socialism, and Democracy*, and its popularization of capitalism as a force of "creative destruction," was an important event. If the epoch were noted for its global village and multipolar profile, then the Declaration of the United Nations (UN) was a major undertaking. If the new era were characterized by a historic commitment to human rights, itself a reaction to the atrocities of the early part of this century, then the German decision at Wannsee, near Berlin, to adopt a Final Solution and exterminate Jewry, was a tragic but key event. If our own understanding of the enemy within us has given this age a more sensitive moral conscience, then the internment of innocent Japanese-Americans was a significant event. In each instance—from Fermi's success to the UN declaration to the internment activity—the year was 1942.

Most of all, if it is America's vision of the world that has marked so much history since the end of World War II, then the allied victories that ensured triumph were unequaled in importance. The battles of 1942, including El Alamein, Midway, and Stalingrad, were the most significant in the prosecution of the war. The events that followed were possible only because of the achievements of that year. The military victories gave confidence to the planning associated with determining how to terminate hostilities and, more important for our discussion here, how to structure the peace. The outcomes of that planning generated early approximations of the world we live in today.[2] Taken together, the events of 1942 represent the end of the beginning. After 1942 a world of economic integration became destiny, and with it, a whole array of business strategies that had been less significant before became essential.

Unquestionably, epochal change would have happened without America's contribution. In politics, for example, Gandhi was effective before he had any attention from the United States. In science, Freud and Einstein were influential before they crossed the Atlantic. Nevertheless, America's activities after 1945 were crucial in stimulating the sentiments and activities that helped give birth to the new emerging epoch. The irony was that the American business community failed to adapt quickly to the very changes it was instrumental in creating.

First Stirrings: Building the Global Economy from Separate Markets

As the end of World War II approached, Susanne K. Langer, a prominent American philosopher, argued for a "new world order." Her contribution was to focus on the role of business in the shape of things to come. She asked, "What is the new 'reality' which is actually shaping the unconscious, instinctive ways of mankind in our emergent age?"[3] She answered her own question: that the "dominant and 'most real' power may be named with one familiar, not very unctuous word: business." The brave, new world, she claimed, was the "business age," where commerce, capital, traffic, distribution, and industry were the driving forces of peace. The call to action was Thomas Watson's early motto for IBM writ large: world peace through world trade. It and like-spirited announcements would encourage a world where neither the structure of global society, the processes of business, nor, as a consequence, the role of leadership would ever be the same again. The new epoch would be built on commerce, peacefully conducted around the world.

The postwar outlook that eventually took shape, with origins actually extending to the internationalists surrounding Woodrow Wilson during World War I (1914–1918), was simple in its fundamental premise. It seemed that the only way to break the cycle of war-defeat-chaos-war was first to accept the notion that every nation was going to act out of its own self-interest. Each nation would eventually do what it thinks will best promote its own economic well-being and national security. The second task was to convince each nation that its self-interest, from consumer goods to security, was best protected by protecting the other fellow's self-interest. In short, the idea was to build international economic interdependence or, in the fashion of today's language, a global economy.

Cordell Hull, as a senator and as Franklin D. Roosevelt's secretary of state, had been arguing this point prior to the war and had sought to show how national prosperity was dependent on a vitality shared among nations. He initiated a series of trade agreements in 1934 that stimulated a liberalization of trade. He wrote in his memoirs as early as 1916 that "unhampered trade dovetailed with peace; high tariffs, trade barriers, and unfair economic competition with war." He reasoned that "if we could get a freer flow of trade—freer in the sense of fewer discriminations and obstructions—so that one country would not be deadly jealous of another, the living standards of all might rise."[4] Implementing this sort of philosophy after 1945 would be as daunting as it had been after the first world war.

The creation of the global order, the early outlines of a new epoch, had to begin with the material rehabilitation of nations injured by the war and an economic system that assured increasing levels of prosperity everywhere. American economic dominance was the first obstacle to making the vision a reality. When the United States entered the war, it held about 80 percent of the world's gold supply. American decision makers realized that the United States accounted for nearly 50 percent of the world's gross national product in 1948. Clearly, for one nation to account for half the dollar value of all goods and services exchanged on the planet was unrealistic. American products needed markets; that required the revitalization of Europe's economic strength. A "dollar shortage," whether real or imagined, was as hurtful to America's self-interest as it was to Europe's.

Second, the rejuvenation and reconstruction of a Europe devastated by war had to proceed against a nightmarish backdrop of deprivation and hopelessness.[5] Millions were homeless.[6] The infrastructure was in shambles even two years after the war. Bridges were still in disrepair (Germany alone had lost more than five thousand bridges). A lack of coal caused a deficit of steel production that inhibited the construction of everything, including, ironically, badly needed coal mines. Skilled workers who had gone off to war had not returned. Long-standing commercial relationships had been destroyed. Inflation had rendered many currencies useless. Agriculture, for lack of fertilizer and neglect of the soil, could not yield the harvests necessary to prevent starvation throughout Europe.[7]

Peter Duignan and L. H. Gann, scholars at the Hoover Institution, put it this way: "The Americans were crucial in restoring confidence, providing money, food, fuel, and machinery, and in pushing Europe toward shared defense, economic integration, and the Common Market."[8] Along with the establishment of the World Bank, the International Monetary Fund, the General Agreement on Tariffs and Trade (GATT), the Bretton Woods arrangements, the United Nations, and particularly the Marshall Plan, American efforts were clearly aimed at building a world order of different dimensions. The intention was to demonstrate the power of mutual aid and collective responsibility. It was to restore faith in free market systems and to inspire democratic processes.

The Marshall Plan is often taken as emblematic of both the challenge and the achievement.[9] It was, according to historian

Michael Hogan, an outgrowth of America's "search for a new economic order at home and abroad." In this sense, the plan was an effort to recast Europe in America's own image.[10] The program was tremendous in scope. It provided dollar grants, material aid, food, and machinery, accounting at one point for 10 percent of the entire federal budget (compared to about 2 percent today for nondefense foreign affairs expenditures). American business had a prominent role. Paul Hoffman, president of Studebaker, was put in charge of the Economic Cooperation Administration (ECA), the agency designed to oversee the program. Various business executives served as consultants to the agency, went to Europe to teach methods of production and marketing, and hosted tours of European businessmen in the United States.[11]

The attitude that animated these efforts was expressed in a 1943 bestseller entitled *One World*, written by Wendell Wilkie, a Republican candidate for president. He wrote, "Many reasons may be assigned for the amazing economic development of the United States . . . but in my judgment the greatest factor has been the fact that by happenstance of good fortune there was created here in America the largest area in the world in which there were no barriers to the exchange of goods and ideas."[12] Wilkie spoke for like-thinking internationalists, saying:

> America must choose one of three courses after this war: narrow nationalism, which inevitably means the ultimate loss of our own liberty; international imperialism, which means the sacrifice of some other nation's liberty; or the creation of a world in which there shall be equality of opportunity for every race and every nation.... To make this choice effectively, we must win not only the war, but also the peace.... Economic freedom is as important as political freedom.... It is also inescapably true that to raise the standard of living of any man anywhere in the world is to raise the standard of living by some slight degree of every man everywhere in the world.[13]

Over time, European prosperity and peace, conditioned on diminution of nationalism and promotion of free trade, would be the cornerstone of the new order. The hope was that international cooperation would bring a new kind of vitality to world commerce, a major attribute of the new age.

It is worth repeating that none of this discussion is intended to minimize the significant role that Europeans themselves had in immediate postwar reconstruction and later activities that created the postwar world. Significant among these endeavors were Jean Monnet's dream of a united Europe and his work as head of the Coal and Steel Community, predecessor of the Common Market and European Community; Alcide de Gaspari's defeat of communist advances in the Italian elections of 1948; and the efforts of Konrad Adenauer and Charles De Gaulle toward German and French cooperation. These accomplishments combined with countless other actions by leaders around the world to shape the economic and political arrangements that developed over the next quarter of a century. The brief attention given here to American attitudes and behavior is aimed at putting the conduct of the American business community in the context of government policy and social opinion that it contributed to creating.[14]

Transition in Japan

The task in Japan had been imposing, too. The Japanese had suffered a military defeat, the horrors of nuclear devastation, and ruin of their industrial base. The country faced starvation; it no longer had a merchant marine to bring in needed supplies. In 1945, production was one-tenth of prewar levels.[15] The entire Japanese way of life, feudal though it might have been, was also under attack. Yet because MacArthur preserved the dignity of the emperor when he declined to put him on trial for war crimes, the emperor was available as a figure around which society could rebuild. The direction of that rebuilding was clear. On the day he was nominated by the president to be secretary of state, Dean Acheson commented in regard to U.S. postwar policy, "Japan will be put in a position where it cannot renew aggressive warfare; the present economic and social system in Japan which makes for a will to war will be changed so that it will not continue." The intention was to prepare Japan for entry into a new world order as a self-supporting, democratic trading partner.[16]

There were dollars behind the rhetoric. Appropriations totaled $2 billion by the end of 1951.[17] This amount, although lower than what was spent on Germany on a proportional basis, was generous, partly from the fear of Japan's turning to communism, particularly after the communist victory by Mao Tse-tung in China.

A number of reforms were introduced. Tenant farmers were allowed to buy the land they lived on from their landlords.[18] Health measures implemented to combat typhus, cholera, and other diseases increased the life expectancy of a Japanese man from forty-three years in 1946 (where it had been since 1895) to sixty-one years in 1951.[19] Labor unions, which brought guaranteed rights to collective bargaining, and women's suffrage were introduced. All these activities persuaded the Japanese that a new era had dawned.

Education and training took place as Japanese industry showed foresight in a willingness to learn from Edwards Deming, Joseph Juran, Seymour Sarason, and others in the nascent quality movement. Quality meetings in Japan were eagerly attended by the top executives of the organization, not just the rank and file, staff professionals, and middle managers, as was often the case in the United States some years later. The *zaibatsu*, the monopolistic organizations (including Mitsui, Mitsubishi, Sumitomo, and Yasuda), which had benefited from militarist expansionism and were considered responsible in part for the war, were diminished in their influence, although several became forerunners of today's *kereitsu*.[20] At the same time, the need for the skills, investment capital, and connections of these organizations was offset by their resistance toward developing democratic procedures and a competitive economy. Despite these crosscurrents, the restructuring of Japanese socioeconomic conditions progressed in a historic manner.

At first, Japan was encouraged to trade with Asian partners because the country's economy was not sufficiently developed to absorb American products. Later, Japan would trade vigorously with the West, particularly the United States, as part of a bargain named the Yoshida Doctrine after the postwar prime minister Shigeru Yoshida. Essentially, Japan was to focus on economic development, thus providing America with a vibrant ally in containing the spread of communism throughout Asia. The United States would provide Japan military protection and political leadership for cementing security ties that would encourage business development. The arrangement was a key step in establishing economic growth throughout Asia.

Political Consistency

Immediate American efforts in other areas were less dramatic. As one example, aid in Latin America was modest, with the United States granting $500 million of Export-Import Bank assistance. The argument for assuaging Latin American disappointment and discontent was that a successful Marshall Plan would create new markets for Central and South American goods in Europe. Historian Walter LaFeber quotes the American ambassador to Brazil as explaining that whereas Europe suffered from "a case of smallpox," Latin America only had a "common cold." Unsurprisingly, reaction in Latin America was negative, despite the signing of the charter for the Organization of American States. The demand of these countries for better access to American markets was "flatly refused," and hemispheric relations suffered the consequences.[21]

Generally, however, the American-led recovery was genuine in motivation. In an open letter to the boards of directors of American businesses in June 1947, Henry R. Luce, the editor of *Fortune*, called on American industry to step up to the challenge: "If the U.S. businessman does not thrust the weight of his thoughts, his policies, and his dollars—in short, the whole business process as he has developed it over the years—into helping save the world, the world will not be saved."[22] The British historian Arnold Toynbee referred to the Marshall Plan, one example of this intervention, as the "greatest act of generosity in the history of diplomacy."[23] And more than half of all Americans surveyed in a January 1948 Gallup poll saw its primary motive as humanitarian. Nonetheless, there was also some skepticism concerning the American motivation. Only about a quarter of English and French respondents to the same poll thought

America was acting from humanitarian impulses in conducting the Marshall Plan. The percentage was slightly higher in Italy. All told, about 30 to 40 percent of the Europeans surveyed thought that America's underlying motives were self-serving: a need for profits and markets, and a desire for a stronger Europe to stave off depression and to stop the spread of communism. In spite of these perceptions, strong majorities favored the program in all countries. It was, as one Parisian said, "a chance to feel oneself surrounded by honesty and plenty of smiles."[24]

THE DOUBLE-EDGED SWORD

The primary lesson of epochal change is the obvious one: it requires adaptation. America's success in accelerating global economic interdependence was not matched by its readiness to deal with this new interrelatedness. A nation that held sway over most of the globe at midcentury openly wondered, not more than a generation later, about the decline of its ability to compete internationally. The roller coaster ride of America's international competitiveness provides dramatic evidence that judgment, as well as resources, needs to keep pace with the changes taking place.

The success of various reconstruction activities would have consequences for which industry leaders were not prepared. America's unique position at the end of the war was an anomaly. It was unlikely that 6 percent of the world's population could continue to account for half the world's economic activity. Indeed, by the late 1960s the American share in the world economy had declined to around 25 percent, roughly where it remains today. The surprise that emerged throughout the world was that the changes caused a whole new set of business dynamics to develop. In a phrase, transformation to a global economy forced corporations worldwide to renew and reinvent themselves.

The postwar economic expansion at first bred confidence. The amount of cash that had been saved during the fifteen years of depression and war was huge: between 1939 and the war's end the amount of savings worldwide had grown almost $35 billion, and the American savings rate was close to 25 percent of that.[25]

During the Depression, people didn't have money. During the war, they had money but couldn't find goods to buy. This unmet demand exploded as industrial plants were converted to meet the needs of a peace economy.[26] Housing was required to shelter growing families. The proliferation of automobiles, highways, schools, and consumer goods of all kinds were part of the optimism that marked the times. The GI bill promised fifteen million veterans a better life. By 1958 John Kenneth Galbraith described the United States as "the affluent society."[27]

Within a decade, however, Americans watched a great wave of inflation devalue their savings. Government decision makers worried about the decline in productivity, which deteriorated dramatically after the oil shocks of 1973. Business and labor grew more contentious, and by the 1980s corporate earnings plunged and downsizings were the rule. After the mid 1960s it became increasingly difficult to attribute the declining performance of American industry to government meddling or other externalities.[28] These could not explain inept management decisions, poor product quality, shoddy service, and the failure to translate basic research into product development. A whole debate eventually began about the decline of American economic power: Was it real? Who was to blame? Is there a way out? By 1989 the prestigious MIT Commission on National Productivity had concluded that American industry was suffering from deep, systemic problems that thwarted its success.

Yet some economists viewed these evaluations as excessively pessimistic. They argued that U.S. productivity remained the highest in the world. The country's share of world production had changed little since 1939 and the United States had suffered less unemployment and had created more jobs than the European community. It had maintained greater harmony than most other multi-ethnic countries, such as the former Soviet Union, the former Yugoslavia, India, Nigeria, Cyprus, and others. Despite deterioration in the primary and secondary education systems, American universities were respected worldwide.[29]

There were several reasons for the stress on American businesses. These firms had helped create a global environment that would be radically different from the marketplace in which they had earned their success. The most obvious attribute of this new environment was the vastly increased number of foreign competitors, a result that was part and parcel of the global economy. The Marshall Plan, the World Bank, GATT, and other aspects of international planning had worked almost too well. The competition now came not only from Germany and Japan, as it had before the war, but also from newer entrants like Mexico and Singapore. In some cases, foreign competitors had distinct advantages, such as lower labor costs or cheap capital. These offshore firms frequently were working with newer infrastructure, equipment, and tools obtained during the postwar reconstruction. Within the U.S. market they often enjoyed privileges not shared by domestic competition. For most of the postwar period, for example, foreign banks were permitted interstate operations while domestic competitors were not.

The increase in international trade also fostered innovation. New products and services appeared regularly. "New" business techniques used by global competitors during the 1980s, such as just-in-time inventory management, overwhelmed the advantages of typical American practices. Most important, a new kind of competition was developing that would alter the very bases of the buyer-seller relationship. The proliferation of competitors helped undermine the power of sellers over buyers and made quality and service a significant consideration. Customer satisfaction became a major criterion of business success.

Other dynamics were also operating. American corporations had invested heavily in foreign subsidiaries for several decades. Between 1950 and 1980, those investments grew by $180 billion. Nearly a third of all transportation equipment plants and a quarter of chemical plants were situated outside the United States from 1957 through 1967. Meanwhile, production processes—not just the sourcing of raw materials—were being globalized. A new international division of labor developed. These two events—arrival of the transnational corporation and the practice of global production—created an environment that was new to American management and a threat to the dominant position it had achieved immediately after 1945.[30]

The Decline of Mass Production

Epochal change in commerce reverberated in many ways. Americans who built their success on the mass production formula—volume production of standardized goods—were slow to react to the emerging requirement for the more vigorous pursuit of value-added strategies. The centerpoint of mass production is cost reduction.[31] The spread between expenses and income is driven by pressing down cost through various efficiencies. Big business, which had carried the American economy to international stature by 1900, used economies of scale and scope to achieve lower unit costs. It integrated mass production with mass distribution (department and chain stores, catalogs, and national magazines for mass advertising) to help create the mass consumption society. This was doable in America because the country's internal market was relatively homogeneous in language, political tradition, and customs, particularly compared to that of Europe. Relative to homogeneous Japan, the American domestic market was much larger. American business could make a great deal of money selling mass-produced products within its own boundaries.

But conditions began to alter. Gradually, a few companies began to offer more than standardized, commodity-like products and services. By adding personalized service, zero-defect quality, and customization to goods and services, they used "value-added" strategies to transform their product lines. When a company built its reputation on innovation (as did 3M) or with customer service (as did IBM in the 1960s and 1970s), it built with a value-added strategy. The reason these companies come to mind is not merely that they were successful, but that for a long time they were *exceptions* to the rule. As the emerging epoch continued to unfold in the 1970s and 1980s, value-added strategies increasingly became the norm. The intertwining of globalization processes, and the trade liberalization, communication technologies, and transportation advances that accompanied it, changed the game. Given the new level and intensity of competition and customer expectations, the old rules no longer applied.

By the late 1960s, difficulties with the mass production strategy were numerous. The pent-up demand created by the Depression and the war was spent as population growth slowed, thus decreasing the number of prospective buyers. Compounding the problem was a decline in productivity in the 1970s. This structural squeeze limited how far unit costs could be lowered, restricted price reductions, and stunted market expansion.[32]

Another blow to the relevance of mass production came with the segmentation and diversification of markets, brought about as the percentage of nontraditional families grew rapidly. Women entering the work force and married couples divorcing with greater frequency combined to restructure the profile of the average household. American society was becoming more diverse. (As but one example, by the end of the 1980s the fastest growing religion in the United States was Islam.) Income distribution became more uneven, creating additional pressures. The result was an explosion in the variety of tastes and needs of the American market. The market for standardized goods was shrinking. Every business, noted a number of observers, was becoming a fashion business, attempting to meet demands for rapid flexibility, quick retooling, and speedy changeovers.[33]

Finally, a wave of environmental factors upset the security provided by the mass production formula. The most commonly cited external causes for the decline of the mass production model are those identified by Michael Piore and Charles Sabel of The Massachusetts Institute of Technology. These researchers claimed that the social unrest of the 1960s and 1970s (for example, protests against the Vietnam War), floating exchange rates, oil embargoes and shortages, and a worldwide recession (1981–1982) combined to weaken the stability of demand and predictability of needed resources. Furthermore, long product life cycles were jeopardized by technological innovations. The outcomes included increased costs as well as advantages to more nimble competitors.[34]

American companies needed to respond to the new dynamics in a competitive landscape, but they were caught short in some measure by their previous success. In addition, the changes that were required were not merely a function of recent business results or inconvenience. Core ideas were challenged. Poor performance was the tip of the iceberg. The mass production system, for example, diminished the intellectual contribution of a worker to the production process. Division of labor created efficiencies as focused repetition reduced errors and increased speed. However, in a value-added environment, intelligence became the significant production variable. Inadequate attention to the quality of education didn't matter when employees didn't need to puzzle over detailed manuals, execute complex computations, or manage sophisticated technological tools. But the old custom of de-skilling personnel ran counter to what was needed in the new environment.

As the viability of mass production diminished, so did conventional perspectives of work. The notion of wage labor (people doing what they were told to do and no more, for an agreed-upon wage) appeared less relevant in a world that required greater responsibility, creativity, and involvement among people at all levels. One writer has even argued that "more than hierarchy, more than middle managers, wage labor and all the psychological baggage that went with it defined the parameters of 20th century business."[35]

Mass production, moreover, required integrating forward (into marketing) and backward (sourcing supplies); it meant bigness and giantism. After years of complacency, many large firms proved incapable of rapid adjustment. New industries were thus frequently pioneered by small enterprise—contrary to Marxist, Fordist, and corporatist predictions. Because the effort to create economic interdependencies worked, it now became imperative for companies to start thinking globally and not nationally, just as it had been necessary for companies to stop thinking regionally earlier in the century. Thus, American business had to relinquish what had been the cornerstone of its success—and because the old approach had worked so wonderfully in the past, American business had great difficulty dropping the formula.

President Coolidge declared in the period between the two world wars that the business of America was business. America was the country where things worked. Whereas the Great Depression of the 1930s had made business executives look incompetent or selfish, the performance of business during the war looked positively heroic.[36] After the war, foreign firms seemed unlikely to generate much competition, considering the state of destruction of their countries. This attitude kept American business from reacting to the changes that were beginning to occur.

Thus, American business leaders often lost a sense of perspective. Technological advances were often ignored out of intellectual arrogance. Innovations such as the basic oxygen furnace and continuous casters were adopted and used to competitive advantage by steel companies in Europe and Japan long before they appeared in the United States. In 1948, three Americans working in the old Bell Laboratories won the Nobel Prize for the invention of the transistor. In 1953, Sony bought the rights to that transistor for less than $24,000 dollars and began their assault on American consumer electronics with a portable radio.

As long as it was imprisoned in the attitudes and methodologies of the previous era, business could not sustain adequate competitiveness or growth in the emerging epoch, regardless of its size and power. The lesson is that the force of epochal change must be accommodated regardless of the level of past success.

GOING FORWARD

Business leaders in every country are now beginning to understand that they are in the middle of something big. The proportions of the change are immense. An organization's response has to be equally imposing. Managers are starting to appreciate that they will not only have to get their organizations to take different actions but will also have to rethink management itself. All organizational decisions and processes will be affected. Taken together, the demands for organizational change will make up a new agenda, a need to move from one pattern of performance to another, from one kind of leadership role to another.

Resistance to change is a familiar problem, but recognizing that we are in the middle of a global transformation should be a powerful motivator for making change happen. The awareness that underlies the need for change is an essential beginning; it opens the opportunity for a wider vision. James Baughman, head of management development for General Electric, has said that where leaders eventually "get productivity leaps is in the minds and hearts of people."[37] While writing an insightful little book on leadership, Herman Miller Chairman Max DePree remarked that practice without belief is a forlorn existence.[38] Cardinal Newman went even further when he observed that a man would give his life for a dogma but would not budge for a conclusion. The implication is the same in each case: more than macroeconomic frameworks and industry analyses are needed to imagine and implement solutions for challenges occasioned by historic change.

There are many reasons for optimism. Change doesn't just "happen." It is created; it can be deliberate. After all, the energetic participation of internationalist leaders was the force that accelerated the development of the globalized economy. Similarly, the outcome of change, if it occurs within the proper strategic choices, can be a boom in productivity and innovation that will dwarf gains already obtained. This, in turn, will increase the availability and diversity of goods and services while providing a panorama of business opportunities not yet imagined. The potential for the improvement of human existence is staggering. Once again, however, to make all this occur requires more than understanding the global crosscurrents highlighted here. It also means having a game plan to make things happen, the subject of the remainder of this book.

3

Rising to the Occasion:
New Roles for New Times

Think like a man of action, act like a man of thought.
—Henri-Louis Bergson

Everyone's role perception tells you their assumptions
about how things are supposed to operate around
here. To reengineer a company those perceptions
have to be aligned with today's realities,
not wistful memories of yesterday.
Charles Geschke
President, Adobe Systems

In the 1990s and beyond, the major hurdle for managers will be their disidentification with the new era and with the new behaviors that are necessary to succeed in it. The way many of us manage today, the way many of us define ourselves as managers, is what led to success yesterday, but has also helped create the problems we now face—a consequence of the success itself.

Consider two questions: Given the quantum changes in market conditions and societal structures, is it reasonable for us to conclude that we can remain in our familiar, traditional roles as we manage our enterprises? Is it reasonable for us to decide that while our societies and businesses are being completely reshaped, we have the luxury of maintaining traditional habits, behaviors, strategies, and priorities as we attempt to guide our organizations through the unfamiliar turbulence going on around us?

These are not rhetorical questions. For the individual manager nothing may be more important than recognizing that the management roles that were fruitful in the past will not be effective as the modern era ends and a new era begins. If, as managers, we can prepare now to live in ways appropriate to and harmonious with the emerging era rather than the passing one, we will have a tremendous advantage. We will be all the more successful and able to prepare our enterprises for even greater success.

What AT&T executive vice president Bill Marx said to his people about the "new AT&T" has been voiced often in recent years in other industries: "I don't know about you, but I got the way I am through years of practice reinforced because it worked. Well, it may not work anymore. This is a very different company than the one most of us joined."

Not only is the company different; the *world* is different, too. Industrial capitalism, the mass production economy, and other aspects of business that have evolved since the eighteenth century carry with them a set of truisms about the way organizations should be run. Many of these assumptions are now being challenged, including the following:

- The cornerstones of business success are standardized and undifferentiated products (instead of segmentation and customization).

- Quality is best managed as assurance applied at the end of the process (instead of being designed in at the beginning).

- Demand is stable and predictable (as opposed to fast changing and erratic).

- Competition within the firm produces the most effective work force (versus the idea that cooperation within an organization is essential).

- Inflation will be around to bail us out of poor investments (despite the clear intention of central banks to avoid the hyperinflation of the 1970s).

- Raw national economic power can provide cover for lack of competitiveness in overseas markets (yet global economies level the playing field and make "value added" supreme).

- Most employees are clear on what it is they are supposed to do (the reality is that reorganizations and market turmoil have left people confused or uncommitted).

- The critical success factors for a business are tangible assets like size of facilities and number of employees (as opposed to intangibles like the creativity and intelligence of its work force).

The most pervasive truism may well be the master-servant idea, originally described by Aristotle and modified repeatedly to accommodate changes in the structure of society and business. Over the past few years, however, the employer-employee dichotomy—the one person invested with rights and privileges, the other with the burden of unquestioning obedience—has gradually been reshaped to diminish the traditional authority of "bosses," middle managers, and professionals.[1] No one today would seriously question the need for greater participation of everyone in an organization, with all moving to higher and higher levels of responsibility and performance. The question for the leader is how to accomplish this involvement within the framework of traditionally maintained roles. The answer is that it can't be done. Something has to give.

RESPONDING TO CHANGE

In 1987, in a sympathetic review of Tom Peters's newly released *Thriving on Chaos*, John Case wrote:

> Businesspeople feel in their gut that Peters has something to tell them.... Whether businesses want to do what Peters recommends, however, is another question entirely.... It is hard to convince anyone to do anything differently from the way they did it yesterday or the day before. Think about the reactions that often greet even the smallest managerial initiative: cynicism, foot-dragging, outright defiance.... And the obstacles aren't just inertia and insecurity; people may see no reason to try changing things. If the company's in trouble, they'll be too busy plugging holes (or looking for

new jobs). If business is good, why should they bother? Transforming even a small organization's patterns and routines can be a wrenching, threatening undertaking.[2]

Since Case wrote his comments, the world has convoluted further. The height of the crossbar has been raised. For many managers today, a tough fact of life is that the world is growing permanently and starkly different from the world they knew and where they expected to finish their careers. It is as if they were hired to play baseball in the major leagues, and with supreme effort they all developed into fantastic players with batting averages around .300. One day the manager shows up dribbling a basketball, announcing that the era of baseball is ending. To the players, his behavior might appear shocking and unfair. But if the manager reflects the real world, is it reasonable to assume that the players will succeed in the new era by putting in additional hours honing their batting and fielding skills, or by denying the realities of basketball hoops and man-to-man defense, or by hoping that speed on the base paths and a strong throwing arm will help them camouflage their deficiencies until retirement?

Ironically, such dramatic changes are not new; the Modern Age has consistently overturned the truths that it inherited from the past: The world is flat. What goes up must come down. One race is genetically superior to another. We came to obliterate these truths with new facts, new ideas. In this way, the modern era reflected Lewis Mumford's observation: "Every goal man reaches provides a new starting point, and the sum of all man's days is just the beginning."[3]

CURRENT WISDOM
ON PERFORMANCE

Even the so-called truths about the critical arena of individual performance are now being questioned. Traditionally, performance has been viewed as a function of two variables, ability and motivation. Expressed as a formula, P (performance) equals A (ability) times M (motivation), or $P = A \times M$.[4] Ability includes intelligence, talents, aptitudes, and skills. When managers talk about getting "back to the basics," they are talking about basic competencies. Motivation, on the other hand, is about desires, goals, interests, incentives, and needs. When we say someone is motivated, we usually mean he or she is ready to work vigorously toward some goal. We usually associate commitment with motivation as well, sometimes using the two words interchangeably. Despite the conventional perspective on performance, however, the clearest lesson from our research is that it is not useful to conceptualize performance as a function of ability and motivation only.

Consider ability. The CEO of a large urban hospital was delighted after successfully recruiting his number one choice to take over the vice presidency of nursing. The new manager had impeccable clinical credentials, a history of impressive turn-arounds of inefficient nursing units, and a reputation for innovation. During the first year, all went well. The nursing department reported impressive movement on internal efficiency (such as scheduling and meeting regulatory standards) and on stalled negotiations with the nurses' unions. The difficulties started when the CEO began to move away from the hospital's costly and sluggish multilayered functional management structure toward a decentralized product- and service-line design with an emphasis on cross-disciplinary self-managed teams. The nursing vice president was highly critical of the new structure, giving numerous explanations for why the results would be wasteful and chaotic. She repeatedly asserted that such approaches had failed in other hospitals where she had worked. She also reminded the CEO and other senior managers that she had been hired to clean up the nursing department and was doing that job capably and vigorously, which in fact she was. Since her reputation in the field gave her credibility with her colleagues (and with the nursing department, the largest department in the hospital), her reactions served to slowly undermine the CEO's efforts in building the new structure and culture. He eventually realized that the vice president of nursing was indeed innovative and effective, but only in her familiar turf of a hierarchical nursing department. Once the organizational mind-set shifted and she was no longer dealing only with nurses or only with an orderly chain of command, her "ability" became a liability.

There are other situations in which established ability can work counter to the organization's purposes. One chain of franchised retail computer outlets did some internal research and was puzzled to find that the more successful salespeople were those who had less experience in the store. Further probing resulted in an intriguing finding: young inexperienced salespeople listened attentively to customers and tried hard to accommodate their sometimes quirky desires. The more experience they accrued, the more arrogant they became. They tended to size up customers quickly and needed to hear just a few words before they "knew" exactly what was best for that person. They spent more time trying to sell the customers on their (the salespeople's) solutions than on developing solutions that fit the customers' needs.

Obviously, ability is critical for management performance. Since it does not guarantee high performance, however, we must ask, What is the contribution of motivation, that second factor? Thousands of articles in the organizational psychology literature agree that motivation, the effort one is willing to spend toward achieving some goal, is crucial to performance. Organizational psychologists and executives often speak of two types of motivation. One is *extrinsic*, a motivation due to external incentives such as pay, recognition, or promotion. The other is *intrinsic*, a motivation due to internal variables such as personal work ethic, an interest in the task, or the excitement in learning new skills.

Motivation involves tenacity and persistence. It is about trying harder to attain something. If ability is held constant in the $P = A \times M$ equation, we assume that greater motivation yields greater performance. For example, if paying more attention to someone results in that person's being more productive, it is because, everything else being equal, the individual was somehow motivated to greater productivity by the special treatment.

On the other hand, we all know competent people who work hard—some are even workaholics—but whose performance is shaky. We know men and women who have all the "fire in the belly" one could imagine, but they still fall short on their numbers. We are saddened to speak of a diligent manager for whom it must be said: "His company outgrew him." The most painful dilemma we may face as managers is what to do with a dedicated loyal employee whose performance is not up to par. What all this suggests is that motivation alone, ability alone, or even a motivation-ability interaction will not explain performance.

We are reminded of a sixty-two-year-old CEO of a $70 million company, a parts supplier to some of the major industrial firms in the United States. He decided that he would spend the final three years of his career overhauling his organization. He understood that decentralizing and eliminating hierarchy in the firm would create massive changes and conflicts and would necessitate tremendous energy on his part to overcome a forty-year-old anachronistic corporate culture. At the time, we were impressed with his determination and vigor because he didn't have to do any of this. Three years before retirement, esteemed by the board and the community, he could have bided his time in peace. Yet as he told us, he "had" to do it because it was the only "right" thing to do if he wanted to leave his firm positioned for the rest of the decade and beyond.

Was the man motivated? Yes, indeed. Ability? He had more than thirty years' experience in the business, twelve of them as CEO. He was recognized in the industry for his competence and visionary thinking and served by invitation on several industry councils. His bottom-line track record was solid in a tough competitive nuts-and-bolts industry. On top of that, he called in the services of one of the nation's most reputable consulting firms to help him guide the transition.

Two years later, he was gone, forced into early retirement by the board of directors. He had set in motion a process the board had initially endorsed but one which he proved utterly incapable of directing. Insiders said that he seemed paralyzed in the face of unfolding events. There were times when he apparently "knew" the right action to take and wanted to do it, but always stopped short. The dysfunctional chaos that emerged in response to his leadership vacuum seriously jeopardized the company's survival. He had to be removed. Obviously, ability and motivation, as traditionally viewed, are not always sufficient for success and peak performance.

Accuracy of Role Perception

The missing variable in the equation is an accuracy of role perception. Increasingly, the failure to boost or change performance is due neither to a lack of motivation nor to ability but rather to an inaccurate reading of the roles that need to be enacted to confront today's realities. To rephrase our opening point, successful management roles for the coming era will not be the same as those that led to success in the era we are leaving behind. This shift compounds the difficulty in assessing accurately the role a manager needs to play. Nonetheless, the proper formula for creating performance is this:

$$\text{Performance} = \text{Ability} \times \text{Motivation} \times \text{Accuracy of Role Perception}$$

Although we do not intend the use of a formula to imply a mechanical precision or scientific exactness in predicting performance, expressing the constructs in this way serves a purpose. The multiplication signs indicate that the effects of ability, motivation, and role perception are noncompensating: a high score in one dimension can't compensate for a low score in another. In the extreme, if both ability and motivation were a 10 and accuracy of role perception were a 0, performance would be wiped out.

There is an overarching element in the accuracy of role perception: the individual manager *sees himself or herself as an agent of change in an environment of new and emerging realities.* Accuracy means getting a sense of today's pressing upheavals while energizing a readiness to respond to them boldly and unequivocally. The people we have in mind as effective change agents believe—in fact, know—that their personal responsibility is to plan and act proactively in the face of these challenges. The extensive and growing literature on mastering change, transformational leadership, and similar topics evidences consensus on the meaning and necessity for accuracy of role perception.[5]

Findings from Our Research on Accuracy of Role Perception

In defining the characteristics of accuracy of role perception, we rely in large part on research we have conducted during the past few years. In one study, Oren Harari and Linda Mukai interviewed executives in a variety of industries and asked them to identify specifically their most effective, promotable middle managers and their least effective, nonpromotable middle managers.[6] Then they asked the executives what made these effective and ineffective managers stand out, and followed up with interviews and observations of the managers themselves. Finally, they cataloged the differences between the two groups of middle managers.

The results showed that experience, education, and motivation did not differentiate the two groups. The most important differentiating factor was what the researchers then labeled "role of the manager." This factor included attitudes about change, attention, power, coaching, and responsibility, each of which is a component of the idea of being an agent of change.

At about the same time Harari and Mukai were beginning their research, Nicholas Imparato conducted a series of in-house studies and workshops with private and public sector groups.[7] In addition to supporting the findings of Harari and Mukai, Imparato's data suggest five more attributes that bear on the issue of how people see their roles as agents of change: attitudes toward expertise, fear, and entrepreneurism, as well as a sense of balance and of continuity. Imparato's study also revealed three additional factors that reflected the different role perceptions of effective and ineffective managers: demonstrating emotional maturity, providing the long view, and standing for an idea. Combining the results of both studies, we now can examine each of the attributes that generate accuracy of role perception. They are presented in abbreviated form in Table 3.1.

■ *Embracing change.* In our research, less-effective managers did not like change. They sought predictability, order, and stability. Many believed that turbulence in their firms was temporary or the fault of senior management, and that they should wait until "things settle down" before tackling big problems. In contrast, effective managers recognized that turbulence, flux, and ambiguity are facts of life and that the environment will

Table 3.1. Factors Determining Accuracy of Role Perception.

Factors	How Effective Managers View the Factors
Embracing Change	See change as presenting opportunities.
Attending to external realities	Focus attention on external issues, customers, and suppliers (versus internal organization).
Creating Power	See formal authority and power as distinct from each other. Managers create power by their actions and decisions.
Promoting a coaching style	Encourage challenging the system and demonstrating self-reliance.
Expanding job responsibilities	Continuously reshape job and attendant responsibilities.
Developing expertise	See role as developing experts and expertise throughout the organization.
Driving out fear	Are committed to reducing fear that enervates and thwarts change.
Exhibiting readiness for an entrepreneurial environment	Strive constantly to help motivate and enable everyone to act as an owner of the business, through both leadership styles and policy.
Keeping balance	Are able to recognize what changes have considerable consequence versus marginal impact.
Maintaining a sense of continuity	Are flexible enough to connect the past and present.
Demonstrating emotional maturity	Understand what the organization needs and are ready to do it, putting aside personal agenda and habits.
Providing the long view	Are able to provide context and a broad perspective, complete with hard assessments.
Standing for an idea	Project an unequivocal and consistent message about what is important.

never "settle down." Many were energized by these conditions because they saw them as opportunities. They said they would soon be bored if life were predictable and stable.

■ *Attending to external realities.* The less-effective managers focused their attention and calendar time primarily on the routine of the internal organization. Their memos and meetings revolved around budget variances, paper flow, procedures, and personnel. They were hypersensitive to shifts in company politics. To the extent that the effective managers attended to the internal organization, they were more concerned with how to speed it up and debureaucratize it. In addition, much of their attention, including that directed at meetings and memos, was focused on external issues such as shifts in markets and technology. Many took it on themselves to schedule regular chunks of time with customers and suppliers.

■ *Creating power.* The less-effective managers believed that their own power to get things done was severely limited and that real power was held only by people in top management. They said things like, "It doesn't pay to try to get things done until senior management gets its act together." They also believed that the power they do have comes with their job title and position on the organization chart. The effective managers saw a distinction between formal authority and power. They recognized that top management had more of the former, but they believed that power, like respect, is earned rather than given out. These managers viewed power as the ability to influence people and get things done, a perception that means anyone can have power. Several stated that managers create power by their actions and decisions, not by holding a job title.

■ *Promoting a coaching style.* Less-effective managers did not spend as much time coaching their people as did their more-effective counterparts; further, the groups differed on what the coaching should be about. Less-effective managers saw coaching in terms of delegation: giving people well-defined tasks and following up carefully. Effective managers wanted people to think of new ways of doing things. They encouraged people to "challenge the system" with an eye to improving efficiency of operations, cost-containment, and revenue-line enhancement. Once they outlined the boundaries of fundamental do's and don'ts, these managers got out of the way.

■ *Expanding job responsibilities.* Less-effective managers saw their primary responsibility as meeting the demands of their bosses, their job descriptions, and their annual goals. They assumed that it was up to someone else (usually their boss) to expand their job responsibilities and goals. When this expansion did occur, several complained that they were overburdened. When it did not occur, they complained that they were in a dead-end position. In contrast, the effective managers did not wait for someone to expand their jobs. They envisioned opportunities and accomplishments and thus looked for—and grabbed—new responsibilities. They were constantly thinking about what they could do to make things better. In effect, they themselves reshaped their jobs continually.

■ *Creating expertise.* Less-effective managers knew the importance of expertise but were "too busy" to grow (or hire) it; often, they saw responsibility for developing expertise as someone else's job. They tended to discourage curiosity, calling their actions "keeping people focused," and were inclined to diminish efforts to keep people abreast of developments in both the company and the industry. In dealing with lower levels and other departments, they saw their role as moderating information flow, with the assumption that filtered information represented what people needed to know in order to do "most things right."

In contrast, effective managers saw their roles as developing experts and expertise throughout the organization. They sought to promote specific skills and "deep talent" in everything from computer knowledge to business literacy. They encouraged people to search out applications of new technologies and promoted mentoring and education programs to ensure professional vitality. They concentrated on getting people to understand the business. They emphasized the importance of widening information flow and building internal systems to leverage more knowledge throughout the organization.

■ *Driving out fear*. Less-effective managers worked from a philosophy that said that these are times that separate the men from the boys and that fear, with the possible exception of greed, is the best motivator. Intimidation, rudeness and abruptness, broken promises, a rush to judgment, and a general tone that implied the workplace is a jungle were elements of the ineffective manager's style. Ironically, even as they used fear to "motivate" others, the less-effective managers often demonstrated their own fears by dampening others' ideas—especially when those ideas differed from their own or from standard operating procedures.

Effective managers acknowledged the corrosive effect of fear.[8] While they kept high standards and a sense of urgency, the top priority they saw was reducing the fear of challenging the process on behalf of organizational goals. They were comfortable in working with individuals whose ideas and value-adds were quite different from their own. They also saw part of their role as defusing people's more common personal fears regarding confrontation, loss of influence, and being left behind by technology or organizational changes.[9] They used a variety of techniques, including open-door policies, supportive feedback, and training programs; but most important was their prevailing perception that the leader must be committed to reducing fear that might enervate the workplace and thwart change.

■ *Exhibiting readiness for an entrepreneurial environment*. In some manner, this factor cut through all the others we found. Ineffective and effective managers alike wanted initiative and creativity to characterize their work associates. They all spoke of their employees' need to "think and act like businesspeople." Yet managers who were described as less effective typically shied away from sharing income statement or balance sheet information with other levels and departments. They guarded closely the processes used to allocate resources and ensured that decisions about alliance opportunities and results of marketing or competitive analysis studies were thoroughly scrubbed before being shared.

Effective managers looked on their role as one dedicated to developing a culture in which everyone not only had the information to make decisions and take risks but also was compensated for doing so. These managers recognized that this approach flew in the face of traditional compensation schemes based on the wage-labor model. Gain sharing, bonus plans, and incentive pay were popular compensation techniques used by effective managers. They also organized work to encourage ownership and accountability by the group doing the work—for example, in variations of self-directed work teams. They saw their job as demanding constant effort to find and strengthen ways everyone in the organization could be enabled and motivated to act like an owner of the business.

■ *Keeping balance.* Less-effective managers frequently did not distinguish between changes that had a great deal of consequence from those that promised little impact. Often the intention was to "play it safe" while appearing to be busy. For example, one director saw switching to a different vendor as a high-impact change even as he kept the same unresponsive distribution channel. In general, less-effective managers tended to fiddle around the edges of a problem, psychologically hanging out in the old familiar places.

Effective managers differentiated between high- and low-impact interventions. They recognized that high-impact change often involved a restructuring of operations, not just manipulation of superficial forms. For example, effective managers were reluctant to layer new technology on old systems, generally calling for process overhaul first.

■ *Maintaining a sense of continuity.* Less-effective managers operated strictly in the here and now. They did not demonstrate an appreciation of the impact the past was having on the present. Their interest in how prior conditions (markets, corporate culture, investment decisions, leadership styles) might have influenced today's organizational processes was limited. In contrast, effective managers thought it was important to connect past circumstances to the current situation with which people were contending.[10] Simultaneously, they were generally able to separate appreciating the past from clinging to it. Finally, they could explain prior circumstances without rationalizing and justifying past errors or missed opportunities in a way that might create a "victim" mentality.

These ten factors make up the vital "agent of change" component of accuracy of role perception. As mentioned, we identified three additional ways that accuracy of role perception can be defined beyond what is directly involved in serving as an agent of change. These additional factors complement the need for leaders to serve as agents of change and embellish the idea of accuracy of role perception. Although each factor has a change agency element within it, the final attributes were judged to represent something more as well. In general, they dealt with steadfastness and resoluteness in vision and style.

■ *Demonstrating emotional maturity.* There were two components to this factor. First, less-effective managers had difficulty maintaining a sense of composure during stressful periods and difficult transitions. Their perceptions of their roles as managers were often distorted and overwhelmed by their immediate personal needs. Second, they were also very turf and status conscious. They saw little value in mingling with people in "lower" levels, or in pitching in to perform either "menial" tasks (answering the phone, stuffing envelopes) or nontraditional tasks (going into the field to help a salesperson make a sale) during a crunch period.

Effective managers projected a combination of urgency, passion, composure, and confidence during tough times. Unlike their less-effective counterparts, they did not shy away from working collegially with anyone (regardless of department or level), or doing whatever tasks were required in order to get the job done. Some of the more-effective managers voiced the attitude that their primary tasks would be defined by "What would the customer be happy to pay me to do now?"

■ *Providing the long view.* Less-effective managers, even those who talked about "vision," seemed unable to provide a coherent, practical "big picture" context for themselves or their colleagues. They doubted the value of providing shape and overview to the events that were occurring. Effective managers also talked about vision, but their approach was to make and share best bets about where the world was going, where the organization ought to go, and how all that might affect what people do daily. Effective managers felt concerned about helping others avoid terminal vision and managerial myopia. Accordingly, they frequently invited discussions that revolved around hard assessments of change in technology, markets, and the overall business environment.

■ *Standing for an idea.* Less-effective managers were unaware of what values they represented, short of "making plan" or "meeting budget." There was little coherence in the pattern of decisions they made. On one hand, they seemed to be in favor of everything—cost-reduction, quality, innovation, service—but their decisions lacked either consistency or continuity. Indeed, they often took contradictory positions, depending on the political circumstances. They were susceptible to fads and programs of the month.

Effective managers defined themselves as standing for one or two particular ideas—self-management or speed, for example—and they were tough, persistent, and consistent in their subsequent decisions in order to give expression to those ideas. They were also eager to enroll others in the same point of view. They went to great lengths to avoid acting expediently or appearing to be opportunistic.

In summary, accuracy begins when we acknowledge that the tumultuous changes we see around us demand new behaviors and actions, a new way of defining our role as manager. Without the appropriate role perception, performance is depressed, ability and motivation notwithstanding, because managers do not take on the responsibility to act in ways that are in harmony with the demands of the emerging epoch. Without accuracy of role perception, all the advice and how-to's in the world have little impact. An inaccurate role perception explains why so many managers who attend seminars and listen to management tapes can't translate their knowledge into higher performance back on the job. Additionally, without proper role perception, managers find it difficult to accumulate the right skills and capacities and to channel their motivation in the right direction, let alone to influence the ability and motivation of others toward the proper goals.

The Devil in the Detail

Let us go back to the sixty-two-year-old CEO of the industrial products firm described earlier. A year and a half into the change process, he invited us to come in and provide an independent opinion about why the process had stalled. He was genuinely baffled. As far as he was concerned, all the pieces were in place: the vision (he had articulated it well), the awareness of why change was important (this had been made public to the 100-person management team and the 800-person exempt work force), the desire for change (most managers ranged from open to sympathetic to passionate; only a few were openly skeptical, and besides, the CEO supported change), the capabilities for change (the CEO rated the majority of the managers as above average to excellent), and the tools for change (the consultants had provided a series of training workshops, decision models, and action blueprints). Why then was there so little progress? Why was there so much backbiting and hostility?

Since we had not been intimately involved with the change process in this company, we gave the CEO and the five managers who reported directly to him two questions to ponder as they prepared for our arrival. The questions were these:

1. Why don't things in this company change the way we want them to?

2. What prevents us from leaving the past behind and moving on to confront the realities of the future?

Here were the responses:

- There is a lack of strong, effective top leadership. (This was stated by two senior managers. When we gently pointed out that our assumption was that the six of them were top leadership, there was an embarrassed silence, followed by the next confession.)

- Basically, we wait for Bill (the CEO) or the consultants to fix things and tell us what to do. And when that doesn't happen, we don't do anything except get cynical.

- We avoid tough issues and difficult decisions because we avoid confrontation. We're not comfortable in challenging business as usual. We do not yell "foul" when one of us does something that does not fit with the new culture. Bill doesn't challenge us and we don't challenge each other. We don't even challenge our direct reports the way we ought to.

- None of us are living the new culture and processes. We "support" it by giving it lip service, but basically we attend to it when we have time, which means we spend most of our time doing the old work. Our people do the same. The message is that the change is an add-on to our work; it is not our real work. The message is that this new stuff is "nice to do" but it's not expected, certainly not vital.

- We do a lousy job coaching and helping our people in their new roles. We follow up on their progress in the old system, not toward the new one. We are reluctant to accept responsibility for reinforcing the new culture with our direct reports and we don't hold them accountable for results.

- We still tolerate managers who are inflexible, territorial, and coplike. We tolerate managers who don't let go and who don't believe their people are creative. The message is that we're not really serious.

- We've hired and promoted a few managers over the past few months who are terrible role models and are not committed to our new organization. Again, that sends the wrong message.

- There's no incentive for risk taking and ground-breaking performance. Our measurements and rewards are still based on old responsibilities. So is our budgeting process.

- We do not support and protect the middle managers who are cutting across departmental lines and trying new things.

- There have been several small but important victories over the past few months—people who have succeeded in working together to make changes and improvements in line with what we've been learning. But we're not playing them up and we're not recognizing the people who have done it.

- We're not showing enough emotion. We don't truly agonize over cost overruns or poor quality or botched customer transactions. We're not showing enough impatience when we see people doing the same old routines. We don't show that we're thrilled over small victories. We're not seen as fanatics on this change process.

- We seem more comfortable with evolutionary than with revolutionary. We're not personally taking the bull by the horns.

The common thread through these remarks was easy to see. Over the span of two days, the six senior managers, including the CEO, came to recognize with excruciating detail that their conclusions illustrated a counterproductive role perception. Bluntly, they failed to take on personal responsibility for being an agent of change. They also failed to exemplify the other elements of accuracy of role perception that we have discussed. As long as they held on to a role perception that failed to identify with the needs of the emerging environment, and protected it with abdication or blame gaming or other excuses, all their abilities and motivations were not sufficient to carry them through. In a more general sense, they had shown that they still identified with an out-of-date mind-set, usually referred to as managerialism.

MOVING AWAY
FROM MANAGERIALISM

Managerialism represents the belief system behind the prevailing practice of traditional management. It is an ideology that grew in the twentieth century to become the most influential force in how we view organizations, how we achieve performance, and what we should expect of those in positions of responsibility. It developed simultaneously with the restructuring of American society from an agrarian economy to an industrial economy at the end of the last century.

As the methodology behind bureaucracy, managerialism brought value to commercial organizations in its time. It diminished the corrosive effects of nepotism, cronyism, and privilege. It established merit as the criterion for success. Competence replaced arbitrary decisions. Working within the hierarchical structure, the managerialist mind focused on financial controls and defining the work of others. It led through a chain of command, by obedience and functional authority. Because it was rational, managerialism encouraged the discovery of management principles. It fostered planning and forecasting techniques.

At the same time, managerialism promoted an elite. It emphasized the distinction between members of a managerial class and others, including employees and customers. It isolated value-added knowledge within the ranks of senior management and corporate staff. It generated a culture where managers presumed to speak not only for themselves but also for other constituencies, particularly shareholders. It also promoted the value of generalists whose talent was in working the bureaucracy rather than in providing understanding of the product or customer needs.

Now, however, managerialism is exhausted.[11] It has degenerated to a set of operating principles and business priorities that no longer fit the current stage of social and business development. In a world where controls are increasingly decentralized, managerialism is the ideology of the power to control others. It emphasizes size at a time when scale appears less relevant than innovation. When high service, quality, and customer satisfaction are the price of entry into a market, managerialism permits poor coordination in handling customer needs. It promotes "me first" individualism at a time when productivity depends on teams and alliances. Its systems are reactive when the marketplace demands being first. Its bureaucracy creates high real costs in unnecessary overhead and inventory at a time when the environment is sensitive to price. The organization it creates is oriented toward mass production and mass consumption in an environment that requires "agile production" and customized flexibility. It orients managers' attention toward internal procedures when quantum changes are occurring externally. It emphasizes prediction and planning, even as planning premises are upended daily. It focuses on analysis when speed, pilots, and proaction are required. Managerialism is grounded in a search for order and stability in a business world that is becoming more unruly and ephemeral.

The deficiencies of managerialism are already apparent in the commonplace distinctions made between the role of a manager and the role of a leader. In the last ten years, much of the writing on how to run organizations has stressed managing less and leading more. There are dozens of prescriptions outlining the distinction between a manager's behavior and a leader's behavior. A manager controls, a leader builds commitment; a manager sanctions, a leader inspires; a manager administers, a leader creates; a manager focuses on the routine, a leader focuses on vision.

At the core, the real challenge of accuracy in role perception is to stimulate leadership that can bring optimism to fruition in organizations. For this to occur, alternatives to the premises of managerialism must be offered. New management styles won't develop from only a rejection of what exists today. The leader who is ready to confront the challenges and opportunities of the emerging epoch must have something else, a frame of reference, something to work toward.

JUMPING THE CURVE

There is an evolutionary flow to history to be sure. One stage builds on another; each creates precedence for the next. Yet as we have seen, change does not always evolve as a smooth continuum. History has shown us several periods characterized by sharp breaks with the past and entirely new sets of realities and demands. As participants in an epochal transition, we are in the midst of such a period today. For the leader, historical breaks require a leap from the conventional into the untried. If epochal transitions were part of one smooth continuum of change, we could argue that conventional managerialism would require little more than continuous improvement to ensure effectiveness. This is not the case. Epochal transitions show discontinuity with the past even as they are dependent on it; the world that evolved from Gutenberg's printing presses became fundamentally different from the world that had existed before his invention. For business leaders, historical breaks require a dramatic shift in the very premises of how organizations are managed. Leaders today are challenged to deal with new realities in ways that are radically and qualitatively different from anything they have known. They are asked to "jump the curve."

Jumping the curve means leaving one stage of development for another, leaving one pattern of behavior for another. Each stage or pattern is based on a different set of priorities and assumptions about where the world is going and how organizations must function. For both the individual and the organization, jumping the curve involves leaving the comfort and familiarity of the old world of conventional wisdom, processes, traditions, leadership styles, and products. If that were not intimidating enough, those who do jump will find that the next curve does not even exist yet. It is not already "out there" like a treasure chest to open or a Shangri-La destination ready for us to find. In fact, it is being created by the leaders who are in the very process of guiding their organizations through "midair"—the gap between the requirements of today's fading epoch and the demands of the new era that is still unsettled and in evolution.

In the remainder of this book we offer four organizing principles that will help leaders accommodate—indeed, capitalize on—the moment. Our goal is to present leaders with tools that will help them facilitate and accelerate their organization's capacity to jump the curve, and thereby truncate the time it takes to move successfully from one "side" to the other. Leaders who engage this role will be best able to position their organizations to confront and thrive in the emerging business environment.

Each organizing principle represents a way to integrate the processes and goals of the organization as it jumps the curve. It is the basis on which leaders can pull together the resources of the organization even as the world demands the process of disorganization. An organizing principle is more than a program, technique, or policy. It is so fundamental that once implemented, dozens of other decisions will already be made. It is a strategic choice, ratcheting through all aspects of the organization, affecting all functions, all levels, and all processes. If properly adopted, it will affect the way leaders structure business units, choose investments, design compensation programs, conduct recruitment and training, and select marketing initiatives. Nothing in the organization will be untouched.

THE FOUR ORGANIZING PRINCIPLES

Jumping the curve first requires organizations to shift their priorities from stabilizing to innovating. That is, the first priority is to recognize that innovation and creativity rather than controls, order, and predictability are the key dynamics needed to achieve market leadership and profitability. The dilemma for most organizations is that they need to look toward tomorrow's products, markets, and technologies even as they cope with today's challenges. Often this will mean leaving behind today's successful products and services in pursuit of tomorrow's opportunities. Often, too, this will mean creating markets rather than trying to anticipate them. Consequently, the first organizing principle is this: *Look a customer ahead.*

The emphasis in the new work environment is on information and knowledge. The "balance sheet" perspective, where the bigger organization is better and more tangible assets mean more strength, is being replaced by the perspective in which an organization's "intangible" assets—collaborative brainpower of employees, managers, partners, and stakeholders—are the most crucial component of sustainable competitive advantage. Jumping the curve thus requires a change in priorities, from building mass and size to growing organizational competence. Successful organizations will see themselves as "brains" or reservoirs of the accumulated intelligence of their employees and business partners—focused toward best serving their customers. The "brains" metaphor is the foundation for the second organizing principle: *Build the company around the software and build the software around the customer.*

Traditional perspectives on information flow and control fragment the organization with mechanisms like hierarchy, "need to know," departmental boundaries, manager as "conduit" of information, and policies. The new organizational forms unleash information flow, blur vertical and horizontal boundaries, and encourage initiative and diversity in decision making. Within that turbulent context, the challenge for the leader becomes how to maintain organizationwide unity, focus, and control. Where open collaboration and diversity replace tight supervision and insular thinking, the approach shifts from fragmenting to cohering. The organization that jumps the curve must harness the diversity of its collective talents, backgrounds, and locales with one cohesive set of values and priorities. The way this is done must generate an organizationwide trust that comes from a sense of justice consistent with the organization's stated ideals. Thus, the third principle is this: *Ensure that those who live the values and ideals of the organization are the most rewarded and the most satisfied.*

In the traditional perspective of commerce, the vendor's obligation to the customer is met when the vendor meets formal contractual obligations associated with the sale of a product or service to the customer. In the new perspective, this sort of legalistic relationship is no longer sufficient. Organizations that will succeed in the future are those that have developed both the structure and culture to support an organizationwide responsibility not merely to sell a product or service but also to ensure that the customer will be fully and completely satisfied. The attitude thus moves from sufficing to guaranteeing. By insisting on customers' total satisfaction, the newer perspective builds organizations around *enlightened* self-interest as opposed to the adversarial self-aggrandizement of the managerialist era. An outgrowth of this perspective is a renewed recognition of personal responsibility to one's customers as the bedrock of sustained customer loyalty. Instead of vague statements about excellence or convoluted measurements about quality, businesses that jump the curve will organize operations, processes, and decisions around this notion of customer-sensitive responsibility. Hence, the fourth organizing principle: *Treat the customer as the final arbiter of service and product quality by offering an unconditional guarantee of complete satisfaction.*

Beginning with the next chapter, each organizing principle is discussed within a pair of chapters. The even-numbered chapter in each pair provides the intellectual, strategic, and utilitarian rationales for the organizing principle. The corresponding odd-numbered chapter provides a set of specific initiatives the leader can use to implement effectively the organizing principle under question.

One caveat: we make no claim that what we propose is the end point of organizational transformation. Indeed, if history is any guide, the creation of the postmodern organization will be a messy, trial-and-error process over an extended time. It may demand two steps forward and one step back, but we have no choice. Many business leaders, regardless of their past successes, have already come to the same conclusion.

Today's dynamics reflect the crossings our society experiences as it moves from one age to another. These crossings unquestionably affect values and ideas about the most fundamental matters. They affect the premises and assumptions, the patterns of thought and the mental models we use to see the world, including our world of work. By influencing our worldview, they shape our image about ourselves and what we can do.

Intellectual discomfort and spiritual disquiet, current consequences of epochal transformation, spur leaders to seek approaches that can set the way to a future where all corporate constituencies—shareholders, employees, customers, and society—are enriched by the experience. We see substance in a handful of organizing principles that reflect broader trends and indicate specific action initiatives. These are now our focus.

PART TWO

Making the Leap

Strategic Choices for the Emerging Epoch

4

The Innovation Imperative

*There is no happiness that is secure and
nothing that does not change.*
—Saint Teresa of Avila

*Everyday the world turns upside down on someone
who thought they were sitting on top of it.*
—Glen Tullman
President, CCC Information Services

The underlying drivers of change today—globalization and technology—compel an innovation imperative. Globalization breeds diversity in the marketplace, innumerable competitors, more choices for the customer, and a wealth of new opportunities. Technology introduces speed as a basis for competition and pressures organizations to dismantle processes that were formerly effective. Contributing further to this turmoil, the organization's critical constituencies—customers, shareholders, partners, managers, and employees—are simultaneously more informed and more demanding.

Innovative energy today is apparent in every domain of business life. MCI's Dick Liebhaber estimates that two new significant technology and product developments occur every day in his industry. Every year sees the introduction of ten thousand new software packages and sixteen thousand new grocery and drugstore products. Technologies that were startling innovations yesterday, such as personal computers and phone-fax-answering machines, are rapidly becoming low-margin commodities.

Processes are altered as well. Factory designs are often outdated in fewer than five years. Intel discovered that an assembly design it had under construction was out-of-date before it was even completed, and a major food retailer recently saw its brand-new 300,000 square foot warehouse made virtually obsolete by new outsourcing possibilities and an electronic data interchange (EDI) system linked to suppliers.

Paralleling the compression of product and process life cycles is the rapid life-cycle shrinkage of organizations themselves. According to a study done by Royal Dutch/Shell, the average lifetime of the largest industrial organizations is fewer than forty years, roughly half the lifetime of a human being.[1] Harvard's Michael Jensen observes that the numerous economic dislocations of the recent past have left many organizations today marked by "excess capacity, and—ultimately—downsizing and exit."[2]

The death knell of organizations is being sounded at an ever-quickening pace. Seventy percent of the largest industrial firms in the United States and Europe in 1955 no longer exist; 40 percent of the 1980 Fortune 500 have disappeared through acquisition, breakup, or bankruptcy.[3] Divisions and subsidiaries are being liquidated regularly; witness NCR's abrupt disappearance as an independent business unit in the AT&T family in the fall of 1993. Even the organizational turnaround cycle has shrunk. The late Bill McGowan, founder of MCI, once noted that the cycle of American business—of rags to riches to rags again—that used to take seventy years now occurs in fewer than five.[4] An even more extreme example is Compaq Computer's champ-to-chump-to-champ changes that took place within an eighteen-month period beginning in 1990.

And yet, as companies die, many more are born. In the 1980s a huge surge in startup entrepreneurial activity began and is continuing today. As the aggressive use of technology in navigation allowed a tiny country like Portugal to dominate global exploration in the fifteenth century, technology today reduces global barriers to entry in many industries. Smart technology and smart global outsourcing allow many small upstart companies to throw their hats into the international ring and be taken seriously as international competitors.

Entirely new industries emerge daily. Just as the beginning of the Modern Age stimulated the exploration of uncharted oceans and continents (historian E. R. Chamberlain described this period as an age of experiment), today's uncharted waters include the cyberspace of Internet, America Online, WELL (Whole Earth 'Lectronic Link), Genie, CompuServe, and Prodigy. Most analysts agree with Harvard's Jensen when he says that "fundamental technological, political, regulatory and economic forces are radically changing the worldwide competitive environment. . . . The scope and pace of the changes over the past two decades qualify this period as a modern industrial revolution, and I predict it will take decades for these forces to be fully worked out in the worldwide economy."[5]

In this kind of environment it is organizational suicide to focus primarily on the routine of today's requirements. As many vendors have found, efficient production and distribution count for naught if the product is becoming obsolete, irrelevant, or unexciting to the customer. Change comes with such rapidity that businesses must anticipate tomorrow's needs today because the distinction between today and tomorrow is increasingly blurred. Innovation as a way of life, central to how an organization conducts itself, becomes fundamental to corporate survival. It is the primary requirement in jumping the curve.

By *innovation*, we mean something other than the meaning historically applied in industry. True, the tremendous growth in the world economy from the late 1940s to the 1960s was fueled by American-led innovations throughout the emerging global economy. Yet there was a sense of predictability about new products. New car models, as an example, were introduced once a year in September. Innovation was viewed as an orderly process with a steady, nearly linear set of expectations. Companies and organizations had time to "groove" their methodologies and operations, even if they were imperfect or wanting. Bottlenecks and cumbersome procedures were layered on processes that already existed. Costs of inefficiencies were passed on to customers. Today, of course, such processes would lead to quick disaster. Today, change is frequently discontinuous and unpredictable, often reducing carefully developed sales and cost projections to the status of wish lists. Innovation in the context of jumping the curve refers less to a plan or procedure than to the organization's ability to capitalize on constant turbulence. To add to the pressure, total quality and turbo speed are today natural adjuncts to innovation. Thus, Motorola can combine its adherence to Six Sigma quality standards (99.9997 percent defect free) with dramatic reductions in cycle time (for example, from three weeks to two days in turnaround time for orders of customized pagers), even as it churns out four new or improved products every day.

Obviously, cost-sensitive operations are important to any organization's survival. However, in chaotic times and crowded marketplaces, innovation forms the essence of sustainable competitive advantage. In the unfolding epoch, successful organizations will be those that can *continually differentiate* themselves in the marketplace. The most important strategic questions that any company must confront today revolve around the organization's ability to innovate quickly and continuously—to wit:

- How are we different from other organizations?

- In what unique ways do we add value to customers?

- What are we doing today to ensure that we remain different, unique, and special in the future?

In the remainder of this chapter and in Chapter Five, we describe the organizational principle that can be used to orient leaders to the task of addressing these questions and meeting the new challenges. Put simply, the organizing principle is this: *Look a customer ahead.* The words are self-explanatory, but their implications for organizations are profound. To introduce the idea of looking a customer ahead, let us move to the boardroom of insurance broker Sedgwick James.

SCANNING
TOMORROW'S HORIZON

In July of 1993, six managers from around the country are in the San Francisco corporate offices talking about improving Sedgwick's service quality. Suddenly they are hit broadside with a message they never anticipated. President Don Morford is challenging not only their conception of quality, but the entire service mix of the company as well. He agrees that quality improvements in current services and operations are called for, but argues that what is defined as quality today within Sedgwick might be undermined by advances in information technology that could eliminate 30 percent of Sedgwick's market within five years.

"Customers would just as soon eliminate brokers," he explains. "They see middlemen as a value-detracting cost factor. Right now, two groups of people want us out of business: the client and the insurance company. Technology will give them the means to do exactly that. We can spend all the time we want on improving current services, but if those services become obsolete, we are doing little more than improving the quality of buggy whips."

A few managers are skeptical. Their group sales are solid, as are the net written premium volume and net income figures of the company as a whole. But Morford is relentless. He begins to tick off potential lost chunks of business, suggesting that client institutions in the future will use their own computer power to scan a comprehensive database and select an optimal insurance package for themselves, in the process cutting out as many people as possible in the distribution chain.

Warming to his theme of technology-as-competition, Morford cites an unpublished study that shows that airlines are concerned that teleconferencing technology will be so effective by the next decade that significantly fewer businesspeople will need to fly as often as they do today. Further, he notes, travel agents are beginning to realize that advances in information technology are such that many of their current services can be duplicated by cost-conscious customers who can access the same database and come to their own informed conclusions. Catching on to Morford's argument, one manager observes that overnight mail carriers have already lost significant domestic market share to technologies such as facsimile transmission and on-line services. Another manager chimes in, pointing out that mass retailers are already cutting out middlemen by installing electronic data interchanges (EDI) that connect point-of-sale information directly with suppliers. Inevitably, the discussion homes in on a sobering reality: from EDI and shared databases to phone and television retailing, the trends lean relentlessly toward diminishing the distance between vendor and customer. For a broker, or any middleman, the time bomb is ticking.

Morford's charge is clear: if responsiveness and quality are to mean anything, they must include responsiveness and quality for tomorrow's customer, who will have entirely new demands and an increasing number of choices. Morford is encouraging his people to look a customer ahead because the alternative holds no place for today's insurance broker; even high-quality obsolete services are still obsolete. At the end of the discussion, an energized group begins to redefine Sedgwick's services to include fast, customized solutions to client's emerging business problems, new kinds of value-adding information, new specialized niche services, and significant improvements in personalized customer service across all Sedgwick offices.

From the vantage point of Morford's vision, the bottom line was clear: Sedgwick James must embrace new market realities—providing services that tomorrow's clients will not be able to obtain on their own. By doing so, Sedgwick will be positioned for success tomorrow. But there's more. By focusing on meeting tomorrow's realities, Sedgwick will also be able to delight (not merely satisfy) today's customers with exciting, unanticipated offerings, and will be able to differentiate itself quickly from other brokers and from generic information technologies.

The essence of looking a customer ahead is a continual focus on tomorrow's markets, technologies, and customers. The focus is not expressed in isolated periodic bursts but as an integral and ongoing part of management at all levels. The reason is simple: beyond incessant technological advances, customer preferences and choices among competing vendors are constantly evolving and changing. Thus, product and service offerings must also be constantly evolving and changing. That is why the most successful organizations have based their achievement on a regular stream of original, often breakthrough products, services, and niches. Many, like Hewlett-Packard, find that more than 50 percent of their revenues and earnings come from products introduced over the prior two to four years. Small, entrepreneurially driven companies often outperform large firms for this reason: note the astounding market and earnings growth of those on the *Inc.* 500 or *Forbes* 200 lists.

Among companies known for breakthrough outputs, strong earnings potential, and distinctive organizational personas, the evidence on behalf of innovation is clear. Eight hundred new athletic shoe and clothing styles emerge from Nike each year. From Rubbermaid comes one new product per day. Wal-Mart is so successful at changing the way it conducts its operations to capitalize on external opportunities—almost on an hourly basis—that executives from around the world come to spend time at its Arkansas headquarters to learn how to meld technology and employee participation for rapid change. Merrill Lynch reinvented the financial services industry by offering its asset management accounts, thus combining the primary services provided separately up to that point by the brokerage industry (stock investments) and the banking sector (savings accounts).

On the other side of the coin, the failure to look a customer ahead can have severe consequences. In free markets, companies that fail as a result of blatantly poor management are numerous. More intriguing is when failure follows success and, ostensibly, good management; consider the prior successes and current woes of blue-chip companies like IBM, Sears, Westinghouse, Eastman Kodak, and American Express. Track the history of individual companies and you'll find that a good predictor of today's business failure is yesterday's business *success*: almost inevitably, complacency, arrogance, or smugness worm their way into the corporate outlook. Mind-sets that reflect the structures, practices, and products that led to the company's successes can be devastating because they sabotage any potential for looking a customer ahead. The typical scenario is something like this: a product or service breakthrough propels the company to a leadership position. As the financial benefits roll in, management begins to assume that with reasonable care and feeding, the goose will lay golden eggs indefinitely. In effect, the numbers that a company achieves today—say, market share or earnings—can easily anesthetize that business into believing that its future success is ensured. A strong revenue stream and impressive profit margins can easily undermine anyone's inclination to challenge the status quo. If it's working, says the old refrain, don't fix it. Yet time and time again, this reasoning leaves yesterday's winner in the dust. The numbers are a consequence of what management did *yesterday*, but *tomorrow's* numbers are a reflection of what management does *today*. There's always a delayed reaction in the marketplace.[6] What may have been good management yesterday—hence good numbers today—is often *not* what is good management today—hence bad numbers tomorrow. In short, the need to look a customer ahead *today*—especially given the chaos of fragmented ephemeral global markets—becomes an urgent priority for organizational survival and renewal.

The focus on tomorrow's customer does not preclude the importance of continuous improvement efforts. As companies like Hewlett-Packard, Dell Computer, and CNN have demonstrated, initial product breakthroughs (Laserjet printers, mail-order computers, and 24-hour news service, respectively) must be supplemented by visible customer-driven improvements in features, performance, and after-sale service—even as the organization prepares the launch of next-generation products and services.

On its own, however, continuous improvement of current offerings is ultimately a dead end. Peter Drucker has argued that one of the deadliest of business sins is "slaughtering tomorrow's opportunity on the altar of yesterday."[7] Paradoxically, even as a company pursues perfection of what it is doing today by means of continuous improvement, it must encourage risk and creativity in pursuit of the destruction of the status quo and the creation of the new—on behalf of tomorrow's customer.[8] Tokyo's SANNO Management Development Research Center issued a comprehensive report in 1992 that concluded, "Management is a repeating cycle of demolishing and creating, making smooth-running situations impossible. . . . Growth in the twenty-first century will require companies to both accept the challenges involved in changing trends and to themselves generate new trends."[9]

FOCUS ON THE FUTURE

Innovation in the form of looking a customer ahead is a foundation for attractive earnings, shareholder returns, and corporate reputation. Why should this be so? Let us begin by making a commonsense financial case on behalf of the organizing principle.

The Bottom Line of Looking a Customer Ahead

Consider this scenario: if we were to say that General Motors made a million dollars profit last year and that our little, one-year-old, six-person software company made a million dollars profit last year, one might assume that we were talking about the difference between how much money the companies took in and how much they had to spend.

But no one would really say that General Motors (GM) and our software company were equally profitable. The size and stature of GM relative to our company makes its one million dollars net seem inconsequential. One million dollars for half a dozen men and women working at their desktops, on the other hand, sounds like a windfall. The difference is in the resources the companies have at their disposal to generate more business and profit. The usual presumption is that the more resources a company has, the more money it should make. For this reason the choice measure of profitability is return on equity, or ROE, a measure of how well a company uses its resources or assets.

ROE is ordinarily computed as net income divided by total equity. ROE can also be conceptualized as a result of multiplying return on assets (ROA) by leverage; thus, $ROE = ROA \times leverage$.[10] Based on this formula, there are several ways to increase profit. One way is simply to increase leverage—how much we borrow to finance what we buy or operate—while holding everything else constant. Our leverage is greater if our mortgage is 90 percent of a house purchase than if it is 80 percent. The 1970s and early to mid 1980s saw a great deal of leveraging—essentially, using other people's money to finance one's objectives.

Yet adding debt has its own difficulties. First, there is heightened exposure if the market value of the asset falls. Second, the organization may run out of debt capacity, and thus not be able to raise capital to take advantage of new opportunities. Bankers, venture capitalists, and other lenders may wonder if a new loan is prudent when the potential borrower is already carrying a large debt load. Businesses are thus urged to "clean up" their balance sheets and reduce debt. Lending institutions themselves can be subject to a tightening of regulations that can cause a credit crunch (as we saw in the early 1990s) and that make a leveraging strategy less viable. The pursuit of profit, in short, can no longer depend on leverage after a certain point.

Profit is ultimately dependent on ROA, return on assets: the higher the ROA, the greater the profitability, or ROE. ROA represents the net income an organization makes relative to its assets (computers, buildings, trucks, goodwill). Thus, one opportunity to increase profitability lies in the opportunity to decrease assets, or at least assets that aren't significant income producers. Executives took up this strategy with a vengeance in the late 1980s. They sold real estate, even the buildings that housed corporate headquarters, as a way of reducing the asset base. Closing plants in the United States and contracting with overseas vendors was another alternative. Like leveraging, however, this strategy has significant limitations. At some point, one begins to throw out the baby along with the bathwater. In 1989, Eastern Airlines employees—machinists, flight attendants, pilots—publicly reported that their deepest feelings of anger and despair occurred as they watched helplessly while Texas Air Chairman Frank Lorenzo and his team systematically dismantled the organization by selling valuable assets in an unsuccessful attempt to recoup shrinking revenues.[11]

The same kind of logic exists regarding net income. Volume has failed to save many companies, and too many mergers have not produced the synergies and expected economies of scale needed for profit targets. Price competition has reduced margins for large and small companies alike. Accordingly, many managers have concentrated on reducing internal expenses.

Presumably, lower expenses produce greater net income. However, some expenses are absolutely necessary for the production of income. Payroll can be cut, marketing budgets reduced, training curtailed, and research and development funds slashed—up to a point. Eventually, one cuts into the heart of the business. Its competitiveness suffers from the retrenchment in resources available to the work force to do its job. Furthermore, overreliance on cost cutting is a risky strategy during economic slowdowns. For example, it is often harder to cut expenses as quickly as revenues deteriorate.

Since the 1981–1983 recession, corporations have made a steady effort to reduce overhead. Most feel they have cut away all the fat and are now down to the bone. Numerous surveys have shown that the majority of the companies that reported gains in productivity in the early 1990s attributed the rise to such resource constraint factors. Few executives, however, believe that shrinking resources or improving operating systems can on their own maintain competitive advantage or bring about breakthrough opportunities for sustained profitability.

Thus, business now has a real dilemma. It must find a way to raise profits without undue increases in leverage and without reducing expenses and assets to the point of crippling its capacity to produce the required income stream. In other words, the issue is how to get more out of the assets that are still held and deemed necessary. Clever financial manipulation and "paper entrepreneurialism" are used up. The emphasis now must be on genuine productivity.

Looking a customer ahead encourages managers to eschew an overreliance on conventional approaches. It encourages them to concentrate on future offerings. To look a customer ahead, the organization has to reexamine its purpose, evaluate different opportunities, shift resources, eliminate functions, and strengthen promising openings. It must move beyond the tradition of cost accounting and look for new ways of allocating its remaining resources as well as new ways of assessing the market and customers' needs.

Interventions like total quality management (TQM), organization reengineering, and time-based strategies also require innovation and are both valuable and necessary. But if taken on their own and without being embedded in a focused context of looking a customer ahead, they merely buy the organization a little time. An organization that cannot provide the market with a steady stream of market-responsive new products and services—including breakthroughs for the future—can no longer hope to survive for long, regardless of the number of cost-reducing, systems-improving, and "restructuring" interventions it attempts. Canon reengineered its semiconductor equipment processes in order to reduce development costs by 30 percent and development time by half. And even as Hewlett-Packard continues to pare down its bureaucracy and make improvements on its LaserJet printers, *Business Week* reports that the company is investing a third of its total budget toward developing "fundamentally new products . . . the kind that will put an old industry instantly out of business, as HP's calculators blew away slide rules in the early 1970s."[12]

Being First

At the start of the 1990s, consultants and analysts were arguing that leading companies would have to bring to market each year two to three times the number of commercialized products as their competitors. Minimally, therefore, one of the key manifestations of looking a customer ahead is rapid, first-to-market commercialization of a new product or service that delights today's customers. In discussing profitability, consultants McKinsey & Co. showed that products that came out six months late but on budget generated about 33 percent less profits over a five-year span than they would have if they had come out on schedule. On the other hand, products that came out on schedule and 50 percent over budget showed a shortfall of only 4 percent in profits for the same time span.[13] Those who get to market first enhance the revenue side of the equation. Moreover, in order to get to market first, these companies have had to reconfigure their internal structure, technology, and culture to improve speed, flexibility, quality, and accountability—thus cleaning up the cost and efficiency side of the equation as well.

Looking a customer ahead drives the organization toward a healthy obsession about being first to market. The company that is first defines the market on terms consistent with its own capacities; it sets customer expectations about service, product definition, and price. For a period, the company is free to charge a premium for the "monopoly" its innovation creates. The impact on operating margins can be substantial. When an organization looks a customer ahead, top- and bottom-line increases are accompanied by increases in market share. In February 1993, the Food and Drug Administration approved Medtronic's cardiac device to treat racing heartbeats. Shortly thereafter, the following appeared in a *Wall Street Journal* article: "Analysts have predicted at least $1 billion in annual sales of devices . . . [and] a jump toward possibly becoming the industry leader in a major new business."[14]

Products as diverse as 3M's Post-it notepads, Asahi's Super Dry Beer, Sony's Walkmans, and Sun Microsystem's workstations, by virtue of being first to market with a breakthrough offering, have snared significant market share and sharply boosted the organization's earnings.[15] Among service providers, discount brokerage provider Charles Schwab Corporation is notable. The company's early foray into discount brokerage benefitted from the elimination of fixed transaction fees in the mid 1970s. It foresaw a new breed of customer. By substituting a low-cost operation for traditional research and advisory services, the company appealed to people who preferred, because of increased access to information, to choose on their own what stocks to buy and sell. Almost twenty years later, in the face of numerous challengers, Schwab maintains a dominant position in discount brokerage, and is continually reshaping the dynamics of retail financial services with new products.

The pattern holds even within the ephemeral, topsy-turvy world of television. Jim Packer, vice president of Disney subsidiary Buena Vista Television, tells us that *Wheel of Fortune* and *Jeopardy* (the first post-1960s game shows) have maintained their number one positions in global market share, profitability, and popularity, in spite of numerous imitators and clones. The same status applies to *Entertainment Tonight* (the first entertainment news magazine for television) and *60 Minutes* (the first prime time weekly news magazine). The years have not diminished the audience lock that these "firsts" maintain. (In Chapter Seven we will discuss the importance of "share of customer"— getting a greater share of each customer's business. Nonetheless, the drive to acquire more customers—that is, to increase market share—is still a benchmark of competitive success.)

Do not presume, however, that being first to market provides any long-term guarantee; quality improvements and continuous next-generation enhancements are a fact of life for maintaining position in any industry. Even Intel, in its quest for the post-486 chip generation, is now being confronted with a swarm of competitors—from large companies to tiny clone upstarts—snapping away at its traditional near-monopoly on microprocessors with new RISC technologies and lower prices.

Looking a customer ahead is a never-ending process rich with opportunities. For example, AMR's SABRE system, launched on the open market in 1986, still enjoys a 40 percent market share, but SABRE's strength has not led to complacency at AMR. Instead, it has generated a new corporate spinoff: the lucrative SABRE Technology Group, five information-based units revolving around travel services, computer services, consulting, and risk management.[16]

The power of looking a customer ahead is especially applicable for start-ups. In 1981, a physician and engineer started Nellcor, a company with one product: the N-100 pulse oximeter, which for the first time automatically monitored oxygen flow in patients who were under anesthesia in operating rooms. Three years (1981–1983) were spent developing and testing the product, and in late 1983 the first revenue units were launched. The 1984 returns were indicative of typical first-year startups: $2 million in revenues and a $4.4 million net loss. But by 1986, revenue had soared to $46 million and net income had increased to $9.6 million. As of May 1994, with more than twenty-five competitors worldwide, Nellcor, with revenues of $200 million, still had 50 percent of the market share for monitors, and, if one includes accessories, more than 75 percent of the total oximetry market.

Processes and Tomorrow's Customer

A critical but often overlooked advantage of the ability to look a customer ahead is that the organization forms an innovation infrastructure (design, systems, knowledge base, competencies, networks, relationships, leadership, vision) that sets up momentum for further innovation.[17]

Nellcor's knowledge base and organizational systems have served not only to make continuous improvements on the N-100 but also to stimulate a steady flow of new products (like disposable sensors and lightweight electronic carbon dioxide detectors), new global joint ventures, and new original equipment manufacturer (OEM) relationships—all aimed at increasing its penetration of the anesthesiology and operating room market niches. In the 1960s, Honda revolutionized the motorcycle business with its high-quality, user-friendly small bikes. The resulting financial successes provided the resources and core competencies that Honda began to apply to entirely new markets. As professors Gary Hamel and C. K. Prahalad note: "Even as Honda was selling 50cc motorcycles in the United States, it was already racing larger bikes in Europe—assembling the designs, skills and technologies it would need for a systematic expansion across the entire spectrum of motor-related businesses."[18]

Quad/Graphics, the award-winning $700 million printer based in Pewaukee, Wisconsin, has four huge printing-production plants in the Milwaukee area and prepress operations in California, Georgia, and New York. The company continually improves its already masterful printing operations by pouring resources into the purchase and continuous improvement of presses and other state-of-the-art equipment, and by investing in *weekly* training for everyone in the company. In addition, product division Quad/Tech develops specialized cutting-edge printing equipment that is tested and used in Quad plants and sold on the open market, including to competitors. By the time the competitors of Quad/Graphics integrate the technology into their organization system, Quad/Tech is already well into the development of next-generation technology. In effect, competitors fund Quad/Tech's research and development (R&D) efforts and subsidize Quad/Graphics's efforts to look a customer ahead. By systematically developing an innovation infrastructure that builds on prior learning and prior successes, Quad/Graphics can maintain its 20–30 percent annual growth rate and allow chairman Harry Quadracchi to assert: "Change is our bread and butter. We eat change for breakfast."[19]

The importance of an innovation infrastructure can be seen from another perspective. John Butler of the University of Washington correctly notes that research findings show a statistically nonsignificant relationship between research and development and performance. Butler attributes this finding to "the probabalistic nature of innovation."[20] True as this may be, it is insufficient as an explanation. Too often, research and development investments are assumed to be indicative of the organization's innovative strength. But if those investments simply create a large internal research bureaucracy or an in-house academic think tank with few commercial outcomes to its credit, then the low correlation between the research effort and performance is understandable. In fact, the absurdity of the conventional line of reasoning was brought home to us at a recent shareholder meeting. The chairman described how research and development expenditures were increasing as a percentage of revenue, thus demonstrating that the company's traditional profile as an innovative company was still intact. The absolute expenditures had actually declined, but sales had declined even faster because of a series of faulty and uninspired products. The ratio looked good, but it had little to do with gauging innovation at the company.

By definition, looking a customer ahead focuses an organization's attention on breakthrough, value-adding outcomes as perceived by the customer. Hence, even measurements of organization systems must be primarily outcome based, not input based. The research and development budget is important, but less so than the company's number of patents or number of commercial successes. Businesses that look a customer ahead understand the significance of outcome-based measurements. At 3M, 25 percent of the revenues of each division general manager must come from new products introduced over the previous five years. Among the key measurements used at Manco (a manufacturer of industrial tape) are the dollar volume and percentage of sales from new product introductions.

Be it Nellcor, Quad/Graphics, or 3M, a firm's ability to develop a learning, innovation-based organizational process that continually pumps next-generation advancements into the marketplace allows it to sustain the advantage it grabbed in the first place.

A Closer Look at Jumping the Curve

The case for looking a customer ahead can be made not only on the basis of utilitarian business outcomes but also in terms of the broader perspective lent by history. Jonas Salk, the major figure in eradicating the nightmare of polio, offered a model that spoke to deeper undercurrents of change and innovation. Salk used an S-curve as a way to "reflect a law of nature that governs growth in living systems . . . and reflects the transformational character of change in our times."[21] Though he initially used the curve to describe bioevolutionary trends, he proposed that it could be used to describe historical macroshifts in values, attitudes, and behavior.[22]

Salk cut the S-curve in the middle and spoke of the two segments as epochs, the first where growth is occurring and the second where it begins to diminish (see Figure 4.1). The growth issue is not our concern here as much as Salk's proposal of a major break in the evolution of a society. In terms of our discussions thus far, the split in the curve might represent the socioeconomic upheavals engendered by the printing press or the personal computer. It might represent the shift in business context from gramophones and three-channel black-and-white TV to CD-ROM, videocassette recorders (VCRs), and digital interactivity.

Figure 4.1. Salk's S-Curve.

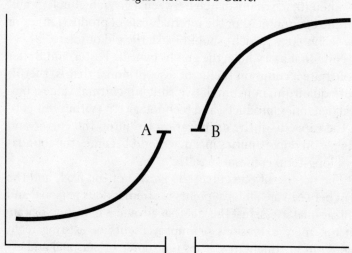

Source: Salk, J., and Salk, J. *World Population and Human Values: A New Reality*. New York: HarperCollins, 1981, p.77.

It might represent the radical changes in organizational structure as memos and messengers are challenged by fax, E-mail, and groupware. It might represent massive changes in trade patterns from the Atlantic to the Pacific. In each case, the gap between the curves signifies a lack of direct linkage: one cannot get from the old to the new curve by proceeding on the same road.

This is indeed a moment of crisis. For a species, argued Salk, the moment demands new action and adaptation to ensure its survival. The same is true for an organization. Just as Salk used the S-curve to describe transformations in cultures and species, others have used variations of the curve to deal with issues more directly germane to business—in particular, upheavals in technology and products. For two examples, see the curves proposed by Richard Foster and John Butler, shown in Figure 4.2.

Foster, for example, observes that "behind conventional management wisdom is the implicit assumption that the more effort put in, the more progress that results. In fact, this is only the case in the first half of the S-curve. In the other half it is wrong . . . The gap between the pair of S-curves represents a discontinuity—a point when one technology replaces another."[23]

Similarly, Butler points out that the break in the curve occurs "when there is a mismatch between a given technology and either the environment or the internal scale of production . . . or a new technology [which] should make the old obsolete."[24]

Note that as a whole, the graphs by Salk, Foster, and Butler demonstrate a common theme of discontinuity; that is, they illustrate quantum, noncumulative shifts in cultural values, biological dynamics, products, and technologies.[25] Within this context, the capacity of the organization to "jump the curve" and capitalize on opportunities in a new world becomes the foundation of long-term corporate health.

The demise of one curve, the growth of the next, and the void in between are all focal points for tremendous personal and organizational stress. Just the fact that advances in technology are often not mere extensions or improvements of existing technologies but are qualitative leaps is a source of personal and career trauma for many managers—and a source of inspiration for others. But it is a stressful experience under any circumstances. The experience of chaos, the sense of feeling overwhelmed, or the

Figure 4.2. Variations on the S-Curve.

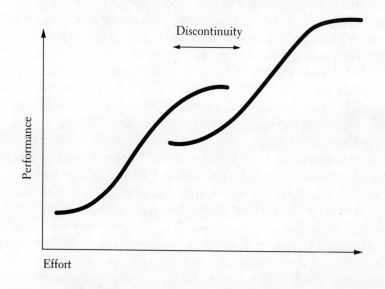

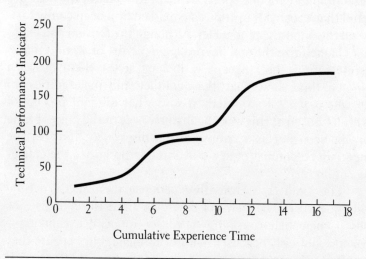

Source: Foster, R. N. *Innovation: The Attacker's Advantage.* New York: Simon & Schuster, 1986, p. 102.

Source: Butler, J. "Theories of Technological Innovation as Useful Tools for Corporate Strategy." *Strategic Management Journal,* 1988, 9, p. 19. Copyright 1988 by John Wiley & Sons Ltd. Reprinted by permission.

exhilarating rush of an adrenaline surge—these are all natural reactions to finding oneself in mid-flight, going across the abyss.

Unsurprisingly, Salk observed that transformation generates resistance. Because transformations are unfamiliar, they
are threatening for many people, especially when their initial
payoff is limited. When one is jumping curves, the old, comfortable, successful patterns of the past look very appealing, especially when you can't be sure what the patterns of success in
the new world will be. Today for example, the movement toward
five-hundred channel, interactive multimedia is proceeding,
even though there is obviously no mass "demand" for the specific products and services that have yet to be developed.

As many leaders can testify, the conflicts between the
protectors of the old and the pathbreakers of the new are legendary. The in-house struggles among existing and emerging
technologies are a case in point: consider bias-ply and radial
tires, mainframe computers and personal computers (PCs),
supercomputers and massively parallel processing architecture,
and film photo and digital imaging technologies.

Consistent with our discussions of role-perception imperatives in Chapter Three, Salk contended that attitudes and values appropriate for one epoch are inappropriate for the next. He
noted that epochal transitions are marked by a deep conflict between the opposing tendencies. Although the tension and chaos
that characterize the conflict present a picture of a world that is
disintegrating, the longer view, looking at the S-curve over a
period of time, shows that "these conflicts and uncertainties can
be seen as part of an orderly if somewhat difficult process of
nature. Looked at this way, the disturbances of the present time
may be seen not as a symptom of a disease . . . [but as] the
uncertain beginnings of new patterns appropriate to the emerging conditions."[26]

The conflicts we currently experience, then, are the natural
consequence of the new era emerging from the old. As Salk
sees it, new behaviors—the result of innovative thinking—
will arise not only because they are "humane, but because they
are advantageous to the individual and society. . . . Over a period
of time," he concluded, "as values change, so will relationships

and, with them, institutions."[27] Business, we can imagine, will not be excluded.

Like Darwin, Salk found that species threatened with extinction must adapt; they make the qualitative adjustments necessary for their survival or they perish. Successful organizations do the same. This is the root of innovation; in fact, both an economist (Joseph Schumpeter) and an artist (Pablo Picasso) used the same term to describe innovation: *creative destruction.* Creative destruction is central to jumping the curve; this leap requires leaving something behind in the pursuit of the new and uncertain.

Successful organizations continually search for new root ideas that will serve as the bases for new growth curves. Hewlett-Packard's quest for the breakthrough industry, described earlier, is an example. Another comes from Motorola, which has managed to thrive since its 1928 inception, not merely because of its recent quality goals but because its visionary leaders—in particular, Paul Galvin and his son Robert—forced the company to go through the regular trauma of jumping curves which then defined the company's product priorities. Accordingly, Motorola jumped from car radios to walkie-talkies to solid-state TV to integrated circuits to, most recently, microchips and wireless communication. Motorola and Hewlett-Packard, as large companies, are exceptions rather than the rule. Many large companies have not been able to leap the inevitable S-curve progressions as well as nimbler entrepreneurs; by virtue of their age and size, they find it difficult to jettison their old ways of doing things.

A FINAL WORD

Salk observed that a complex series of reactions takes place when sugar is introduced into a potentially reactive bacterial culture. The reaction, or "'ritual' is well established and occurs in a way suggesting the existence of a 'cultural heritage' and of 'great knowledge' on the part of the bacterial cell." According to Salk, this constitutes an "anticipatory biological potential ... *which is not revealed until 'challenged'*" (our emphasis).[28] The scope of this challenge for business is summarized by reengineering experts Michael Hammer and James Champy: "In today's environment nothing is constant or predictable—not market growth, customer demand, product life cycles, the rate of technological change, or the nature of competition. Adam Smith's world and its way of doing business are yesterday's paradigm."[29]

Hence, looking a customer ahead as a regular, ongoing part of management becomes a crucial strategic imperative. Salk's reasoning offers encouragement and optimism; he is saying that to be challenged is not the same as being late. Innovative managers who continuously look a customer ahead can help ensure that their organizations will jump the inevitable series of product, process, and technology curves ahead. The task is to meet the challenge at the appropriate moment, with the full force of one's resources and judgment.

C H A P T E R

5

Practicing Creative Destruction

*What we have to do is to be forever curiously testing new
opinions and courting new impressions.*
—Walter Pater

Not being ahead of time is not being on time.
—Javier Moreno Valle
President, Grupo Promotor de Empresas

Unconventional times call for unconventional strategies. Sustainable competitive advantage will accrue to those organizations that can clearly and unequivocally differentiate themselves from the rest of the global pack. Organizing around looking a customer ahead can help the organization do precisely that.

FOCUSING THE
ORGANIZATION ON THE FUTURE

Since tomorrow's financials are a function of today's decisions, how can a manager position the organization to look a customer ahead and thus attain good numbers both today and tomorrow?

The first critical task for the leader is to confront and transcend three major barriers that are primarily attitudinal. These barriers are adherence to a mind-set appropriate to the past, acceptance of a corporate culture of mediocrity, and conviction that a quick fix can be found. The following sections address each one in turn.

The Outdated Mind-Set

Willingness to look a customer ahead is the exception rather than the rule among managers in established organizations. Arnold Cooper of Purdue University and Clayton Smith of Notre Dame University note that "where established firms enter young industries, they do not pursue the new product aggressively, and they continue to make substantial commitments to their old product even after its sales begin to decline."[1] They and other researchers attribute the trend less to technical expertise than to internal politics, ego defensiveness among managers who are comfortable with the status quo, and the rationalization of sunk costs.[2] Thus, even though IBM labs turned out critical breakthroughs in microprocessors, microcomputers, and personal computer (PC) software in the 1980s, the company's "soul" remained firmly entrenched in mainframes.[3]

Sometimes the failure to look a customer ahead occurs because managers' familiarity with an existing product or technology blinds them to the possibilities inherent in newer developments. Prior to the Time-Warner merger, Time Inc. was undervalued by $6 billion. One insider at Warner told us, "Time had the resources to be a CNN. And they could have locked up the home video market with HBO. But the management grew up in print and saw the world in print. They didn't understand the revolution in technology." Apparently, the market came to the same conclusion.

Because of their inability to look a customer ahead, those who appear to be best positioned to get into a new business are often among the last. This reluctance frequently yields new opportunities for upstart competitors and entrepreneurs who are burdened with little of the old baggage and who have neither the time nor the money to be preoccupied by conventional thinking.

The Culture of Mediocrity

If an anachronistic mind-set is the most common obstacle to looking a customer ahead, the most pernicious mind-set is an organizational culture of mediocrity. Mediocrity can permeate an entire organization, producing acceptance of missed deadlines and quality deficits, aimless meetings that begin late, reports and presentations long on flash but short on substance. In a culture of mediocrity, complaining, blaming, and making excuses replace accountability. Lethargy and complacency take the place of action. Reactivity and defensiveness rather than initiative and risk proliferate. Sloppy internal processes are tolerated despite the sense of urgency that charges the air. Personal irresponsibility is sheltered by the same bureaucracy that smothers customer complaints.

The result of all this is that many corporate reorganizations are really about satisfying the need to do something while at the same time not actually changing the underlying fundamentals of how the business operates. One company we studied had reorganized itself five times in three years, with little to show for its efforts. The major impediment, the requirement for an endless series of approvals for almost any kind of line decision, was always left intact. Despite massive convulsions in reporting relationships, the basic premise of the business stayed the same. The company's ambition for superior performance was thwarted continuously by its failure to get rid of the unnecessary command-and-control mentality.

Part of the problem is the emotional attraction of predictability, even if the predictability is not very pleasant. In business environments, complaining about the negative consequences of a mediocre but predictable culture often seems preferable to plunging into the ambiguity and uncertainty of innovation. Everyone knows that certain processes or products are not adding value, but people perpetuate them because doing things in the familiar way avoids the fear of change and the unknown. In large measure, mediocrity endures because it becomes a habit.

One can see the mediocrity addiction in the way people hang on to wasteful, unproductive work routines. It is there in the busywork that is used to escape the hard questions of "What am I doing that adds value?" Research conducted by George Stalk and Tom Hout of the Boston Consulting Group suggests that in most organizations, "most products and many services are actually receiving value for only .05 percent to 5 percent of the time they are in the value delivery systems of their companies."[4] Stalk and Hout note that it takes twenty-two days for the average insurance company to process a customer's application, but the actual work spent within the organization to complete the job involves only seventeen minutes. Similarly, the order turnaround cycle of a heavy equipment manufacturer is forty-five days even though the actual assembling time is sixteen hours.

The research of Stalk and Hout suggests that over 95 percent of in-house activities add little value in terms of the deliverables that matter to the customer. The plethora of in-house operating procedures and control systems often do little but add weeks to the time cycle. Consider the debilitating impact of all the committee meetings, reports, memos, sign-off requirements, and interdepartmental pass-offs that are typically part of a manager's daily ordeal. In a mediocre culture, each of these steps may add no value but nevertheless winds up with a life of its own and passionate defenders who will swear that the entire company will collapse if it is eliminated.

Ultimately, mediocrity diminishes innovation for two reasons. One, it unquestioningly holds tradition and habit sacred, and thus buries questions that challenge the comfortable or the familiar. Two, it continues providing support for the customary low performance expectations: marginal increments in sales or profits, diluted measurements of customer satisfaction, and hedged bets on department or group objectives.

The Quick Fix

Those who have suffered through the Program of the Month Syndrome can attest to management's frequent attraction to fads or fashions that offer the elusive promise of painless and immediate change. Whether for quality, speed, partnerships, customer service, reengineering, empowerment, or diversity—all worthwhile goals—the search for the quick fix is predicated on the desire to avoid uncertainty and risk. That is why it is not uncommon to see scenarios where management rolls out a new business priority and everyone groans. Employees know what follows. After some pretty speeches and balloons in the atrium, everything gradually goes back to normal. Until, of course, the manager reads another book or attends another seminar. Then he or she roars into the office with the next idea while everyone else dives for cover. The cycle begins anew.

The reluctance to confront uncertainty operates at the macrovariable level, too. Many planners and line managers grow uncomfortable as innovation becomes a greater element in the economic system and undermines the system's ability to predict and control. Since the 1970s, many econometric models have failed to predict economic behavior because the effects of innovation and risk taking were not included as part of the models; it is difficult to subject the surprise of innovation to mathematical notations and forecasting models.[5] Further, as the mathematics of chaos theory reveal, the idea of "inherent uncertainty" is a predominant fact of life.[6]

Businesspeople often have difficulty accepting that message, and thus they enmesh themselves in a perpetual search for the program or technique that will magically protect them against the vagaries of chance and uncertainty. They continue to search for elixirs with the hope that risk taking and entrepreneurial innovation will somehow be mysteriously accounted for.

One recent variant of this quest is the inclination of senior managers to search for a "hot" industry and get into it as the surest, most painless way to position for tomorrow's customer. Antipollution technologies and services are being touted as tomorrow's winners, as are health care (especially home health care), physical infrastructure (roads, bridges, harbors), leisure and entertainment, biotechnology, investment products for retirement and old age, technologies that integrate entertainment and education, and technologies that merge the functions of telephone, computer, and television.

But even in hot markets there are no guarantees for individual companies. Quite the contrary. All the data really do is identify which markets are sure to become extremely crowded with frenetic competition.[7] In our work with the Country Radio Broadcasters' Association, we found that the sharp growth in the popularity of country music led to a parallel growth in the number of radio stations that switched to that format. This trend led to market saturation and flattened ratings in many localities. From low tech to high tech, hot industries attract a vast multitude of fierce competitors.

The existence of a hot list might imply that "nonhot" businesses offer no opportunities. Many of the fastest growing companies in the United States have succeeded by providing breakthrough innovations in so-called mundane industries—for example, Charter Golf (apparel), Ultra Pac (containers), and Staples (office supplies).[8] Our personal favorite is Weaver Popcorn, which, as its name implies, makes only one product. Yet by obsessing on quality (its standards are at least six times higher than those of the Federal Grain Inspection Service's best grade) and customization (of hybrid crops, packaging, coloring, and delivery) for individual customers in the snack foods and concession industries, the highly profitable family firm dominates the popcorn business in the United States and sells popcorn in thirty countries, enjoying a 25 percent global market share.

Overcoming the obstacles of an outdated mind-set, a culture of mediocrity, and the desire for quick fixes is a key prerequisite for looking a customer ahead. Doing so depends on the leader's capacity to accept, even embrace, the inevitability of constant disorder and irregularity, and to perceive market chaos as *the* opportunity in business. As Robert Ferchat, president of Northern Telecom Canada, noted: "Order, the opposite of chaos, is by definition concerned with the status quo. Chaos is the random spark that defies the status quo, that creates change . . . that frees people to innovate. . . . We must develop within ourselves a new mind-set that exploits the creative power of chaos."[9]

Action Amid Chaos

One company that has exploited the creative power of chaos to look a customer ahead is Chicago-based CCC Information

Services. The $93 million, 900-person company has entered—actually, created—three lines of business that should logically have been the domain of much larger competitors. In 1980, the new upstart reinvented the "total loss valuation" market. Traditionally, when a car was stolen or damaged beyond repair, insurance companies would use a "blue book" or "red book" to get an appraisal of the full value of that car. Since some of the books were published quarterly, and others were published monthly, but with a three-month lag, the data were often not current, nor were they specific to region and state. CCC's first business was the development of the largest computerized used-car database in the world. The data were much more specific than industry standards, breaking down information on the basis of mileage, style, options, engine, and the price for which a local car dealer in the area in question would actually sell the car. And the data were continually updated. Not surprisingly, insurance companies found that using the database saved significant research time for their adjustors and provided valuations that were more acceptable to their policyholders and more verifiable to regulators.

Today, CCC's total loss-value business is $45 million in revenues, which translates into a 90 percent share of the computerized total loss evaluation market. Seven thousand computerized valuations are processed every day, or one valuation every six seconds, twelve hours per day. According to President Glen Tullman, the powerful vendors of the "blue" and "red" books "would have been naturals for creating this market, but they missed the whole idea that a computer could provide better information than a manual system."

Next, CCC entered the much larger collision-estimating market. Here, they went head to head with billion-dollar players like ADP and Mitchellmatix, both of whom were mainframe driven. The old way required back-and-forth mailings of adjustors' spec sheets and computer evaluations. CCC developed EZEst, a collision-estimating software product that would operate on a stand-alone portable computer. With this program an adjustor could write the estimate in the field, even while he was looking at the damaged car. Insurance companies found that EZEst led to more accurate estimates, faster turnaround times (saving days or weeks), and an immediate 30 percent cost reduction in the estimating process.

Within eighteen months of entering this business, the little company had gained more than a 30 percent share of the computerized collision-estimating market and a business exceeding $28 million in revenues. Once again, the established players were caught flat-footed because, as Tullman points out, "they were comfortable with the status quo and very profitable. They had no real drive or incentive to obsolete their own significant investment. . . . They also didn't understand the significance of notebook computer technology and the value their customers would place on immediate access to information."

CCC's most recent foray has begun to revolutionize the entire industry: installing CCC systems—EZEst and a new EZNet—in body shops so that the body shop employees themselves can do the estimates. Traditionally, the owner of the damaged car is inconvenienced by the insurance company's requirement of getting several estimates. The usual assumption in the industry is that body shops overestimate and adjustors underestimate, then they haggle on the final price. In CCC's business scenario, the body shops are brought in as partners from the beginning. In this arrangement, an owner of a damaged car calls his insurance company, which gives him the names of four or five shops located in his area that are on the CCC network. The owner picks one and by the time he gets to the shop, a rental car is waiting for him. In the new environment, there is no need for an adjustor, trust between insurers and shops replaces arguments, and the body shop turns into a claims office. "We're now selling networks, not estimates," says Tullman. Within one year, the reward for their fledgling efforts has been a $20 million business, which translates into a 50 percent share of the market of collision repair shops with computerized estimating systems.

CCC's initiatives have led to more than a tripling of sales from 1989 to 1992, and a projected doubling of sales from 1992 ($62 million) to 1994 ($122 million). The company has also found that looking a customer ahead provides the dual bonus of positioning the company's priorities and infrastructure for tomorrow's opportunities while creating exciting options and fresh possibilities to attract today's customers.

FORESIGHT IN ACTION

Looking a customer ahead demands entrepreneurial thinking, calculated risk, and a strong dose of courage and fortitude. But the call to look a customer ahead is not license for visionary recklessness and fiscal irresponsibility; it demands discipline and prudence. We propose four initiatives that speak to these demands and that will quicken a leader's imagination about what is possible with tomorrow's customer. The initiatives represent a call to action, as well as a strategic and tactical road map for leaders who are serious about preparing themselves and their organizations to look a customer ahead.

Each of the four organizing principles in this book, presented in this and subsequent chapters, will have its own set of initiatives. The purpose of the initiatives is to provide the leader with a set of definitive techniques and tools he or she can use to effectively implement the organizing principle under discussion. Within this context, the creative leader can then fashion specific tactics and decisions that are appropriate for the specific circumstances he or she faces.

In that spirit, we begin with four initiatives for looking a customer ahead: continually prepare for obsolescence, run your shop with bifocal vision, create a vigilant organization, and insist on all-hands, organizationwide strategic listening. In the remainder of this chapter, we discuss each of these four initiatives. The initiatives and the organizing principle they support are summarized in Table 5.1.

Initiative 1: Continually Prepare for Obsolescence.

The concept of deliberately making success obsolete is alien and unsettling. It strains conventional wisdom to hear one Japanese executive say, "The quicker we can abandon a successful product, the stronger and more profitable we'll be." On the other hand, in a global, free market economy, whatever your company produces and sells will be obsolete someday and, given the pace of change, that someday will be sooner rather than later.

If obsolescence is inevitable, then Polaroid founder Edwin Land's advice is wise: you, rather than your competitor, should be the one to obsolete your product. The rationale for preparing

Table 5.1. Look a Customer Ahead.

Initiative 1: Continually prepare for obsolescence.

- Encourage everyone to think the unthinkable.
- Maintain an air of urgency.
- Prepare to be resisted by others in your organization.
- Assume that all products and services are experiments.

Initiative 2: Run your shop with bifocal vision.

- Insist that each management decision be bifocal.
- Require that all levels and functions engage in bifocal vision.

Initiative 3: Create a vigilant organization.

- Refuse to be shackled by familiar markets.
- Go beyond traditional decision rules in investment and pricing.
- Treat test failures as learning opportunities.
- Sensitize people to the importance of an organization structure that is fleet, flexible, and liberating.

Initiative 4: Insist on all-hands, organizationwide, strategic listening.

- Make listening a universal responsibility.
- Insist that listening take precedence over many traditional activities.
- Listen especially closely to the end user.
- Listen with particular care to pathfinder customers—those who are innovative and demand cutting-edge products.

yourself and your company for obsolescence is straightforward: you want to do it before someone else does it to you. But as we have seen, the tantalizing feeling of security in today's success (even if it's just pseudo-success, as in "we're no worse than anyone else") precludes many established companies from systematically obsoleting their market offerings and jumping the curve.

Many firms try to get by with pretend jumps. They limit their creative attempts to changes in features and services that are so small as to be unnoticed or inconsequential in the confusion of the marketplace or so insignificant and infrequent as to be easily copied by competitors. They maintain that they are being sufficiently innovative by sticking to continuous improvement of current products and processes. Continuous improvement is a valuable process for any organization and is the basis for many TQM interventions. However, as discussed earlier, the rapid acceleration of jagged, nonincremental changes in the marketplace may at any time make obsolete the entire product or process that the company is continuously improving.

Today, continuous improvement is fundamental; without it, an organization cannot survive in today's ball game, much less tomorrow's. But continuous improvement of today's products does not offer the manager either the mind-set or the means to jump the curve and hence create the new products, new customers, and new markets that form the basis of sustainable competitive advantage.[10] Tamara Erickson of Arthur D. Little cogently observes that "automobile manufacturers strive to improve fuel efficiency. Detergent makers become intent on improving the whitening power of their products. While these certainly are not unwise targets for improvement, they are unlikely to move a second-tier firm into a leadership position."[11]

There are, however, companies that do embrace the initiative of obsolescence. The Woolworth Corporation is an example. Its transformation from antiquated dime store and bland discounter to versatile global specialty retailer in the span of three years has been nothing less than remarkable. The new Woolworth is a collection of smaller, feisty, independent companies in more than forty different store formats, including Foot Locker (and spinoffs Kids Foot Locker, Lady Foot Locker, and World Foot Locker), Northern Reflections (women's outdoor apparel), Champs Sports (sporting goods), Athletic X-Press (footwear and apparel), and San Francisco Music Box (specialty musical gifts). The company has so many new and varied faces, mostly in the sports and leisure niches, that mall customers often don't even know they are shopping at Woolworth's. Moreover, "perhaps more than any other U.S. retailer, Woolworth has realized the potential of foreign markets, which in 1991 accounted for 42 percent of sales."[12]

The results of these transformations include sharp boosts in earnings (59 percent in 1992) and stock value for Woolworth since 1991. The company anticipates that by the year 2002, earnings should double to $20 billion. Just as impressive is ex-Chairman Harold Sells's understanding that Woolworth's obsolescence will be a perpetual event; he anticipates thirteen thousand specialty stores by the year 2000 but confesses he has no idea what they will look like. "The best predictor of our success will be our ability to change," he says.[13]

Lars Kolind would certainly agree. In 1988, Kolind was brought in as CEO to turn around the fortunes of the ailing $60 million hearing aid manufacturer Oticon, based in Copenhagen. Kolind spent the first two years cleaning out organizational inefficiencies and improving product quality, steps that squeezed out some pretax profits in 1989 and 1990. But in 1991, he realized that "the course we were following would never allow us a sustainable competitive advantage." He concluded that there was no percentage in going head to head with the large established players (such as Sony, Panasonic, Siemens, 3M, AT&T) who were investing heavily in the hearing aid market. "Me-too" products and services would get Oticon nowhere; established companies had goodwill, brand equity, and economies of scale on their side.

Accordingly, Kolind decided to obsolete the company that was a mass producer of conventional hearing aids. He began to conceptualize an Oticon based on "fast and creative *integration* of all existing expertise in the field," including chip development, circuitry, anatomics, and audiology. The company organized around multidisciplinary project teams focused on knowledge acquisition, speedy creative design, and first-to-market priority. The teams redefined a new product under development as the first fully automatic "computer at the ear." A marketing concept was generated, with the aim of taking the "handicapped" image away from the hearing aid and repositioning it as a modern communication system. Similar shifts were made with other products, each requiring a reconfiguration of planning and organization.

Defying conventional wisdom (and market research) indicating that users wanted only flesh-colored aids well hidden from anyone's sight, Oticon successfully launched a variety of models in different shapes, sizes, and fashionable colors and with an assortment of features. One of the biggest winners was the world's first fully self-adjusting "in-the-ear" multifocal hearing aid. Oticon sells this aid, which has an outstanding digitalized sound system and user friendliness, to dispensers for $600, generating the kinds of high margins it now looks for (the typical hearing aid is sold to dispensers at $200). As of June 1993, the next two generations of the multifocal hearing aid were already on the market, thus positioning Oticon two years ahead of its competitors in product development. The company's self-induced obsolescence has resulted, as of 1993, in a fivefold increase in pretax profit since 1991, a 23 percent increase in net sales over 1992, and a 13 percent return on sales—an industry record.

While stories of companies like Woolworth and Oticon are inspiring, moving toward obsolescence and subsequent reinvention represents a hard, rigorous route—and there are no guarantees of success. At Atlantic City Medical Center (ACMC), a $180 million, 581-bed two-hospital system, ex-CEO George Lynn says, "We have re-invented ourselves" in such a way as to increase both opportunity and exposure. In September 1993, Lynn resigned his position as CEO to take over the newly formed holding company, AtlantiCare Health System, of which ACMC is now a part. The other "parts" of the new health delivery system include a network of health care providers in the southern New Jersey region, such as other independent hospitals, physicians, and home care providers, whose specialized services AtlantiCare will broker and manage. Also included in the new system is a set of managed care health plans and a foundation whose aim is to have an impact on the health of surrounding communities by dealing with issues ranging from obesity and pollution to the importance of wearing seat belts.

The rationale for creating an AtlantiCare, says Lynn, lay in "the fundamental problem that, despite most efforts at the state and national level, health care costs continue to rise and people's health status continues to decline. Since health care is essentially a regional product, we believed it was not in the best interests of the Medical Center or our community to wait for some government initiative to determine our future." Lynn confesses that in the cautious world of health care management, AtlantiCare is simultaneously groundbreaking and risky. But apart from his confidence in the concept and his people, he argues that there is far greater risk in simply being reactive.

To the discerning manager who wants to plan for obsolescence and reinvention, we have the following advice:

■ *Encourage everyone to think the unthinkable.* Greeting both employee and visitor to Oticon's Copenhagen headquarters is a large marble column inscribed with "Cogitate incognita"—Latin for "think the unthinkable." When everyone is expected to ask (and follow up on) "why not?" and "what if?" questions, and when such questions are a regular part of ordinary management meetings, obsoleting alternatives begin to emerge.

■ *Maintain an air of urgency.* Talk passionately about the dangers of complacency and arrogance. Educate people about the delay in the marketplace between decisions and numbers. Lay out the reasons and rationale for the urgency. Keep the issue on the table with full disclosure of all organizational information so people can become as scared as you are. Don't automatically assume that people will get it on their own. Nellcor CEO Ray Larkin told us, "One of the hardest things I learned was that the facts don't speak for themselves. People are capable of rationalizing the most damning facts. Data can't replace leadership." So talk to your people about the implications of the data, and then relentlessly continue to prod and inform. Insist on creative movement from people, *especially* when the company's numbers look good.

Understand that urgency is different from panic. Urgency inspires deliberate, focused risk taking. It reflects commitment to a clear direction. It is about alertness and priorities. In contrast, panic is diffuse and unfocused, occurring when crises overtake the organization, usually after a long spell of complacency. The panic reaction is noted in organizations that commit to sweeping knee-jerk decisions and "desperation projects"—announced at the eleventh hour when the old ways have failed. Apart from its other benefits, maintaining a sense of urgency becomes the best insurance against the destructive cycle of stop-go-stop-go. It helps ensure forward progress, even against the tide.

■ *Prepare to be resisted by others in your organization.* We have seen managers with the noblest of intentions give up too early, or become impatient when people resist the plunge into the "de-learning" process. Or managers are taken aback and flustered when others do not share the same urgency for change, even when the evidence is right in front of them. Preparing for obsolescence will invariably generate some negative reactions and even personal attacks. Leaders planning for obsolescence must therefore expect and be able to take heat.

■ *Assume that all products and services are experiments.* The idea of "everything as experiment" spurs the development of a culture of continuous innovation, where anything is open to tries and tinkering, where bold upheavals are encouraged, and where nothing in the organization is absolved from improvement or abandonment. Yet to consider everything an experiment is disquieting for many managers. The tantalizing promise of managerialism tells us that good management means creating conditions of stability, order, and predictability. Accordingly, managers spend a lot of time looking for the home run product that will generate a long-term, stable stream of revenue. Concurrently, they try to devise a tidy, sensible, nonexperimental organizational world by developing a stable, orderly infrastructure of formal procedures, job descriptions, functions, and systems. Within this dream of a well-buffered world, the reluctance to make anything obsolete is comfortably reinforced. Meanwhile, outside, all hell is breaking loose. It takes a major commitment to defy conventional thinking and insist that everyone approach everything as an experiment. But that is just what preparing for obsolescence demands.

Initiative 2: Run Your Shop with Bifocal Vision.

Management gurus tout the importance of vision for leadership. We have no quarrel with that, but we suggest that in order to meet today's requirements effectively and look a customer ahead, a leader's vision must be bifocal. To meet responsibilities to today's customers and investors, a leader must insist that today's products and processes be perfected. Simultaneously, to successfully meet the responsibilities to tomorrow's customers and investors, the company must work toward destroying the status quo in pursuit of the new.

Bifocal vision is demonstrated in a number of companies. Microsoft, for example, has a higher stock market value than Caterpillar, Gillette, Time-Warner, Texaco, Boeing, and BankAmerica, even though Microsoft's sales and physical assets are a fraction of those sales and assets of these companies. Investors anticipate that Microsoft's earning strength will be higher, in large part because the company consistently and creatively destroys its current offerings and replaces them with new products and features that tomorrow's customers will gobble up. Likewise, the investment community knows that in Microsoft's judicious joint ventures with companies in the entertainment, telecommunications, and education industries, the company is positioning itself for tomorrow's breakthrough technologies. Its top priority is to accelerate the development cycle for new, sometimes groundbreaking, user-friendly products. Microsoft's attention to cost efficiency, continuous improvement, and zero defects represents one necessary aspect of bifocal vision. But, as the investment community understands, market-driven entrepreneurialism and innovation—looking a customer ahead—are the primary elevators of stock value.

Among other companies, bifocal vision is reflected in a disciplined attention to today's curve while leaping to the next. Disney continues to improve and add to its lucrative theme parks even as it aggressively moves into the arenas of software, movies, and video entertainment. Kinko's Copy Centers is continually improving its core copying services with necessary investments in equipment and customer service, while at the same time continually venturing into new business opportunities ranging from textbook and desktop publishing to a full line of services for its office-away-from-the-office concept.

Bifocal vision should be an integral part of strategic thinking, which in turn should be a responsibility of every person holding a management position. Managers at all levels must continually confront questions like these: How do we invest in our current products and markets while building the resources to develop tomorrow's opportunities? What specifically do we need to do *today* to thrive both today and tomorrow?

Bifocal vision as part of strategic *thinking* is different from conventional strategic *planning*. The latter can undermine the potential of bifocal vision. The fundamental premise of strategic planning is that the discontinuities of the future can be forecast in a logical, systematic manner. Nobel Laureate Frederich Hayek called this assumption "the fatal conceit" of managers.[14]

Writing in the *American Economic Review*, Hayek argued that "economists must understand that the complex phenomena of the market will hardly ever be fully known or measurable, unlike most of the factors that determine events observed in the physical sciences."[15] Complex algorithms, sophisticated models, and brilliant arguments often camouflage the fact that the premises themselves are a foundation of sand. As rational human beings, we behave and think as if the world of tomorrow will look much like the world of today. Thus, our thinking becomes rather narrow and linear, limiting the possibilities of bifocal vision. In 1900, Daimler Benz planners grossly underestimated a worldwide demand for cars, primarily because of the limitation of available chauffeurs. Within two decades, the Ford Model T had revolutionized and democratized the entire industry. More recently, Japan, Inc.'s high-profile developmental progress on high-definition television had U.S. pundits predicting that Japanese companies would lock up the U.S. market for television sets forever. But while Japanese developers were immersed in analog techniques, U.S. researchers were delving into the more advanced digital technology. The emergence of a viable digital format for television now means that a new American-led technology has leapfrogged over years of Japanese efforts and investments exceeding $10 billion.[16]

We offer two tips for managers who want to encourage bifocal vision in their shops:

■ *Insist that each management decision be bifocal.* Every meeting agenda, memo, report, and final decision should have a bifocal dimension. That is, it should explicitly consider the impact on today's customers and tomorrow's. The weight in management meetings, even so-called routine meetings, should be on tomorrow. Even as managers efficiently attend to the routines and improvements of today's activities, the prevailing mind-set should be on the future.

■ *Require that all levels and functions engage in bifocal vision.* In many organizations, the responsibility for "today" is delegated to groups such as operations and customer service, while "tomorrow" is the domain of those in the planning and research and development functions. Or today is the responsibility of middle management, while their bosses deal with tomorrow. Nothing could be more counterproductive. To stimulate a culture that looks a customer ahead, every manager on the payroll must take responsibility for bifocal thinking. Every manager must have opportunities to participate in total systems improvement and strategic thinking exercises. Every manager must be exposed to all data quality, sales, earnings, margins, market, and econometric trends—and participate in discussions about what the numbers mean and what the company ought to do in response today, and tomorrow.

Initiative 3: Create a Vigilant Organization.

To look a customer ahead, a corporate culture must be characterized by speed, proaction, and risk taking. These attributes are necessary but not sufficient. Directionless speed and proactivity can simply exhaust a company. Directionless risk can ruin it. The organization must therefore become vigilant, that is, alert and ever-watchful in order to capitalize immediately on the fleeting opportunities the marketplace continually provides.

Plano Moldings Company makes tough plastic fishing tackle boxes. Back in 1979, the company and some of the retail stores selling the product received periodic queries from makeup artists and models as to whether Plano sold large cosmetics boxes. In most companies, such queries would have been lost in a mountain of other business correspondence. At Plano, an opportunity was seized, and a new division called Caboodles was spun off to develop and market a line of cosmetics organizers— variations of the basic tackle boxes but colored pink and lavender. Plano hired a former Estee Lauder executive to run the division, assuring her of no interference from a corporate headquarters that understood only fishing. Today, Caboodles offers twenty-three products in fifty-four colors. The products are sold in more than twenty thousand stores, and the division's annual sales have topped those of the core tackle box division. Plano has quickly followed up on Caboodles's success by spinning off five divisions, each targeting a niche with the company's core competency of storing and containing: fishing tackle, cosmetics (Caboodles), toolboxes, cassette and CD storage, and the new Jammers, which provides storage for children's toys, including a special subdivision for holding Barbie and Ken doll accessories.

In another demonstration of vigilance in action, on November 21, 1987, the *Miami Herald* responded to the growing Hispanic population in south Florida (nearly 50 percent in Miami's Dade County) and launched a full sister Spanish-language newspaper called *El Nuevo Herald*. The award-winning *El Nuevo* is not merely a translation of the *Miami Herald*. Though it is delivered with the English *Herald* as an optional package, its articles emphasize Hispanic, Cuban, and Latin American news and sports. (In fact, it is clandestinely distributed as an underground information source within Cuba itself.) From 1987 to 1993, daily circulation increased from 60,000 to 105,000 and Sunday circulation grew from 70,000 to 130,000. The paper has already achieved profitability.

Like Knight-Ridder (which owns the *Herald*), many organizations are discovering that tomorrow's customers are not necessarily native-born of European stock. By the year 2000, more than 50 percent of Californians will not speak English as their first language. By early next century, less than half the U.S. population will be of European ancestry.[17] As if to drive the point home, the *El Nuevo* story, like that of Caboodles, has become a classic case of the tail wagging the dog. *El Nuevo* has boosted the flat earnings and subscriptions of the *Herald* to such an extent that the *Herald*'s health now relies on the well-being of *El Nuevo*, not the reverse.

The essence of vigilance involves grabbing opportunities and creating the future, regardless of what current competitors are doing. "Competitor analysis" as a quick, occasional scan of what today's official competitors are doing is useful benchmarking, especially as a vehicle to stimulate urgency and quick response. But problems arise if executives are mesmerized into following the movements of today's "official" well-established competitors who themselves are often lodged in yesterday's solutions for yesterday's customers. As CCC's Glen Tullman says, "We didn't want to imitate our competitors. We wanted to change the rules of the whole game." In a world where everything is up for grabs, seeking the future while wearing the glasses of conventional competitive analysis is tantamount to driving a car on a highway and looking only side to side while ignoring the road ahead. Vigilance means always looking ahead at vast untapped possibilities.

Vigilance provides substance and direction to innovative efforts. When companies are not vigilant, even impressive research and development expenditures are more likely to generate their own internal bureaucracies than to spawn a rapid commercialization of customer-delighting products and services. When companies are not vigilant, moreover, organizational decisions revolve around today's customers and processes, not tomorrow's opportunities. Hence, hardware-and-mainframe-driven IBM refused Microsoft Chairman Bill Gates's offer to let IBM buy the DOS operating system in 1980 for $75,000, and in 1986, to let IBM buy 10 percent of Microsoft (worth $70 million at the time).[18]

Finally, when companies are not vigilant, their employees who do look a customer ahead often become frustrated and strike out on their own. In our work with health care systems, for example, we have seen visionary health care professionals voluntarily leave hospital employment to start their own clinics and labs because their new ideas for increasing revenue had been repeatedly blindsided by entrenched bureaucracies.

To the executive who wishes to stimulate a vigilant organization, we offer four quick pieces of advice:

■ *Refuse to be shackled by familiar markets.* Like Plano, vigilant companies avoid getting locked into narrow business charters; they search for the unconventional opportunities that can be confronted within the domain of their core competencies. Motorola and AT&T are plunging into wireless communication using their brainpower and proprietary technology and that of their numerous strategic partnerships. At 3M, generous incentives encourage scientists to transfer knowledge gained in one subsidiary toward the development of a new product that might one day have enough market viability to ultimately warrant its own division. 3M's entry into health care is an illustration. Group vice president Ron Baukol explains that 3M entered the hospital market through its masking tape line: "Hospitals used [the tape] to wrap bundles for steam sterilizers. From there, someone [at 3M] got the idea of putting indicator ink on the back of the tape that would turn color after sterilization." Thus another product line was born. 3M gradually expanded into other products and services such as new tapes, infection control, and wound management.[19]

Vigilant companies add entirely new functions to well-known products (as Yamaha did with digital recording pianos), develop novel applications of a well-known service (as Banc One and Citicorp did with ATMs), or deliver a new functionality through an entirely new product concept (as GE and Imatron did with CT scanners). There are no limits on efforts to wring out new possibilities for existing outputs. When the news trickles in that a few innovative Japanese ranchers are experimenting with herding their cattle by equipping them with pocket pagers (the cows are conditioned to come home upon hearing the beeper), the vigilant vendor recognizes new opportunities that would certainly have been missed by competitor analysis or strategic planning.

■ *Go beyond traditional decision rules in investment and pricing.* Vigilant companies rely a great deal on intuition and close-to-the-market "feel." For three years, the *Miami Herald* delivered *El Nuevo* free to any interested subscriber to the *Herald* in the interest of testing and developing a new market. From a traditional price/performance perspective, this move might have appeared unjustifiable. Traditional approaches like net present value analyses make large and fast payback demands on new product ideas. Many entrepreneurial success stories were once rejected as unworkable by discounted cash-flow proofs conducted by analytically detached experts. Glen Tullman recalls that the initial development and application of CCC's EZEst software system cost $25 million, which means that "we bet the company." Had they done a net present value, he says, CCC "would never have developed the system." President Mike Weaver of Weaver Popcorn recalls that in order to try to crack the Japanese market, the company made a huge capital investment in optical scanners that actually "look" at each kernel of corn passing through their processing facilities. When asked how he could justify the investment, he admits, "We never did an analysis. We just knew we had to do it if we were to get into Japan." And Weaver Popcorn has since "gone from a zero share to 70 percent of the Japanese market."

We are not endorsing reckless expenditures, but we do note that vigilance is often scuttled by overly cautious executives who use statistical models to justify a "wait and see" attitude. Or they delude themselves into thinking they can save big investment dollars by simply imitating the new products or services of those who have taken the early research heat. Either approach invites slowness to market. On top of that, the imitation approach also invites lawsuits, as Kodak learned when its "aggressive following" strategy led to its being ordered to pay $909.5 million in damages for too closely "following" Polaroid's instant camera technology.

■ *Treat test failures as learning opportunities.* Arie de Guess, former chief planner at Royal Dutch/Shell, has suggested that the key to business success is the ability to learn faster than competitors, and that the key to learning faster is to run plenty of "experiments on the margins."[20] Learning is as much an outcome of failures as of successes, as Apple's earlier Lisa computer demonstrates. Although Lisa failed in the marketplace and caused dislocations within the company, it provided the technological base and learning infrastructure that ultimately resulted in the Macintosh. The marketplace will always punish product failures. If, however, leaders punish individuals and work groups for trying something new, vigilance is doomed. In contrast, creating a culture where people who take prudent risks and publicly share their learning from setbacks receive rewards—not retribution—is a daunting yet vital task for any executive.

■ *Sensitize people to the importance of an organization structure that is fleet, flexible, and liberating.* This is a crucial prerequisite, one to which we allude throughout the book.[21] Regardless of its strategic goals and noble intentions, there is literally no way for a company to seize opportunities if it is saddled with an overly layered, overly centralized, and overly functionalized structure. However great its desire, an organization cannot look a customer ahead if it is bloated with autocracy, fiefdoms, and bureaucracy. As former 3M CEO Lewis Lehr has said, "If you place too many fences around people, they can easily become a pasture of sheep. And how many patents are assigned to sheep?"[22]
If individuals feel they are constrained from taking speedy action, be it by a morass of sign-off and approval requirements

or a smothering blanket of policies and procedures, then all the reading and training about vigilance is futile. An out-of-shape man who reads every running book available and buys the ultimate in high-tech clothing is still out of shape when he steps up to the starting line in a 10-kilometer race.

Initiative 4: Insist On All-Hands, Organizationwide, Strategic Listening.

According to President Glen Tullman, the most important part of the CCC Information Systems story is that "we knew nothing about collision estimating, so we went to the clients and asked them 'what do you need'? Our competitors were established, so they told our clients: 'We're experts, here's what you need.'" No one requested EZEst software or integrated electronic claims management networks—because they had never considered them as possibilities. Clients did, however, air their problems, concerns, and frustrations about traditional collision-estimating services; CCC's innovative efforts provided the solutions.

Listening begets innovation in many ways: it provides the fuel for vigilance. It uncovers market opportunities. It generates the feelings of urgency necessary to overcome complacency. It stimulates people's creativity by opening up practical possibilities. It provides the direction and focus for speedy proactive impulses.

Finally, listening unearths "latent needs," what MIT's Peter Senge describes as "what customers might truly value but have never experienced or would never think to ask for."[23] At 3M, one of the major roadblocks to the release of the Post-it notepad was the marketing department. Since nobody was explicitly asking for semi-sticky little yellow pieces of paper, there were no hard data suggesting a market for them. Surely there was nothing to predict the current $600 million market that has made Post-its among the three most commonly used office products today (along with paper clips and staples), and that has spawned a steady stream of variations of the product. Nobody was *asking for* compact discs or desktop publishing either—and for the same reason: "nobody" thought of it. But the needs were heard by those who really listened.

It is no surprise that strategic listening is an obsession at CCC Information Services. There are no market research or customer service departments. The company insists that everyone, including senior people, be out in the field regularly—interviewing clients, observing them, jointly problem solving with them, coming up with new ideas with them, bringing those ideas back to headquarters. Tullman explains the success of his company succinctly: "We all did a lot of listening in order to understand why the insurance companies were unhappy with the old systems."

The CCC philosophy can be contrasted with two major roadblocks to strategic listening that exist in many organizations: too many people are not expected to do it as an integral part of their jobs, and too much emphasis is placed on market research. Let us consider each hurdle.

Too many people in too many organizations are buffered from external realities. They "do their jobs," with scant attention to or knowledge of marketplace realities. We have talked to managers who could not describe their own company's product or service except in the most superficial terms. We have talked to employees who were blissfully oblivious of competitive pressures facing their company. We have talked to staff professionals who had never had a significant conversation with a paying customer—and who didn't even see the need. Yet no one—staff or line, manager or nonmanager—should be exempt from regular interactions with real people who are, should be, or might one day be customers. For this reason, Nellcor CEO Ray Larkin has eliminated the term *internal customer* from the corporate lexicon. "*Everyone* is expected to help us better serve the people who use our products in hospitals," he says. "We can no longer support people who believe that their job is somehow absolved from listening to our customers in the field."

For another example of effective strategic listening, we look to $50 million packaging materials distributor Conifer Crent. Secretaries, warehousepeople, and truck drivers are expected to deal directly with customers, come up with innovative ideas, and work quickly with management in collaboratively implementing new service concepts. This working philosophy has helped the little company snare large accounts throughout northern and central California and has resulted in an average annual growth rate of 15 percent—even in the midst of the California recession.

Another major roadblock to strategic listening is an overreliance on market research. The truth is that breakthroughs have almost always deviated from the conventional wisdom tapped by market research. As one Detroit executive commented, "You could never produce the Mazda Miata solely from market research. It required a leap of imagination to see what the customer *might* want."[24] Likewise, designer Hal Sperlich couldn't sell Ford on the concept of the now wildly successful minivan and thus moved to a more receptive Chrysler. His experience led him to note a fundamental flaw in Detroit's product development paradigm. Market research probed likes and dislikes among existing products; hence executives didn't believe there was a market for the minivan because the product didn't exist. "In ten years of developing the minivan, we never once got a letter from a housewife asking us to invent one. To the skeptics, that proved there wasn't a market out there."[25]

Successful innovative companies such as Benneton, Rubbermaid, CCC, and Weaver Popcorn eschew a traditional reliance on market research for management decisions. Their goal is not so much to be driven by the market as to drive the market and in the process position themselves as truly unique. For a goal of this caliber, market research has inherent limitations.[26]

For the executive who wishes to generate an organization-wide strategic listening process, we offer the following advice:

■ *Make listening a universal responsibility.* A true listening strategy entails frequent, focused, two-way, collaborative, problem-solving verbal interactions—ideally face-to-face—done by everyone on the payroll. In dealing with clients who complain about the dearth of fresh creative ideas in the pipeline, we have often recommended actions that initially raised eyebrows and occasionally resistance, but which proved successful once implemented. They included the following: engineers and marketers invite end users to participate throughout the development cycle—from prototype discussions to test marketing; purchasers and planners accompany salespeople on sales calls; accountants and materials managers participate in customer focus groups; maintenance engineers and lawyers answer the 800 customer-service phone number; personnel managers and food services people attend trade shows; MIS people and controllers attend user club meetings; hourly-paid employees and executives visit customer sites; and designers and software coders live on customer sites. The idea is not merely to hear passively. Rather, it is to *listen*—to pay close attention to what frustrates or excites customers, to observe what might make their lives easier, to solve problems with them in a partnership mode, to build collaborative relationships for future innovation, and to gain new thoughts and ideas for future possibilities. Assuming a vigilant culture, these possibilities can be quickly implemented as product/service pilots.

■ *Insist that listening take precedence over many traditional activities.* A listening strategy of any kind requires a commitment of managers' most precious resource: time. If some of your managers and professionals protest that listening—on the phone, at a customer site, in focus groups—will take them away from their work, then they are probably doing the wrong work. Some form of frequent, regular listening (and follow-up) will keep every manager and professional busy enough to force them to eliminate non-value-adding activities from their calendars. Listening will help them concentrate their time and efforts on creating quality and value as the marketplace sees it and championing the projects that will allow the organization to meet the demands of tomorrow's customers.

■ *Listen especially closely to the end user.* Most organizations can identify multiple categories of customers in each line of business. Companies obviously have to listen to each constituency. Television stations, for example, must listen to advertisers and independent studios as well as to viewers, while food distributors must listen to wholesalers and retailers as well as to the final consumer. Even so, the priority has to rest with the end user. The end user is not only the foundation for all current revenue streams, but is also likely to be the best weathervane for future opportunities. To illustrate the point, a few months ago a division general manager of a major pharmaceutical company confessed to us that his division "blew it" in the disposable contact lens arena. Instead of listening to the wearers of contact lenses, his group listened solely to the dispensers (opticians and ophthalmologists), most of whom predicted a meager market in disposables. This company fell far behind market leader Vistakon when the so-called meager market turned out to be a burgeoning billion dollar business. The market has exploded because an increasing number of end users are defining price-value consistent with the utility and ease afforded by disposables.

■ *Listen with particular care to pathfinder customers—those who are innovative and demand cutting-edge products.* MIT researcher Eric A. von Hippel has found that innovative ideas frequently come from users who need something different or better and are willing to adopt prototypes that might address those needs.[27] In fact, his research suggests that 75 percent to 90 percent of innovations in certain sectors of plastics and scientific instruments emerge from the demands of these aggressive end users.

Gordon Radley, president of Lucasfilm, Ltd., spoke to the value of strategic listening, particularly with respect to innovative customers. In talking about Lucasfilm's relationship with customer-partner Silicon Graphics, a leader in digital imaging, he said: "We push [Silicon Graphics'] equipment harder than any other of their major customers. We're making the *Terminator II*s and the *Jurassic Park*s and we go to them and say, why doesn't the equipment do this or do that? They love it, because we're not satisfied with anything. They want someone who will push it, show them things they didn't even realize their equipment could do. As soon as we show them what their equipment can do, they can put it in their next model and make more sales."[28]

Smart vendors are receptive to the demands of their most innovative customers and make extra efforts for them. When Hewlett-Packard and Andersen Consulting joined forces to create a customized open-systems software for Oticon, they charged a minimal price for their services. They recognized their little customer as an industry groundbreaker and future powerhouse, and thus wanted to establish a relationship early on. Further, in an emerging management world of open information flow, they realized that they could test a valuable prototype, which would no doubt be revised for future audiences as well.

INNOVATIONS:
CHALLENGES AHEAD AND WITHIN

In order to look a customer ahead, the organization has to continually innovate, create, and even reinvent itself. This mind-set begins with a readiness to ask questions—often unpopular, unnerving, and irreverent questions. The challenge is in building an organization that has the culture of continually asking very hard questions about the soul and fate of the organization, with the premise that things *are* going to change, always.

There are implications for organizations and for leaders. Let us consider organizations first and reflect on what a successful one in the emerging epoch might look like. Organizations that look a customer ahead become good at group learning processes (for example, brainstorming and debriefing); they aggressively seek out ideas and suggestions, and encourage open, constructive conflict (problem analysis, not blame analysis). They provide everyone with the technology necessary to be informed. They allow few, if any, information elites and tolerate even fewer sacred cows. They figuratively break down walls between departments and between organizational "insiders" and "outsiders." They literally break down real walls, forming open spaces in which people can interact with each other. They keep divisions and project teams small, regardless of how large the organization grows. They are clear on the broad responsibilities of the group and the individual while allowing everyone continually to recreate his or her job. They make flexibility and change a way of life, they foster networking and collaboration across departments and disciplines, and they are willing to experiment by spending money on feasibility studies. They provide "bootleg" time; they encourage people to bootleg resources. They shelter new ideas until ready for vigorous evaluation, and they establish "incubators" that can nourish the idea of a few committed champions. They wipe away bureaucratic demands for multiple approvals and double-checking; they share credit and encourage a tolerance for ambiguity. They are fanatics about getting customer feedback. They pool their core competencies with those of other partners for specific, sometimes short-term ("virtual") projects. They foster a climate where action is emphasized over debate, pilots over proposals, tries over analysis, accountability over sign-offs, trust over second guessing. Finally, they reward (not merely tolerate) the risk takers and challengers.

The list of what these future-creating companies don't do is just as important: they don't let size suffocate innovation, they don't get complacent, and they don't retreat to complexity as a way of handling the unknown (listening for zebras when they hear hoofs). They don't foster a sense of arrogance about the old truths. They don't focus unreasonably on the short term, they don't obsess about security, they don't apologize for hard work, and they don't fear failure or success. They don't allow decisions to go unmade, they don't overly restrict resources, and they don't demean the nonspecialists or nonexperts. Most important, they don't shoot those who make mistakes, nor do they expect success of every venture.

The power and potential of the organization that looks a customer ahead are enormous. Even organizations with "bad" numbers today can be investors' darlings if they are perceived to be effectively preparing for tomorrow. Of the five-hundred-some independent, publicly traded biotechnology firms in 1992— many of them enjoying steadily increasing stock value—fewer than 10 percent generated a positive cash flow. Likewise, McCaw Cellular never turned an operating profit prior to its purchase by AT&T, yet it was consistently listed as one of the most valuable companies in the United States. One analyst described Craig McCaw, a dreamer of national cellular networks, as someone who "lives five years into the future."

What does all this mean at the level of the individual leader? The willingness to adopt the new role characteristics, as discussed in Chapter Three, is paramount. Also, leaders who look a customer ahead acknowledge that success from innovation is a result of multiple tries and multiple setbacks.[29] The wisdom of Salk's remark, that "life is an error-making and an error-correcting process," reflects their sentiment.

Since S-curve leaps and transformation involve inherent conflict between old and new, it is not surprising that leaders who look a customer ahead encourage people to have straight, no-holds-barred, creative conflict among alternatives and options. Constructive conflict allows people the freedom to challenge the system and the safety to disequilibriate old, tried and true practices. Managers who fear conflict create cultures where no conflict exists—and thus no innovation, either. And even that statement is not correct, because the conflict merely goes underground and becomes dysfunctional and personal; frustration and lethargy generate political games, back stabbing, and raw power plays. Unsurprisingly, at forward-looking large companies and myriad zesty start-ups, healthy, vigorous, issues-based conflict—and skins thick enough not to be personally devastated by it—are the norm.

Simultaneously, leaders who look a customer ahead make certain that the constructive conflict is embedded in a context of inclusion and cooperation. This context provides support and safety for innovation, which is by definition risky and threatening. As previously mentioned, Salk argued that certain attitudes and behaviors that were appropriate for the epoch we are leaving behind are not as appropriate for the epoch we are entering. Specifically, he suggested that the excessive emphasis on individualism, power, independence, competition, and "either/or" thinking is being replaced by consensus, collaboration, interdependence, and values that embrace both the individual and the group simultaneously. He called this trend *Both/And* thinking, as opposed to the exclusionary Either/Or (Us versus Them) thinking appropriate to the previous epoch. As innovative companies have found, win-win Both/And inclusion in the form of cross-level, cross-disciplinary collaboration is essential to innovation.

To conclude, organizational change driven by looking a customer ahead is not the periodic upheavals seen in the once-a-year, cataclysmic, top-down reorganizations that leave people running around trying to figure out what their jobs are, or have customers calling telephone numbers that no longer function. Instead, it means the day-in, day-out process of challenging what we do and the way we do it. It is ongoing, relentless. It is the waves hitting the shore, over and over again, morning and night, when you're around to supervise and when you're not, when you feel in the mood and when you don't.

The final words are spoken not by a manager but by a historian and a psychologist. For the eminent historian Arnold Toynbee, success arises from inward articulation or self-determination more than from conquering external obstacles.[30] This view is consistent with our earlier discussions, in which we noted that the leader's personal willingness to take on a new role is the necessary precursor for effective, innovative responses to outside factors. As Salk might have put it, the issue is the struggle among values.

Clare Graves, a psychologist writing in *The Futurist* in the early 1970s, made the same point when he wrote that humanity is "learning that values and ways of living which were good for him at one period in his development are no longer good for the changed condition of his existence. He is recognizing that the old values are no longer appropriate, but he has not yet understood the new."[31]

Keeping these thoughts in mind, consider that the final challenge that looking a customer ahead presents to individual managers is whether they have the capacity to overcome fatalism ("I can't impact my environment"; "I'm just a leaf in the wind") and organizational determinism ("Why bother to try to change since the more things change, the more they stay the same?"; "Why fight City Hall?"). In the rebuttal to this attitude, Jonas Salk, Arnold Toynbee, Clare Graves, and others are in agreement. Ultimately, the capacity to look a customer ahead resides in ourselves, our mental models, our curiosity, our tenacity, our vision, and our courage.

C H A P T E R

6

The Intelligence Imperative

*You cannot step twice into the same river, other
and still other waters flow upon them.*
—Heraclitus

*Tell me how a competitor values a set of financial
ratios and you have given me useful information.
Teach me to understand his worldview and you
have given me something that is priceless.*
**—Franco Cremante, Managing Partner
Roland Berger**

Organizations are not the "ends" of business; rather, they are the means by which managers attempt to realize mission, strategy, and values. To paraphrase a question we asked earlier, is it reasonable to assume that, given today's massive transformation in civilization, we can maintain the same organizational "vehicles" that may have been effective in the past? We believe not. Pragmatically, upheavals in the environment require major change in organizational structures and processes.

Yet even as many managers embrace fads and programs of the month, when it comes to the idea of radical surgery on organizations themselves—the structure, the systems, the size, the form—they just as readily lean toward "yeah, but" rationalizations. Managers are often prepared to tinker with the edges— a little decentralization here, a little flattening there—but too frequently reluctant to do much else, even in the face of profit hemorrhaging and severe external dangers. Resistance can entail any of several arguments: we don't really need to change policies and processes (a training program or consultant's report will suffice); bureaucratic controls and size are necessary (otherwise, how can we monitor people?); we can't afford technological investments (we have our quarterly reports to contend with). Each of these rationalizations has been taken to task by a host of writers and executives, and increasingly, those associated with business realize how bankrupt such protestations are.

Our intention in the next two chapters is to describe an alternative point of view. It maintains that when information flow and associated processes are used as an organizing principle—that is, when an organization builds itself and its software around the customer—dramatic improvements result in the way the company operates. This is more than a cheer for designing technology-mediated organizational structures; it is another acknowledgment that the old ways of looking at organizations need to be replaced. First and foremost, it means letting go of an anachronistic metaphor: the organization as machine.

The machine metaphor and the corresponding mechanistic (as opposed to organic) perspective on organizations has been discussed by a variety of researchers for half a century. Writing in 1942 (again, note the bellwether year), Steven Pepper discussed the differences between organic and mechanistic ways of looking at the world and the power of such metaphors.[1] But only recently has the general business community begun to understand the implications for organizational strategy and development.

The mechanistic orientation is evidenced in treating the organization as a machine that has to be "wired," "revved up," or "geared up" if it is to work properly. The assumption is that once we get things "organized," success is on the way. Organizational charts thus become necessary blueprints. So do volumes of policies, standard operating procedures, paper controls, and strict budgetary and hierarchical systems.

The mechanistic approach, as the name implies, tends to dehumanize the organization in the literal sense of the word. Because productivity is presumably enhanced by routinizing work and eliminating deviations from the norm (that is, originality), uniformity is a crucial attribute of the organization. So is the concept of the worker as a cog in the machine. Each person (employee, middle manager, staff specialist) focuses on one "job" and excels in it as a function of repetition and limited vision. As one executive suggested, "the idea seems to be to dumb down everyone to fit the system." It is assumed that the more detailed the job description, pass-off interface, or sign-off process, the better.

In this mind-set, training and education are an expense (a necessary cost in "fine tuning" the machine), not an investment in value-adding creativity. Time and motion studies are de rigueur as are all other efforts to gather up standardization and economies of scale.[2] Professionalism is defined in terms of putting everyone and everything in a neat order. In terms of motivational psychology, a simple input/output model is embraced. Ultimately, people are viewed in the fashion of B. F. Skinner's stimulus-response boxes: for more productivity, one pays people more money, and that should do it.

The ideas that are common to the mechanistic approach are so ingrained in the way we think about organizations that it would be difficult to jettison them entirely. The concept of the division of labor, which was promoted by Adam Smith as early as 1776 as a means of increasing efficiency in manufacturing, still endures in some fashion in even the most innovative companies, at least in terms of primary group responsibilities. Eli Whitney's idea, circa 1800, of interchangeable parts—which accelerated the manufacture of guns and showed the way to mass production—still has relevance in industries that fabricate new products with "off-the-shelf" components. The idea of analyzing work processes, espoused by Frederick Taylor's scientific management, is a part of the reengineering movement that is so popular today. The notion of bureaucracy, as described by Max Weber, was a high achievement of the modernizing process; by emphasizing the importance of accountability and competence while reducing the effects of nepotism and favoritism, classical bureaucracy led to improvements in efficiency and reliability.

But the real source of reluctance to abandon the machine metaphor of organizations is more straightforward: we are inclined to view organizations as machines because that is how we view the world. This is an inheritance from Isaac Newton's proposition during the scientific revolution that the whole world could best be understood as a Great Machine. Newton's model built on the empirical work of Galileo (observation and measurement, not faith, will prove what is true and what is false) and Descartes (the world "out there" can be explained by a great system of geometric equations). Within his metaphor could be found the ideas of predictability, the causal nature of physical phenomena, solid particles, linear thinking, rational thought, and mechanistic determination (the present is an unavoidable consequence of a chain of events in the past). The emphasis was on analysis, and consequently, on the fragmentation of problems into smaller and smaller individual pieces. The view was static, but it worked. The Newtonian and Cartesian ways of thinking, what some have referred to as the Cartesian-Newtonian paradigm, came to dominate Western thought until the beginning of the twentieth century.

At that point, things changed. Science—physics in particular—found that it could not explain subatomic phenomena using Newton's view of the world. Newton's work could be relied on to explain and make predictions about things one could actually see. However, as the preeminent physicist Werner Heisenberg concluded, the language and concepts we use "to describe ordinary physical objects, such as position, velocity, color, size, and so on, become indefinite and problematic" in the new physics. He summarized his position by noting that "for modern natural science there is no longer in the beginning the material object, but form, mathematical symmetry."[3]

For example, in trying to decide whether light was made of particles or waves, physicists found that the answer depended on how one was looking at light. Under one set of circumstances, light would best be described as made of particles. Looked at another way, light appeared to have the properties of electromagnetic waves. In effect, there were not independent "things" out there, in the sense of objects occupying a specific amount of mass or matter; there were also some dependencies on the environment. Light was one or another kind of thing as a function of the environment used to observe it. The focus of study in the emerging physics, therefore, was not so much a concrete object as a set of tendencies or, in the formalism of quantum theory, a set of mathematical probabilities. In contrast to Newtonian thinking, the findings of the new physics stressed the intangible nature of the world we live in.

In business, the relevance of nonmachine intangibles becomes especially clear when we look at the worth of information and values. The market value of companies is usually a significant multiple of book value. So, often, is purchase price. In 1988 Dun & Bradstreet sold the Official Airline Guides for roughly $750 million.[4] Most of the content of the guides is publicly available information about flight schedules. The company was basically selling an intellectual framework, an intangible. Earlier in the same year, Donald Trump paid $365 million for the Eastern airlines shuttle.[5] Comparing these two figures, one could argue that information about when the planes fly is about twice as valuable as the planes themselves.

A similar dynamic was reflected in the $12.9 billion Phillip Morris spent to buy Kraft in 1988. At the closing, after toting up the value of Kraft real estate, the cows in the field, and all the cheese, the total came to less than $2 billion. In other words, Phillip Morris paid more than $11 billion for the intelligence of the work force, the relationships between Kraft and its distributors, and the image value of the name.[6] Phillip Morris paid not for something one could hold and put in a box, but for the intangible.

More recent examples are represented in the interest in acquisition of publicly traded mutual fund companies. Mellon Bank's pursuit of Dreyfus and GE Capital's hostile bid for Kemper reflect the value seen in organizations that produce wealth by knowing how to invest other people's money: their value is in knowledge, distribution, and a host of other intangibles. A recognized name, reflecting the older branding strategy, is a specific consideration germane to the point. Coca-Cola's market value, to take a leading example, has consistently enjoyed a large lift over earnings per share in bad times and good. What investors have come to admire is not only the name recognition but also the market intelligence and business acumen of the Coca-Cola team.[7]

Even the conceptualization of an "organization" or "enterprise" is challenged. Increasingly, leaders stress the reality that an enterprise is more than a collection of fixed assets, and that a merger or acquisition, in order to have any value, must be greater than the simple valuation of consolidated balance sheets. The myriad global partnerships and outsourcing relationships—many temporary—that characterize companies as diverse as Daimler-Benz, Apple, Sony, MCI, and Corning attest to the possibility that organizations themselves are becoming best described as a web of intangible and "virtual" alliances.

The idea of alliances underscores the importance of intangible connectedness. Once again, science converges with business. Astronauts report that when they look down at Earth from out in space, they are struck by the absence of international boundaries, an observation that emphasizes how artificial such boundaries really are. Some quantum physicists have suggested that there is an interconnected wholeness to the universe. Less dramatically, Bertrand Russell has said that the universe is not so much a set of things as a connection of events: "It is true that there are still particles which seem to persist, but these . . . are really to be conceived as strings of connected events, like the successive notes of a song."[8]

Controversial studies reported by Rupert Sheldrake in the field of biochemistry strive to make a similar point. His contention is that organisms somehow draw on the pooled or collective memory of other members of their species. For example, when a fruit fly is caused by some unusual environmental condition to grow abnormally, the likelihood increases that other members of the species will develop abnormally. Somehow the species appears to learn from the experience of one of its members. Likewise, new compounds, which are difficult to crystallize, can take up to months to form for the first time; yet amazingly, regardless of the location where the compounds initially crystallize, "as time goes on, they tend to appear more readily all over the world. . . . A cumulative memory will build up as the pattern becomes more and more habitual."[9] The vision is increasingly of a "nonmechanical reality."

Observations such as these are used to challenge the idea of organizational boundaries (internal and external) and even the historical overemphasis on individual performance. Instead, it is the aggregate that is real. It is the whole, the unity that we cannot see or touch, that we deal with. Separateness, the bedrock of Newtonian physics, and for that matter Lockean political theory (which asserts that the true foundation of a society is the autonomous individual), is considered an illusion. Thus, we are encouraged to think of organizations as webs of interconnections among teams, cross-functional departments, business partners, and vendors.

These webs, as suggested earlier, are not permanent, nor even stable. In contrast to the Aristotelian view that says objects move toward a state of rest, modern physics says that the subatomic world is perpetually restless. Einstein's relativity theory guides us to observations of a dynamism in molecular structures. Particles are "dancing," "jiggling," and "vibrating"[10]: one moment mass, then energy; here matter, there activity. Mass is, in fact, no more than energy bundled up. If we penetrate deeply enough, we find matter to be patterns of energy on the move, constantly changing. The picture is one of an unstable world, of a universe always in flux and change. The mathematics of chaos theory adds to our understanding by positing that events that often seem to be random have an underlying unity and structure that can be explained by mathematical formulas. That is, among many other implications, the theory indicates that while there is order deep within perpetual disorder, the disorder is not the deviation from the norm but the norm itself. The implication for leaders is that the expectation of a stable, predictable world where everything is finally in place is futile.

Thus, when one hears of organizations without boundaries, of spider web structures, of the importance of the intangible and context, and of chaos in the marketplace as a given, one can also hear the protagonists of a new science whispering their description of a new worldview.[11] Systems and subsystems evolve, change, grow, and vibrate in interaction with an evolving, changing, growing, and vibrating environment. For businesspeople, the demand is to deal with a world of greater complexity. The effort to find order within the disorder pivots eventually on the ability to transform information into knowledge and to keep identity in the midst of innovation and adaptation.

THE QUEST FOR
A NEW METAPHOR

A fresh conceptualization of organizations is needed. Organizations designed as machines are most effective when doing the same things over and over again. They are not designed to be constantly innovative, fleet, and flexible. Nor are they designed to deliver customized products and services rapidly across a global marketplace that is best characterized as splintered. The new metaphor, therefore, must efficiently tie together all these priorities, as well as the ideas of interconnectivity, permeable boundaries, and the importance of intangibles. The metaphor of the organization as brain comes to mind. In essence, jumping the curve means negotiating the transition from mass to brain.[12]

Back in the early 1980s, entrepreneur Paul Hawken referred to the changing ratio between mass and information as a critical determinant of business success.[13] Similarly, the relatively new metaphor of organization as brain suggests that the traditional management emphasis on growing the organization's "body" size (mass, tangible assets, personnel roster, centralization, vertical integration) is not only a significant cost drain but often a lethal strategic error. Loyalty to the machine metaphor leads managers to celebrate the huge body and the little brain. This is illustrated when so many organizations try to become larger (through often myopic sales efforts, poorly conceptualized acquisitions, or quickly expedient "strategic alliances"), even as they become slower, "dumber," and less capable of either change or true market responsiveness.

In contrast, the notion of organization as brain emphasizes the reverse priority: reducing the body mass and becoming leaner and more flexible while enlarging the knowledge and competency base of the organization. The image is one of an organization with limited numbers of people and unlimited reservoirs of intelligence, whose body is so gossamery and spread out that it is no longer even constrained by a fixed location. It can quickly appear as a presence anywhere and everywhere in the world. This lighter, nimbler, more intelligent organization finds it easier to jump the curve.

Seen in this metaphor, small but "smart" organizations become powerful global competitors while larger organizations compete by descaling and spinning off small subunits each containing large pools of expertise. Speaking to just this point, a vice president of a major oil company told us that despite his company's retail successes relative to the other oil "majors," the new environment is initiating the trauma of rebirth: "If we're to continue to be successful, each of our businesses needs to look like a small independent, not a major." Acquisitions, alliances, and joint ventures become essential strategic vehicles. However, they are evaluated not with the goal of growing per se (though that may be an immediate consequence) but with the idea of rapidly exploiting a larger base of brainpower anywhere on earth. Moreover, the attention of the "brain" is focused externally: on responding to today's markets and customers, and on anticipating tomorrow's markets and customers.

To help the leader bring the organization-as-brain metaphor to life, we propose the second organizing principle: *Build the organization around the software and build the software around the customer.* Software, in our usage, means more than just technology and programming code. It also refers to the organization's processes, systems, and methodologies that enable it to respond quickly to a changing mix of customer needs and developments in technology. Building the company around the software means organizing production and work around knowledge—knowledge about business and about the business environment. It means using technology to bring flexibility and adaptation—not rigid complex procedures—to the firm's capabilities.

Building the software around the customer means that the customer becomes the central focus of these efforts. It means that the market—the world beyond the inward-looking bureaucracy—determines the roles and processes that need to be played out, the strategies that need to be pursued, and the goals that need to be set.

The recommendation to build the organization and the software around the customer is grounded in an underlying set of assumptions. The first is that organizations must be continually restless and perpetually evolving. Whereas machine-metaphor organizations deal with assumptions of staticness (for example, budgets are expected to have a lifetime of one year, job descriptions, of several years), organizations built around dynamic software assume fluidity and evolution. And with big "brains" and little "mass," such assumptions are easily realizable. Also, the world "outside" the organization is not assumed to be still. Demographics and customer tastes change. Competitors find unexpected opportunities. New technologies are born. Trade rules disappear. Immediate responsiveness becomes a strategic source of opportunity.

The spread of knowledge to every corner of the organization becomes a business priority. The leader's ability to feel fully confident in an aggressive, informed work force becomes an invaluable, intangible asset. Databases that document the turmoil of the market and the organization's response are valuable; databases that can fashion data in a way that employees can access and use immediately are more so. The challenge becomes how to create organizations that permit an easy use and flow of - information.

Another assumption is that the organization is no longer a collection of bodies, capital, building, and other resources. Indeed, a company's home office—bricks, mortar, two-by-fours, land—contributes less added value than the competence and market awareness of its work force. The diffusion of information technology helps knowledge-based activities and organizational intelligence attain strategic importance.

The organization thus becomes something more intangible, a knowledge reservoir that holds the collective wisdom of everyone associated with it: once again, a brain, of sorts. The underlying premise is that responsibility for thinking, judgment, and creativity exists everywhere in the organization. The capacity for renewal is seen as a function of intelligence and openness that characterizes people at all levels of the organization, not just a few in the president's suite. Building the organization around the software and the software around the customer suggests that an organization can regulate itself by constantly monitoring and anticipating the environment, by coordinating multiple parts to perform as a whole and by absorbing both positive and negative feedback to shape action. The implication is that the organization can learn, and must learn, constantly.

The brain metaphor is also relevant to how we come to view the necessity for change. Organizational memory has value in reminding people about what has been learned in the past that is useful for today. Just as important, however, is the requirement to put aside what was learned yesterday because of its lack of relevance today. "Unlearning the organization" includes in great measure a readiness to recognize failures and to try something different. Institutionalizing the process by which that can be done is in part what the organizing principle is about as well. In short, the organization not only has to learn new methods or scout for new data, it also has to learn how to forget.

The flexibility inherent in building the organization and the software around the customer underscores that a key purpose of management is to continually make the brain smarter, faster, and more customer sensitive. By the same token, the purpose of the brain is to enable all employees and managers, from those on the factory floor to those in the executive suite, to do their jobs better and better—that is, more creatively and efficiently on behalf of the customer. Success becomes measured not only by achieving certain productivity goals for a day or a quarter or a year but also by growing the intelligence and capabilities of the organizational brain. To see how such an approach might look in real life, let us first examine a pedestrian, everyday product: cookies.

Smart Cookies

Back in the late 1970s Debbi Fields began selling cookies out of a little store in Palo Alto, California. The quick success of the business led to the possibility of expansion to other locations. There was a problem, however. Debbi was a close, hands-on manager who was a fanatic about quality and the work standards that lead to it. As she and her husband, Randy, looked at the balance of opportunities and risks associated with growth, they often mused that the solution was in taking Debbi's approach to the business, her sense of priorities, for example, and somehow grafting that onto the management style of the people who would work in the different stores. The traditional way of doing that was with training tools, policy and procedure manuals, and periodic field inspections. Such techniques were good as far as they went, but something was missing. For one thing, Debbi disliked the loss of individual contact, the not knowing the specific concerns of a particular store or who was committed to what goal. Randy saw the dangers of hierarchy. He saw the costs of building layers of management just to ensure that the workers in the stores, those who were actually providing the service that customers wanted to buy, were doing their job. The inefficiency—the dilution of purpose—was as bothersome to him as the dollars wasted.

Once they began to sort out the work practices that Debbi actually used, Randy realized that a great deal of what Debbi did could be built into a computer system to help employees see a situation the way she saw it. In addition, employees could influence and shape Debbi's perception based on their own experience and learning. They would learn from the system and the system would learn from them, and all would learn from the customer. This, after all, is how a learning organization can be distinguished.

What Randy and his team envisioned and eventually built was a software system that captured the ideas Debbi and other experts (such as high-performance managers, corporate specialists, and interested employees) had about every aspect of running the business, from baking to selling, from people management to production schedules. The goal was to collect their ideas and incorporate them as a set of recommendations that anyone in the field could call up on a computer and utilize immediately. These suggestions were included within modules, also designed by Randy, Debbi, and the experts for sales reports, scheduling of daily activities, inventory control, financial reporting, and an assortment of other functions. In short, a whole array of traditional management activities was automated. At the same time, advice and coaching were available through instruction sets containing the collective expertise of dozens of managers and authorities, the "best and brightest." The underlying premise in such a system is that every successful business person has a knowledge about his or her job that is partly derived from common sense shared by many and partly derived from a unique set of insights and instincts. The trick is to capture those insights in a way that makes them accessible to other people in the organization.

The intention to create this sort of system carries its own demands. The experts must have an opportunity to revise their recommendations and the rules and assumptions they use to develop those recommendations. This revision can be done once a week or once a year. In a similar fashion, field personnel can contribute knowledge they have gleaned from their work experience, either at the end of the day or at the end of a week. The principle is the same: the system has to be flexible enough to incorporate what is learned about how the business performs—and to do so in a timely manner. Learning can essentially be assessed by how the company changes the way it interacts with the market.

For example, the same pattern of problems might occur across a number of stores during the same week. Then one store manager in Des Moines, let's say, experiments with a solution that has not been tried before. The results are superb. Sales go up. Customers are happy. Facilitated by an expert at home base or at a district level, the new wisdom is spread electronically throughout the system. Since there are minimal buffers like management layers and departmental boundaries, everyone on the payroll can access the new information and translate it to fit his or her own situation.

Telecommunications systems allow peer-to-peer communication so that the idea can be elaborated and polished right away by those who are face to face with the customer. A network becomes more than form or data transmission; it is about coaching and education using live performance information. With it, a new alternative, another solution, can be brought to the repertoire of activities other managers can engage in to be effective. Over time it will be tested by different locations and evaluated for its appropriateness in specific conditions. At some point, assuming its continued validity, the insight is included in revised standards and procedures. The new technique becomes part of the expert advice available to everyone using the corresponding software module. Thus, the insight of one employee not only affects the performance of her store and operations but, through the mechanism of the computerized component of the organizational brain, her insights also assist others in the pursuit of their objectives. Just as mechanical devices could be used to leverage the muscle and physical energy of a laborer in one era, information technology can be used to leverage the knowledge of an entire Mrs. Fields community.

In short, the Fields organization takes the technology in a different direction from what we have normally seen in the past. It is not content just to tell people what to do (or to do it for them); instead, its ambition is to exploit every piece of knowledge the organization acquires in a way that maximizes the effectiveness of the entire system. The goal is not to create "electrocop" but to give people on the line the best information about how to run a business. Information is not used to control but rather to elevate awareness and understanding.

If one were to build an organization around such a system from the beginning, the way it would conduct business would be radically different from the way business is typically managed. Minimally, recruitment would change. In effect, the organization would seek to hire a person to run stores who is different from the kind normally hired today. Administrative skills would be less important than communication skills. The software would do a lot of the information processing and administrative grunt work, freeing the store manager to spend more time coaching employees and being with customers. Listening, communication, and judgment would become more important. The technology would aid the search for ideas and suggestions that might facilitate operations; it would also encourage the creation of innovative solutions and ideas. In short, a different kind of skills hierarchy would be supported by the technology, one that is more outward looking in its orientation. Increasingly, the emphasis would be on innovating, not on managing a list of administrative "to do's."

The cumulative effect all these opportunities have for increasing an employee's sense of significance is immense. The employee gets the feeling from four sources that what he or she does matters. The first is her impact on her own store's performance. A second is the knowledge that she has assisted others in pursuit of their goals. Third, she knows that future employees will benefit from a system she helped create; her influence will continue over time. Fourth, she has demonstrated success in learning about the business; she has proven that her skills and competence are growing.

Significant benefits accrue to the organization. When everyone has access to the collected intelligence of the organization and can input data so that the activity of all other workers will be affected, strategy can begin anywhere in the company. It is no longer the preserve of just the top three or four people in the organization. The knowledge base grows as a shared investment of everyone in the organizational community.

The element of sharing is a confidence builder in itself. Because the data are from people in the field, innovations are more likely to be driven by customer input than by administrative necessity. Problems and opportunities are visible immediately. Issues can be aired before everyone in the company at the same time; informed action can therefore be under way long before a report would be filed, studied, and responded to in the home office. Speed is accentuated and management's role becomes not telling but listening. Layers of management are eliminated, lessening the opportunity for disempowerment by a command and control environment. What is in control, instead, is the knowledge base of the enterprise.

Knowledge flow never stops. The system can be "on" twenty-four hours a day anywhere in the world. In fact, building the organization and the software around the customer liberates spatial restraints; the organization is where the knowledge is and where the customer is. Images of invisible, electronic pathways and a cyberspace pulsing with data come to replace the machine metaphor. The power to make a difference anywhere becomes tangible on a moment-to-moment basis. Randy Fields has said that this is the one true value of all information technology. The intended outcome, he told us, is making it "normal for every employee, but especially for those who are dealing directly with the customers, to be a big player when it comes to deciding the way things should work."

Smart Processes

It is not a large jump to move from seeing the value information plays in integrating a work force within an organization to seeing the role information exchange might have across organizations. Building the organization and the software around the customer is relevant in enhancing interpersonal relationships across organizations. Processes that allow members of two-partner organizations to work off the same database, for example, reduce delays, errors, and the need for hierarchical controls, because the likelihood is increased that information is where it can be employed most efficiently—even in "real time." Yet, when building the organization and the software around the customer, the technology is not used simply to expand the size of either company or to speed old ways of doing things. Its role includes being an integral part of the redefinition of both organizations' processes.

Thinking of the organization as a brain encourages getting all the knowledge one can about the market and using that information appropriately. Information becomes knowledge when the organization uses it to generate new products, enter new niches, and customize services. Economies can be achieved by a customer identification program that indicates who would want to buy what and when, by finding and reaching the "best customer" over and over again. The consequences go beyond the implementation of a marketing program. Advertising and promotion are aligned with financial demands as well as human resource requirements. The knowledge and programs derived from the manipulation and use of data eventually impact all aspects of how the organization is run. Since the knowledge base is about customer behavior, the result is that the customer ends up driving the processes of the organization. The organization—the brain—learns about critical functions and levels of performance from the environment.

Smart processes go beyond technology. In fact, Colin Gilmore, one of the key architects of United Airlines' quality process for engine repair, argues that when outdated assumptions about people, quality, and management systems remain entrenched, new technology either covers up problems, or even worse, aggravates them by building them into the new process. Building a company around software is about much more than picking the correct software product. The problems the strategy confronts are sociotechnical; the solutions have to be as well.

WHEN ORGANIZATIONS
DEPEND ON BRAINS

Despite the transformational promise of communication technology, the sad truth is that in practice it is still used primarily to overlay electronic systems on outdated manual processes. For example, the checker at the grocery counter uses a point-of-sale device (POS) to automate the same process she conducted before the advent of bar codes and computerized inventory systems. Each purchase is picked up by the checker as before, its price is entered into the system as before, and the sum of purchases is totaled as before. Unless it is geared to search for and interact with customer or inventory profiles, the computer adds value only by reading and adding numbers more quickly and accurately. Consistent with Gilmore's warning, one can argue that all too often computerization's major contribution has been to rigidify the procedures and policies that were in place to begin with.

The beginning point, however, for transforming the brain metaphor into concrete results is to examine the processes that the organization currently employs. Many organizations recognize that the activity of redoing their technology infrastructure is the best opportunity to reengineer the processes that exist. As one executive told us, "Having support for redesigning our technology systems gave us the opening to redo all our processes. We came to think of it as the 'main chance' in the long view of the life of the company."

When organizations depend on brains to achieve productivity improvements that customers value, the large number of people needed to work in-house decreases. Labor substitution is one factor. Economies of scale are more reliable with outsourcing and subcontracting to other organizations with special skills. Vertical integration in the end looks less effective than partnering. Alliances are used to acquire needed knowledge quickly. Niche strategies and market focus, spurred by faster dispersion of customer information, also diminish the tolerance for bloated structures.

By encouraging a reduction in sheer size and an expansion of knowledge sources, these trends promote a more open and fluid view of organizations. The emphasis, once again, is on agility and nimbleness. Consequently, networks of small, focused teams become the norm. Information technology provides the coordination across functions and departments that middle managers used to do. Even as the organization grows in size, it breaks itself up into smaller, decentralized units. It essentially disorganizes itself by continually shedding as much "body mass" as possible.

The appetite or readiness for more sophisticated (not necessarily more expensive) use of technological tools generally increases once the orientation of the company as a pool of intelligence begins to take hold. Randy and Debbi Fields, for example, were exploring the area of expert or knowledge-based systems, the legacy of a specialty in software development known as artificial intelligence. Applications that play chess and conduct clinical diagnoses, according to rules and data supplied by masters and respected diagnosticians, are uses of expert systems that actually preceded significant business applications. The business applications themselves have varied widely. Chemical Bank uses an expert system to monitor its currency exchange activity over thousands of international locations. The system scans about a billion dollars of transactions each day in search of suspicious trades, essentially where the exchange rates deviate from rules established by the experts. Once "flagged," a trade is given closer scrutiny. Considering that a single bad trade could cost the bank millions of dollars and that it is impossible for auditors to inspect all the trades, the expert system's contribution to the overall performance of the bank is important.[14]

Expert system software developed by Neuron Data has also helped Sony to reduce the time required to design the chips it uses in the development of its camcorders. The software captures the knowledge of engineers in how to conduct simulations, so people with relatively little experience in running simulations can do them efficiently. The net result is a two-third reduction in the time needed to complete the design process. As product life cycles continue to contract, the impact of the expert system will increase.

Other applications of expert systems have been used by Westinghouse, Fujitsu, Coopers and Lybrand, and Digital, among others. DuPont had some two hundred applications under way by the end of the 1980s. About half of the Fortune 500 companies had some application in use within a few years.

The technology for supporting the organizing principle is not restricted to expert systems. Anything that connects people and information is valuable. For example, client server computing—using a central computer to coordinate droves of smaller desktop or personal computers, a more general description of a network application of what has been described above—will become more commonplace. Furthermore, gains in wireless communications, multimedia, and interactive media will all assert their value.[15] By reducing overhead costs, facilitating customization, spurring creativity, and quickening response times, such techniques will be employed more and more to cope with the sheer volume of new information that overwhelms the marketplace daily.

Just as important, however, will be the continued flow of insights regarding interpersonal issues. Terry Winograd and Fernando Flores describe work as a network or series of conversations. In their view, four elements—what they called workloops—comprise conversation and interpersonal transactions of the kind we commonly see at work: someone requesting an action, someone agreeing to do it, the actual process of getting it done, and the approval or satisfaction of the customer, the person who made the original request. In their approach, the aim of software or any other tool has less to do with tracking material and physical resources than with the coordination of conversations where these action components come to life in what people do and say. Each loop is about commitments two people make; technology is about highlighting these and using them in database and communication software. The work processes of the organization, therefore, can be represented as thousands of workloops that are connected throughout the entire enterprise. On one level the approach is about methodology; on another it is about a philosophy that addresses what makes up workflow in a knowledge or professional services business. In effect, the approach links an understanding of social process to computer technology.[16]

By putting commitment at the center of the model, the Winograd and Flores design not only speaks to the well-being of the organization but also to the integrity of the individual. It intertwines both, in the sense that work becomes a completed workloop—a fulfilled commitment. Similarly, the Fields technology addresses more than the accumulation of facts and figures. The company's consultant-in-a-box is primarily aimed at coordinating the growing skills and creativity of individuals throughout the organization. Feedback is offered on an ongoing, self-managed basis. In both situations the organization treats human intelligence as its basic building block.

In short, it is easy to see the value in building the organization and the software around the customer once organizations appreciate the priority of brains over mass. As a technique for jumping the curve, this organizing principle has implications for all structures and processes, including but not limited to managing performance, collaborating across groups, developing leadership, and customizing new products. Specific initiatives and actions pertaining to these areas are discussed in the next chapter.

7

Growing the Smart Organization

Execution is the chariot of genius.
—**William Blake**

*Given the widespread availability of computing
power now, there will be just two kinds of
companies in the future: smart or dead.*
—**Randall Fields, CEO, Park City Group**

When the organizing principle of building the organization around the software and building the software around the customer is in effect, an organization becomes as much a collection of thoughts and ideas as it is a collection of things. This shift suggests that information technology is not just another resource that has to be "managed." The idea that the information system *is* the management system is closer to the point because of its stress on the centrality of knowledge, particularly if applied in pursuit of both today's and tomorrow's customer.

Implementing the organizing principle capsizes traditional ideas. Typically, the organization—with its attendant structures and systems—is considered a "given." Any software additions are integrated or superimposed into that existing infrastructure. Once everything is in place, the enterprise is presumably ready to attend to the customer. Granted, this is somewhat an unfair stereotype, since events in the world of management are never neatly sequential or black and white. Nevertheless, the description rings true when managerialism, or classical management, drives the process.

The idea of building the organization and the software around the customer transposes the standard order of events completely. The initial assumption is that the important action is "out there," and that the action revolves around the customer. Software—including information technology and supporting social systems—is used or developed to meet the demands of that activity. The software earns its value by enabling the organization to satisfy customer needs. The customer represents the beginning of the entire process, the foundation for everything that follows.

GETTING SMART

Few organizations, if any, have managed to complete the transition described here and jump from mass to brain. But some, as we shall see, are heading in the right direction. There are techniques and approaches that can help leaders in the effort. The idea that a company builds itself around software and that the software is built around the customer means that managers are committed to the aggressive use of information technology in four distinct but related initiatives:

1. Leverage knowledge across the organization.

2. Accelerate the development of collaborative work within the organization and between the organization and "outsiders."

3. Prioritize efforts that lead to mass customization, slenderized marketing, and individualized customer sets.

4. Liberate people from the constraints of the paper-dependent environment.

These initiatives are not exclusive; they are different attributes of the same strategy that facilitates the organization's ability to jump the curve. They have in common the intention to make the organization less "heavy" and, instead, to energize the organization around processes that are driven by the customer environment rather than by custom and bureaucratic tradition. Each of the initiatives, outlined in Table 7.1, is supported with a set of action steps. The aim is to use—as thoroughly, frequently, and quickly as possible—the intelligence and experience of everyone associated with the business, regardless of the roles they play: employee, manager, partner, vendor, or customer.

Initiative 1: Leverage Knowledge Across the Organization.

Robert Haas, CEO of San Francisco–based Levi Strauss, once noted that the idea for the $1 billion-a-year Dockers line was thought up by an employee in Argentina.[1] One wonders what other good business ideas are available in the company's universe—and what business information, insights, and experiences exist in the

**Table 7.1. Build the Organization Around the Software
and the Software Around the Customer.**

Initiative 1: Leverage knowledge across the organization.

- Begin with a statement of compelling need, for *everyone*.
- Be ready to persuade.
- Be clear on the criteria for success.
- Be inclusive and open about inputs into the system.

Initiative 2: Accelerate the development of collaborative work within the organization and between the organization and "outsiders."

- Build in dialogue and feedback from the beginning.
- Prepare for success.
- Start thinking of organizations and careers in terms of networks.

Initiative 3: Prioritize efforts that lead to mass customization, slenderized marketing and individualized customer sets.

- Know your customers, markets, and competition.
- Integrate business and technology strategies.

Initiative 4: Liberate people from the constraints of the paper-dependent environment.

- Deliver on comfort while promoting experimentation.
- Do it now.

organizational system that could be instrumental for other opportunities or improvements. How can such knowledge be moved through the system and become commercialized?

Let's look again at the Mrs. Fields example. A teenager on her first job after a career in baby-sitting walks into a Mrs. Fields Cookies store an hour before it opens and turns on the computer. The computer asks her all sorts of questions: Is it a weekend? Is it raining? Is there school today? And so on. She is still half asleep but dutifully answers each question. Then the computer does something that is a planner's dream. It tells her that based on previous experience over the years at that location, the store's recent performance and certain attributes of the immediate environment—all recorded in the computer's memory—the pattern of answers she gave indicated that she would sell eight hundred cookies and muffins during the day. Further, the computer says, the likely breakdown of cookies is going to be so many chocolate chip cookies, so many oatmeal cookies, and so many muffins. The computer then displays a series of graphs showing how sales will progress during the day. Muffins will go early, before lunch and then taper off. Chocolates will lumber along until the afternoon and then move up. This information is accompanied by recommendations about when to start the baking process and in what quantities for each of the dozen products offered. The production schedule is particularly critical since the Fields policy is to throw out any cookie that doesn't sell after two hours. Thus, if the projection of the number of cookies needed is in error and leads to an overrun, there is considerable waste. If the projection is too low, of course, the business has to turn away customers for lack of cookies to sell. During the course of the day, the actual sales are recorded. The new data are automatically included in the forecasting model. The next day's projections are therefore a revision of the model's predictions based on today's results. The forecast becomes more accurate each day; the organization learns. The data can be compiled on the basis of one store alone, by manager, by region—whatever format is best at providing predictive data for a unit's performance. The effectiveness of the system in proposing production schedules and the ability of store managers to use the system's recommendations wisely are key to the success of Debbi Fields's operation.

There are other applications of leveraging knowledge. When Debbi ran a store, for example, she could "feel" what the sales were going to be like during the course of the day. She would plan a list of chores that a salesperson could attend to when sales began to slow. Sometimes these were sales-driven activities. Taking a sample tray of cookies out in front of the store where people were passing by or onto the main concourse of a shopping mall would guarantee an increase in the number of cookie sales. At other times certain housekeeping chores could be done, such as the periodic inspection of particular equipment. Part of what made Debbi so effective as a manager and business owner was her ability to prioritize what needed to be done during the day, in addition to working on the mainstream activity of selling cookies behind the counter.

Consequently, the system designers instructed the computer program to list alternative chores and the most likely time during the day that they could be accomplished efficiently— along with the dollar impact of each alternative. Again, the computer reported recommendations to the young manager based on a model derived from the accumulated wisdom of experts— the high-performance store managers, employees, specialists, and consultants. Each manager could choose to follow the system's recommendation or ignore it. Regardless of the specific decision that an operator or store manager would make, her performance during the day was maximized by the knowledge that originally had been implicit in the minds of the star performers and that now had been made explicit for everyone in the organization. Moreover, the information was presented to the managers in a way that they could use.

The effort of leveraging customer-relevant information is ongoing, ceaseless. With just a laptop computer, from anywhere in the world, Debbi can see performance scores for any store. Observing the pattern of sales, for example, allows her or any seasoned executive with similar access to evaluate performance of the store with current data. In this way she can provide coaching that is relevant to the store operator's immediate problems or challenges, coaching that is market responsive. The feedback is not meant as coercion, close supervision, or "gotcha!"; rather, it is meant to be an exchange of information about what the customers are buying, what they are not buying, what the store operator thinks the customers would buy, and what the manager is doing about the situation now. Looking at the pattern of other information the system collects about the store can give an expert at a central location additional ideas about what the young manager might be doing wrong and needs to change or what she is doing right but needs to emphasize. In effect, the "coach" can evaluate dozens of stores during the day and offer counsel, suggestions, and advice.

Workflow and processes are affected in other ways, too. A store manager has to have the store open eighty hours per week. Employees are likely to be local high school and college students who have crowded schedules. The unpleasant task for the store manager, a retailer's least favorite chore, is scheduling ten or fifteen part-time employees across the week in a way that accommodates their availability. As if this weren't enough of a challenge, the manager also tries to use the knowledge he or she has gained about a particular group of workers and the demands of the work environment to best utilize the workers' abilities. In every work situation in every industry there is a complement of work skills, a mixture of human talent, that is best for a particular set of circumstances, that is best for delivering services and products to the customer. Some people work well in hectic, noisy circumstances and some in more measured settings; some have superior sales skills, others excel in production work. Even in situations where functional boundaries have collapsed, these differences matter. The manager will try to put the right combination of skills and talents together throughout the week to optimize the store's performance and maximize customer satisfaction, using rules and insights about the process that can be captured and communicated by an information system. In effect, the best and brightest of the store managers can be brought together and debriefed on how they make their work schedules: what guidelines they use, and what variables they weigh to make the different trade-offs. After skills data are collated and put into the information system, a manager can avail himself or herself of the enterprise intelligence that is now made explicit. The manager enters the raw data about who is available and when. The system then provides the best schedule for the operation for that week, matching the number of on-the-job employees against fluctuation in the sales forecast, as well as configuring the optimum set of skills. Notice what has happened. First, the manager is freed from the ugly and time-consuming task of setting up the schedule. He or she now has time, once again, to do the things that probably represent the greatest added value. Second, the manager has developed a schedule that represents the combined wisdom of the organization. The quality of work is enhanced. And it is based on market and consumer shifts, not internally obsessed notions of order, stability, and hierarchical control.

Something else has happened, too. When the experts—the lead performers and advisors—are in a room making up the rules for a particular assignment, they are really having a conversation about how work should be processed during the day, about the priorities that need to be handled. In effect, they are looking at workflow, and their guidelines are as much about redesigning work activity and work processes as they are about anything else. The review of such rules in these circumstances, as well as the incorporation of suggestions and feedback in real time from workers in the field—essentially evaluating and incorporating customer experience—makes the reengineering component of organizational change a daily and market-driven affair. Process transformation is institutionalized as a counterweight to the natural proclivity to postpone change.

Leveraging knowledge throughout the organization on behalf of the customer is about more, therefore, than knowledge transfer or information management. Leveraging knowledge renders hierarchy and giantism, with all the attending layers of management and rules, as less essential for organizational effectiveness. Rigid boundaries are threatened because information flow opens up new ways people can provide added value. Indeed, if we make the decision to jump the curve by going from mass to brains, there is little in process or product that can remain unaffected.

The overall impact of these combined outcomes is significant, even in companies that endure cost pressures from nonoperating sources. During the late 1980s and early 1990s, Mrs.

Fields Cookies was buffeted with a series of economic difficulties. Many of the company's outlets had been in shopping malls where foot traffic had declined significantly. Additionally, its occupancy costs rose dramatically. Senior managers who had left the cookie company by the time we were doing our research told us that the computerized system had been a major factor in sustaining the company during difficult times. The impact it had on helping managers control the controllables and in reinforcing Debbi's business priorities made the difference. Moreover, as the inevitable downsizing began to occur, there was a reliable way to ensure that the knowledge earned by one person stayed in the company when that person left. As the company regained momentum, the acquired wisdom became important for keeping energetic managers focused and coordinated.

Beyond the normal considerations given to the application of information technology, research with the Fields organization and other companies that use similar techniques suggests four considerations in regard to implementation of the first initiative:

■ *Begin with a statement of compelling need, for everyone.* If top management had no other responsibility, it would be required to articulate the necessity for transforming the organization into a smart enterprise, a de-massed, brain-based entity. Some resistance to change is inevitable, but do not underestimate the interest and receptivity of people at all levels of the organization in absorbing information about the broader intellectual, social, and technological processes that are at work. Traditional managerialist elitism could lead managers to conclude that one set of data is good for one group (such as some competitive information for line operators) and that a second set of data (the context/visionary/global piece) is appropriate for another. Not true. Building the smart organization means doing so right from the start. We have found truck drivers and clerks as curious and excited about the implications of the organization-as-brain metaphor, the demise of the industrial model, and the importance of the intangible and knowledge as were polished MBAs in executive suites. Interest in building one vision means giving the same frame of reference as completely as possible to everyone in the organization.

■ *Be ready to persuade.* Drawing forth a compelling need means lots of conversation and discussion. A written treatise or a series of written directives is not worth the paper it is written on for purposes of creating change. Helping people "get it" demands frequent manager and top executive participation in dialogue about the business environment and the new roles that are required for success.

■ *Be clear on the criteria for success.* The challenge is not only in determining architecture strategy but also in deciding what organizational attributes are important for success. Flexibility, accountability, and openness are appropriate across the leading-edge organizations we have dealt with. Technology should be used to promote and nurture these qualities. Additionally, emphasize how one ought to avoid looking at work as a series of separate tasks and focus on how those tasks are linked—that is, how they form a process that allows the organization to achieve its mission and priorities. Before the technology is considered, determine who owns not only the tasks but the overall process for any aspect of any service or product. Establish the metrics with employee involvement to evaluate progress to goal.

Remember that the new processes are being implemented while the organization is still holding on to facets of the old way of operating. For many, the feeling is like trying to fly an airplane at the same time they are building it. No one is sure how to get from here to there safely. Clarity about success criteria can ease the confusion and doubt.

■ *Be inclusive and open about inputs into the system.* The information gained from everyone's dose of reality—from focus groups, site visits, discussions in trade shows, newsletters, industry assessments, and consultant-driven databases—should have a role. The source of the data should be unimportant. The only thing that should matter is the accuracy and utility of the information. It should be irrelevant whether the input comes from a high-priced consultant or from someone working on the shipping dock.

Embedded in these recommendations is the idea that for the individual leader the issue is not about technology alone. It is about understanding the role one has to play in preparing and galvanizing organizations to adopt the new tool sets. If the future of organizations depends on their reaction to the new information technologies, the question is not how the contests among neural networks, parallel processing, multimedia, and wireless techniques will develop. It is about getting people beyond the normal resistance to change, the combination of cultural and psychological attributes that can prevent innovation from occurring no matter how desperately it is needed.

Initiative 2: Accelerate the Development of Collaborative Work Within the Organization and Between the Organization and "Outsiders."

Collaboration is the heart of business success today. Collaboration means more than an individual sharing an insight with co-workers. E-mail might be a necessary component of collaborative procedures in a wired community, but it is not sufficient. Joint synergistic trust-based effort on a common project is at the heart of collaborative work.

Research with companies using collaboration-oriented systems suggests a series of actions that are often overlooked. We turn our attention to these now.

■ *Build in dialogue and feedback from the beginning.* The challenge for organizations is to have systems that facilitate accountability and cooperation throughout an entire project and work environment. Consider what occurs at advertiser Young & Rubicam. Groupware is used by the company to construct a software map of workloops among members of that organization and its clients. The process defines the numerous combinations of commitments and agreements made in connection with a project—who agreed to what, and when. Commentary and annotation, questions, and data sharing are part and parcel of a constant stream of communication that is enabled by the software. In short, feedback is not attached at the end of a process; it is built in from the beginning as an integral part of the workflow. From the start, it is assumed that the organization is going to learn its way through the task at hand, prevailing on all the past and present wisdom it can muster from its own resources and from its customers.

In a project with Chevron, Young & Rubicam chose to automate its own traffic system, a set of traditional procedures used in the advertising industry for controlling the internal administration of a project. By mapping what had to be done by whom, and then overlaying a software program on top of the processes to improve coordination, the advertiser was able to significantly increase quality and decrease turnaround time. The business processes were revised and made explicit as, in the course of identifying and analyzing workloops, people learned for whom they did a particular piece of work, why it was important, and how other workloops were linked to their own. Not least significant, Chevron, whose activities were key elements of many workloops (through requests, evaluations, sign-offs, and so on) learned about its role in the advertiser's processes; communication between the organizations improved significantly. In a sense Young & Rubicam reinterpreted work, according to CIO Nicholas Rudd, to focus on how to move an idea around and between organizations and how to transform and deliver the idea in ways that maximized added value. By so doing, Young & Rubicam explored a key element in jumping the curve.

As it becomes clear who is supposed to do what, roles at Young & Rubicam are more easily distinguished. As more and more workloops are identified and as more information exchange takes place around a project's progress, assignments are clarified. Priorities are better understood and therefore easier to maintain. Knowledge about the customer's needs and objectives is brought directly to people who are doing the work with the greatest impact on customer satisfaction. A client, for example, could look at production estimates or at the first pass of the creative team and provide feedback almost immediately. In this way, by facilitating and clarifying communication, the system brings the customer inside the organization. The immediacy of information exchange between Young & Rubicam and a client can intertwine members of both organizations in the course of a project, giving rise to a "fate sharing" attitude.

Such an approach generates an egalitarian atmosphere that encourages creativity and risk taking. People begin to understand genuinely what they are paid for: high knowledge activities such as judgment and innovation. In the end, they feel more fulfilled and become more sensitive to the larger needs of the project community.

In one study across a varied set of clients, Young & Rubicam found that by using technology in this way, they could increase the number of jobs completed on time by 63 percent and those completed on budget by 19 percent. The agency decreased overtime and duplication of effort. Most significantly, it reduced by 64 percent the need to redo a part of a project because of miscoordination.[2]

As with the Fields example, the Young & Rubicam program created additional intangible consequences that were not obvious at first glance. Because implicit agreements are made explicit, commitments and obligations are better understood. The clarification about what each person is supposed to do and why, particularly when there is customer input to the definitions and requirements of the activities, reinforces the empowerment process. People who provide information and data get better feedback on who uses the information and why.[3]

For these reasons, it is important to reiterate the crucial role of the social factors that are at play in applications of this sort. There is a need to accommodate the realities of how people work together. If collaboration and trust are viewed negatively, the most sophisticated technology will generate only marginal returns. If people feel that by sharing information they hurt their power base or chance for advancement in the organization, for example, all the technology in the world will not induce collaboration or optimum performance. Software that does not accommodate organizational realities becomes much like other bureaucratic mechanisms that are counterproductive: in the end, people spend huge amounts of time and energy trying to find ways "around the system."

■ *Prepare for success.* Serious issues need to be addressed, the earlier the better. The lesson from companies that have been down this path is that extra attention to the emotional aspects of information sharing is necessary. As one executive put it, "The biggest task is to get people to see that sharing information is not a zero sum game. The analogy we promote is about using one candle to light another. Even after it has lit the other, the first still shines brightly."

Collaborative software and processes will raise questions about resources. As the system becomes more widely used, the organization will move to maximize cost savings in record keeping, coordination, and similar activities. To avoid politicizing the process—that is, enervating the organization with turf battles—set out early the new criteria for resource allocation. At the very least, establish a process for establishing resource allocation processes.

Recognize that there will be consternation if people are left out of a collaborative network because of system restraints. For example, a voice mail system can quickly become taxed because of limited memory capacity once people are using it widely around the organization. Opportunities to give customers access to a system can be restrained as well—a major loss. The capacity question is optimistic: prepare for success by planning for tomorrow's expansion potential right from the beginning.

Address the questions that people will have about how to manage electronically. Begin exploring how people might best supervise telecommuters, field service employees, and others who are technologically tethered to the organization. Consider how customer behavior might be managed when face-to-face contact is sometimes replaced with electronic communications. The fact is that we don't know enough about the issue; the minimum requirement is to understand the uniqueness of your organization's culture and anticipate the different ways electronic communication might change it. Attitudes regarding the formality of communications, frequency of communications, precision in language, and expectations of what constitutes timely response are all elements of the new, computer-dependent managerial environment—just as they were part of the pre-computer environment. It is likely, however, that the electronic medium will affect these attitudes: an organization needs to know how, so that managerial effectiveness is improved, not diminished.

■ *Start thinking of organizations and careers in terms of networks.* It would be intellectually dishonest for managers to implement certain technologies without also thinking about the consequence that often matters most: job security. As painful as it may seem, the elimination of positions that are not intimately connected across functions or to outside constituencies—that is, not linked to a process—will continue. Reengineering expert Michael Hammer, in fact, expects a further 75 percent reduction among the current middle-management work force.[4] The important issue is for people to understand that the dynamics are universal across industries. Investments in information technology generally lead to size reductions. One series of studies correlating census data and technology expenditures has shown that the industries that have shrunk the most are those that have made the largest investments in information technology.[5] However, there is some evidence that a decrease in the size of a large firm is frequently paralleled by an increase in a number of smaller firms. The technology permits a decoupling of larger units, often by outsourcing needed services and products so that the net effect might be one of restructuring processes as well as a substitution of labor.

Designing organizations as networks, where communications crisscross boundaries, also makes giantism less attractive. Approaches like the "virtual organization" illustrate the same trend. Companies come together in temporary alliances to take advantage of a brief window of opportunity and then disband to form yet another configuration of customers, vendors, and suppliers. All these activities are made possible by electronic communication where the emphasis is on sharing what has been learned. The impact on careers and organizational life is extensive. Rosabeth Moss Kanter has observed that individuals will focus on "portfolio careers," moving from project to project, in the open and fluid organization. A different set of talents will become more prominent, one with a clear dependence on team skills and cooperation.[6]

One of the most visible technologies for increasing collaboration and networking among organizations—electronic data interchange (EDI)—deserves special attention. Essentially, computers that belong to buyer and seller, customer and vendor, are linked so that the barrage of paperwork that is normally traded between the companies is minimized or eliminated. Electrons substitute for paper versions of purchase orders, accounts-payable, and the assortment of documents that initiate, approve, and confirm a transaction. The logic of EDI is straightforward. According to one specialist, it produces savings of $5 to $50 per document.[7] Speed in stock replenishment, delivery cycles, and payments adds to the benefits that come from reduced administrative costs, fewer errors, and reduced need for storage and warehouse facilities. During the early 1990s, use of EDI doubled in the retail industry;[8] it is often ranked in the top three of likely technology investments by senior executives.

There really is no good reason that any organization should not be actively pursuing applications. Fred Metzgen, an expert in the field, quotes the head of one multinational organization as saying, "Not doing EDI in the 1990s and beyond, will be like not having a telephone today."[9] It is essential for organizations that see speed, accuracy in information exchange, and customer partnering as being crucial to competitive advantage. EDI enhances relationships between supplier and customer and makes the need for vertical integration and heavy, centralized staff controls less important. It makes warehouses and the staff needed to run them less necessary.

A number of major organizations (including RJR Nabisco, Wal-Mart, General Motors, and Sears) already require suppliers to work through EDI. Alcoa uses it to strengthen internal controls and enhance its disbursement process, and Digital Equipment uses the system to reduce the time required to issue a purchase order.[10] Levi Strauss uses its version of EDI—LeviLink—to reduce the order turnaround cycle with retailers, and anticipates that it will run 80 percent of the business with that set of customers within a few years.

As technology—processing power and access—continues to become more affordable, the old mainframe-based EDI systems will increasingly give way to desktop computers, workstations, and personal digital tools. Internet and component networks will expand and become easier to use. On-line services that permit customers to order plane tickets or pay bills from their homes exemplify the trend. The practicality of participation by the smallest organization will become increasingly clear.

All these developments raise new issues for strategic consideration. In addition to assessing potential partners' financial

strength and reputation for product durability, we must now assess the sophistication of their information technology. The focus
is not just on the technological characteristics (intricacies about
such aspects as architectures and default standards, which have
been concerns for a while) but about the purposes and uses of the
systems. Strategic thinking by companies that jump the curve
will include a number of questions: Can we integrate our system
with theirs in such a way as to enhance our abilities to serve our
customers? Are we prepared to be open and trusting with them?
Are we really prepared to take on a win-win philosophy?
Transmission speed is one thing; the access that people around
the enterprise have to the system is something else. Similarly, the
experienced manager would be interested in gauging how the system allows—even encourages—people who regularly deal with
customers to have an impact on the organization's strategy and
implementation processes. If the organization without boundaries really is coming to pass, these concerns about the partner organization are immediately relevant to our own.

Another question concerns the kind of data, information,
and knowledge that companies would want to access. Most discussions of information management revolve around the use of
internal data. Yet, consistent with the organizing principle, the
managerial environment encompasses a lot more, much of
which is external: demographic trends, international trade regulations, environmental data, competitor performance, and
broader economic and societal information. These are all relevant in the topsy-turvy world we are in now.

Initiative 3: Prioritize Efforts That Lead to Mass Customization, Slenderized Marketing, and Individualized Customer Sets.

The root idea behind this initiative is straightforward: success in
business today becomes a function of applying organizational
knowledge to a greater number of smaller and smaller markets.
As one entrepreneur told us, performance comes from finding the
optimum set of niches. Ultimately, the trend leads to the complete individualization of product and service offerings. "The 1:1
future," as Don Pepper and Martha Rogers have expressed it, is
"characterized by customized production, individually addressed

media, and 1:1 marketing. . . . Instead of market share, the goal
of most business competition will be share of customer—one
customer at a time."[11] Accordingly, mass customization involves
the acquisition and manipulation of customer information and
the linking of different parts of the organization so that it recon-
figures itself relative to the requirements of individual customers.

Retailers and manufacturers have for some time used bar
code information to track sales and make adjustments to price,
inventories, and promotion strategies. More recent is the effort
to disaggregate the data and correlate it to the shopping patterns
of specific subgroups of customers so that specially designed
products and programs can be offered to them. The same data
packet might be used again and again in a range of analyses and
predictions about the behavior of widely different groups.
American Airlines, for example, uses databases to generate a
pricing matrix that includes a large, diverse number of fares for
any flight. By anticipating what price can be charged for what
type of customer for what package of variables (length of advance purchase, for example) the company can quickly raise its
revenue per seat.

Retrieving data about the preferences of a particular customer in order to offer additional products is a step closer to genuine mass customization.[12] American Express, for example, has
databases that include information from retailers and shoppers
using its charge card. It can take that data and disassemble and
recombine it to identify a list of customers who likely would be
interested in a retailer's new product or special promotion.
Databases that are used to anticipate customer needs provide another example of the same target marketing idea, as in diaper
sales to pregnant women and then later, toddler clothes to the
same household. Syntex uses half a dozen databases to match a
physician's profile with products that sales representatives can
sell. The databases include information about a physician's practice (prescription information, patients' insurance, Medicaid en-
rollment), HMO affiliation, and HMO formularies (the specific
drugs used by an HMO) among other data to align customer and
product. Coopers & Lybrand takes streams of tax information
and recombines the data so that clients can access a customized

report on the firm's Tax News Network. The same data might be used repeatedly but in different ways, thus allowing customers to get the report that meets their individual interests.

Information technology permits innovations that would have been impossible just a decade ago. McGraw-Hill, for example, has developed a computerized publishing system that lets individual college professors design textbooks by selecting, reordering, and combining chapters from other books under the publisher's banner. They can also request software and customized teaching aids, depending on personal need and interest. If Blockbuster has its way, customized videos won't be far behind. The Ritz Carlton Hotel group keeps information on customer tastes; when a guest registers at one location, her choices during previous stays at other locations are available for customizing particular services.

Basic product design is only one way to mass customize. The notion of total product or service suggests other dimensions. Marketing support that is differentiated according to customer needs illustrates mass customization. Also, training and education programs can be specialized—interactive manuals and computer-aided instruction are tools that can complement efforts at individualizing training content (for example, technical issues versus support questions). Mass-produced products can be customized in packaging and delivery schedules, allowing mass production economies to be teamed with the requirement of giving the customer what she wants.[13]

The manufacturing arena has seen the largest development of mass customization. Motorola, for example, has the capacity to manufacture an almost limitless number of feature/function combinations for its cellular phones. Matsushita reports that twenty employees can produce eleven million variations of mountain, road, and racing bicycles—in 199 colors. A customer's measurements are taken with a special bicycle frame. Then the measurements are transmitted to the factory, where the bicycle is manufactured from a computer-generated blueprint within a matter of hours.[14]

Of course, companies have been able to customize products in the past without resorting to the kind of technology that we have been discussing here. Usually, customization was approached somewhat in the spirit of dealing with exceptions to some standard model or service. *Building the organization and the software around the customer allows a company to switch figure and ground.* Customization becomes the norm, standardization the exception. The process modules are multiplied many times over because the variety of products produced—literally the once-in-a-lifetime combinations that can be devised—are recognized as the source of the company's sustainable advantage. Further, "informating" a product by embedding intelligence into it—for example, via a microprocessor—accentuates the customization orientation. Thousands of instructions and options can be offered to customers instantly so that the market approaches a set of one: the individual actually using the product or service.

The pervasive nature of nichemanship and mass customization demands two fundamental responsibilities:

■ *Know your customers, markets, and competition.* In individualized marketing, the game focuses on getting the maximum "share of customer"—which requires knowing the customer and investing in the customer relationship. The focus shifts from economies of scale to economies of scope. It is not just about cross-selling additional products or services, but knowing what to sell to a particular customer. The consequence is an eagerness to get as much information as possible about the buying behaviors of a specific individual or organization— through frequent usage, members-only and interactive on-line programs, as well as questionnaire data. Emphasize strategic listening as it applies to each customer. Develop a process for identifying the best customers—and budget for it.

Keep what you are doing in perspective. There is some difference between selling multiple products to the same customer and selling multiple variations of a single product to the same customer. Toyota and other companies, for example, have often overwhelmed customers with a "tyranny of choice" by offering nearly every possible combination of product features. The mistaken attitude is that if a feature can be offered, it ought to be. But excessive choice can confuse customers, as vendors in the computer industry have also learned. Instead, the suggestion is to be informed about what product varieties might be sought by or useful to the customer; have customers lead the process by engaging them early in your planning and research process, however nonlinear and chaotic it might appear.

Use new criteria when looking at competitors; start grading them on their *flexibility*. Sociologist Daniel Bell once remarked that a feature of our times is that things are less important than the properties of things. An ore or alloy is less important than its conductivity or tensile strength. Similarly, in the new environment, a company's ability to reconfigure itself becomes as important as its products. The pressure is to think of potential threats from competitors in terms of their capability to recombine modules representing a range of skills, processes, or work components.[15] Examine what this means for your own processes. What restraints are there on your own ability to reconfigure process modules? Contrast your capacity to rearrange tasks, resources, and personnel almost immediately. Expand your definition of what it means to be a low-cost producer by including on a regular basis the costs of coordinating the reorganization of workflow processes, from the gathering of information to the delivery of product components.

■ *Integrate business and technology strategies.* Technical prowess is no substitute for staying focused on business objectives. Keep in mind that mass customization is not the end in and of itself; the goal is still to delight the customer. In addition, be wary of delegating key decisions to technocrats who might have little contact with customers. It is unfair to them and to the organization. Time and time again we have seen good intentions stalled at the starting gate as technicians were intimidated by questions posed by other management. They recognized that the questions were only superficially about the technology and were really about fundamental strategic choices the company could make, choices they felt ill-prepared to decide. Mass customization has a clear prerequisite—despite everyone on the payroll having the opportunity and responsibility to maintain intimate contact with customers and external market realities, top management must be energetically involved in the process changes caused by shifting the focus of marketing and production.

By the same token, advantage based on technology does not go unchallenged. Competitors will respond and imitate; further expenditures are usually necessary to stay in the game. The path of further technological development should be congruent with overall business goals. Development of smart products, for example, changes more than the range of products offered to customers—it includes changes in market positioning and pricing strategy. A long-term perspective is rarely as important as it is in the commitment to mass customization.

Finally, it is most important for a leader to remember that any effort to initiate nichemanship and customization should be treated as a complete transformation of the way work and production will be organized. To treat the effort as simply a matter of manipulating information technology misses the point. When companies organize around customization, large amounts of information moving quickly around the organization create a demand for flexibility not needed before. Flexible manufacturing, adaptive supplier arrangements, responsive advertising and sales programs, contingent compensation systems, and other areas are all shaped by the drive to customize. Additionally, the role of other change programs (particularly those focused on the continuous improvement of existing mass production techniques) are altered. Mass production is a social principle, and disrupting it affects every kind of work relationship.

Initiative 4: Liberate People from the Constraints of the Paper-Dependent Environment.

In varying degrees, the previous three initiatives are about paperless systems. *Paperless* is how, in part, we define information technology. The intention of being paperless, however, can reinforce organizing the business around the customer.

Despite all the talk about paperless offices, paper consumption across organizations doubles about every four years. The problem isn't paper per se but paper-based management systems. Even with monumental efforts to prevent it, the greater the amount of paper that has to be handled, the greater the number of errors that occur.[16] The errors must be corrected, making less time available. Generally, quality and customer responsiveness are severely diminished. An organization bloated with paper can neither reduce its size nor grow its intelligence effectively.

Paper-based systems demand time and energy to coordinate and conduct the collection, tabulation, and distribution of information. When such activities are computer-based instead, the leader's attention and resources can be directed to asking the "what if" questions and to searching for underlying trends or emerging context. For example, computerized training can facilitate measurement of the employee's skill set and simultaneously identify pockets of weakness across a group of employees. Managers can then spend more time evaluating and planning for the skill needs of the future. Words about becoming a state of the art company get some substance. Paperless systems represent tangible efforts to generate innovative and creative environments by freeing time and resources so that people's attention can be focused on activities that customers would find valuable. Managers have the energy and time to explore how they can develop the business for tomorrow. In short, the organization gets smarter.

Bill Macfarlane, vice president of information services at the Disney Stores, the 270-location retail operation of the Disney enterprise, made this point in noting the company's savings from automating manuals. An on-line manual can be revised in very little time by placing the revisions in the existing text and then distributing the new information across the system. The duplication costs associated with a paper-based system, in contrast, can be formidable. The costs and time needed for distributing manuals and the endless updates are more imposing given the expansion Disney plans to undertake throughout Europe and Japan. Significantly, on-line information is readily usable at the same time to everyone in the system. When everyone is "in" simultaneously, the goals, direction, and priorities of the organization are not confused by contradictions between outdated and recent communications. The focus stays with the customer.

The use of software to replace paper manuals is, as Macfarlane has described it, "a fairly mundane and unexciting effort," even if it produces benefits that are substantial. The real excitement comes in the application of programs that eventually transform how the organization works on behalf of its customers. Macfarlane's strategy in the beginning was to put all the paper forms that existed in the company in electronic format. In this way he defused the usual resistance to automation projects. The second stage involved going back and asking which forms were really necessary and eliminating those that were not. The hiring process, for example, had originally involved the use of more than twenty forms with overlapping information. After the process was initiated, the number of forms shrunk to six, three mandated by federal regulators. More important, the hiring process was reduced from two weeks to one day.

The activity of questioning what forms are needed is basically about asking what is good in the current process and what needs to be changed. Coupled with an expert scheduling program, reflecting the input of an ongoing series of "collective work group focus groups," Macfarlane says he will have "institutionalized the processes of continuous improvement and reengineering." People throughout the organization will be able to challenge the way work gets done. They can provide constant input in answer to a fundamental question, "How can we best run our stores?" as well as all the derivative questions regarding how to improve services and react to customer patterns. These are important issues: the organizing principle emphasizes wrapping the software around the customer, not an internal set of efficiency standards. The net of this kind of activity, according to Macfarlane, is that the "credibility of the mission is enhanced. There is real proof that we are trying to do everything possible to be the best. The immediacy of the system and the linkages of one component with another makes an impression that no amount of razzle dazzle executive presentations and paper memos can match. An improvement psychology takes hold and an assistance methodology is provided. It is an unbeatable combination." This sort of program is a matter of corporate courage and will as much as it is about technology. In a manner of speaking, the company challenges the unknown every day.

Consistent with viewing the organization as brain, the aim of paperless management systems, including applications for financial and inventory systems, is not simply to replace the paper system with electronic communication, but to alter the way business is conducted. Every aspect of the enterprise, from performance expectations to human resource strategy to cooperative alliances, is transformed.

Authorities are pushed lower and lower as approval processes appear less and less relevant to creating added value in the customer's eyes. Business literacy grows throughout the enterprise as everyone gets to learn the price of goods, the risks associated with different decisions, customer priorities, the costs of distribution or manufacturing, and the challenges in channel management, with real-time data that can be accessed by anyone.

The emphasis on controls is loosened as everyone learns that improvements in administrative tasks can be achieved in shorter time frames with fewer people. Span of control, as it exists, increases; the logistics of managing multiple locations become easier. Management time is liberated for building consensus among newly empowered employees and for creating cohesion among ad hoc teams that spring up with new insights. More energy is available to generate commitment to a vision that can be understood by people inside the organization and out. In short, the use of paperless systems produces more than savings on the physical requirements of moving and storing paper. It establishes a basis upon which to adopt a new view of the organization.

J. Galleberg, a Norwegian retailer, has moved to a paperless system and seen positive motivational benefits for employees at all levels. Its sales representatives use pen-based computers to order products and to show clients new product information. The system is on-line, permitting immediate verification regarding fulfillment of orders, and allowing the representative to show a store manager how shelf space might be configured with the ordered product being displayed. With the immediately accessed data bank, the representative can tell a customer how different products have sold at that individual store and give year-to-year comparisons, complete with clever graphics for easy understanding. The interactive nature of the system allows quick and flexible response; its user-friendly profile encourages a partnership between vendor and buyer. The feeling grows among employees, as well as among J. Galleberg's vendors and clients, that the company is working hard to "do things the right way."

A multitude of technology-oriented books on the market provide recommendations on how to implement information technology within a firm.[17] There is no need to repeat all of their suggestions here. Instead, we propose two tactical action steps that are especially relevant to using paperless management as part of building the organization and the software around the customer.

■ *Deliver on comfort while promoting experimentation.* If people are not comfortable with the system you choose or the approach you take to implement it, little good will come of your efforts to go paperless. You want to create an environment in which people can see the utility of a new approach, get excited about trying it, and not fear retaliation for mistakes. Alain Pinel Realtors floundered with their early efforts to use computers for competitive advantage in Northern California. The end users—the real estate agents—were either computer-phobic or too pressured to take the time to learn all the interface protocols and commands. After spending several hundred thousand dollars on the system, they decided to reinvest within six months in an alternative that used easy to understand commands. But they had to feel their way. No trade organization or software provider had what they needed. They would have to forge new ground with a corporatewide system that conventional thinking said could not be developed economically. But just two programmers working closely with interested agents began a development process that now includes more than twenty-five modules. They took the "batch processing" approach of traditional real estate systems and moved to something that operators in the field would find more practical; they ended up with a friendly interface, relational databases, and an interactive, seamless system that could not be found at any of the dozens of exploratory site visits company officials had made to other organizations over a six-month period.

The payoff was quick. By networking agents in the firm electronically, as well as connecting the agency to partner organizations such as title companies, synergies were created for securing new listings, establishing pertinent databases, and speeding timely response. As an example, think about an agent who is told by her client that he is willing to drop the price of his home.

Immediately, using a notebook computer, the agent puts the new data into the company's database, its knowledge reservoir. Within moments every agent in the organization has the news—and can make it available to other clients who are interested in purchasing a home in that price range. In contrast, another company would be subject to a more cumbersome process: an agent would inform a secretary, who would enter the change on a paper form that would be retyped or duplicated the next day, in the best situations, and distributed in mailboxes. It might be two or three days before every agent gets apprised of the change in the seller's position—long after the Alain Pinel agents have had the opportunity to reach their customers. The immediacy of the paperless environment, according to company president Helen Pastorino, was "a value that more than compensated for the effort in building an entirely new system."

The Alain Pinel experience also shows how experimentation and comfort are not exclusive. When the real estate agents key in information about a client or property on their keyboards, they are performing a basic data entry task, not what people imagine real estate work to be about. But this new role is adopted regularly throughout the day because it is transparent—using the system is easy and functional. Emphasizing various measures Pastorino assesses per-person productivity to be about twice what it is for her competitors, such that thirty-eight agents now can do the work of what seventy can do in a different environment.

The company also learned that experimentation and comfort have trade-offs, but comfort is the floor requirement. As an example, programmers wanted to place a query or field in the upper right corner of a form, because that is where "logically" or from a technical point of view it should be; but real estate agents wanted to place the same information in the bottom left corner, just because that is where it had always been. Inevitably the query and data were placed at the bottom left. Decision making reflected the idea that there was no value—no experiment, as we would say—unless the system was turned on. Comfort doesn't impede experimentation; it makes experimentation happen.

By a variety of measures—number and average value of listings, agent commissions, customer satisfaction—the young, recent entrant into the California market has been hugely successful. Based on listings and sales, it aims to dominate any market it chooses to enter within a year; it is rated as one of the fastest growing privately held companies in the San Francisco Bay Area. The key element according to Pastorino, however, was the "decision to do something different with the technology that would make it easy and worthwhile to use by agents in the field—and that would have practical value for how we satisfied customer needs."

Another way to promote both comfort and experimentation is to start small. Coopers & Lybrand's network got started as a pilot project with a loan of a few dozen laptops from a manufacturer. Now the company uses an expert system to disseminate a wide variety of knowledge about specific technical and business issues among staff consultants. In-house "experts" (anyone who has something valuable to contribute) in these areas log in their knowledge, ideas, and experiences, and other Coopers & Lybrand professionals across the world access the information. As a result, a comprehensive knowledge menu is continually kept up-to-date and useful to all. As extensive as the system is, however, it began with an initial experiment.

Using advocacy centers can also generate a sense of comfort with the system while promoting experimentation. The centers are comprised of people who are experts on the technology and who have the competence and vision to help translate vague ideas into workable programs. They can facilitate the review of internal processes. The people who are selected for this role should have great team skills, an optimistic attitude, analytical skills, knowledge about benchmarking, quality control and service management, a knowledge about the business fundamentals (for example, the dynamics of the industry), and excellent project management skills. Since these individuals will not only deal with technology problems but also with a more general resistance to change, it is absolutely essential that they have credibility from the very beginning. In effect, have your efforts in paperless systems "sanctified" by association with the opinion leaders at all points around the organization.

■ *Do it now.* There is a learning curve to innovation, regardless of ease of use or comfort. No matter how much the technology changes, no matter what opportunities there are to leapfrog over the technical features of some competitor's system, there is still a set of issues that require active engagement on the human or social level. How to listen to a customer and how to incorporate what one hears in processes and information flow are tasks most organizations need to work at. When Federal Express calls customers to apprise them that their packages will be delayed because of flooding or closed airports, the company is reacting to what it has learned about how to use the technology to manage products and services *according to the customer.* Their actions reflect what they have learned about how to interface the technology with customer needs.

Dealing with people's fears about being able to keep up in a dynamic environment is another skill organizations get better at with practice. Once the issues of ease of use, computing power, and access have been resolved, the success of paperless systems is contingent on how one looks at work. "The issue is only partly about the technology," says one executive. "It is about the meaning of work and how that meaning changes with new processes and systems. The question is basically philosophical. Your worldview gets affected—you start thinking about how fluid events are, you start thinking about change differently. So there is a time requirement for the organization to 'get it.'"

Learning to unlearn is also an activity that requires time. No matter how sophisticated the technology, the organization has to be ready and disposed to let go of old ways of behaving. The issue is not fear of failure but fear of success. The comfortable and the routine will be out. A tolerance for ambiguity and change does not materialize overnight. Some of the most technologically sophisticated organizations have been slow to move because they mistook the replacement of tools as being the same as changing the firm's attitudes and core strategies that needed to be put aside.

Finally, there isn't much substance to the attitudes that push for delay. As an illustration, the argument that faster technology will be available next year is irrelevant to most situations. Relative to other trade-offs, there isn't enough perceived value for users in the nanosecond improvement to justify not having a value-adding system operating immediately. A distinction between eight megabytes and sixteen megabytes is a big yawn to most operators in the field who need help today. The argument for delaying a purchase until something better comes along is also empty. As Helen Pastorino said, "You have got to jump on the technology time line sometime. And no matter when you do it, you will always be six months from the latest and greatest model."

IMPLICATIONS OF
THE ORGANIZING PRINCIPLE

As we have suggested, building the organization and the software around the customer is obviously about more than the selection of the proper software product or the application package with the most attractive functionality or price. It is about issues of culture, leadership, strategy, and courage.

Technology can be used to reinforce a command-and-control environment just as it can be used to flatten hierarchy. Supervision can be drawn tighter around a work group. Access to information can be restricted. Privacy can be invaded. Processes can be made inflexible. To avoid such outcomes a fundamental truth needs to be acknowledged: the direction that an organization takes is a function of leadership and values more than it is a function of processing speed and elegant protocols.

Growing the organization's intelligence needs to be recognized for the social activity that it is. Leaders must insist on change, knowing that technology can produce only the change that the enterprise is ready to accept. For example, as alluded to earlier, if a culture diminishes team efforts, or if it eschews the idea of colleagues and customers as trustworthy allies, then groupware and EDI that facilitate collaboration won't be of much help. As another example, distributive computing is effective to the extent that the organization permits empowerment and assures that people know how to use that power and newly found decision-making opportunities for the benefit of all stakeholders.

Similarly, the technology can be used to create the perception that the organization has been remade, just when it needs to be unusually vigilant about the changes still needed. Reengineering, for example, is a double-edged sword. On the one hand, it has value in removing cumbersome and wasteful processes. On the other, it can mesmerize people around the enterprise into thinking that some kind of permanent solution has been achieved. It might imply a promise of stability ("once we get things right") at a time when things are unlikely to settle down. *Positioned as technological efforts, interventions like reengineering do not go far enough.* The significant increase in productivity comes from a leader-led commitment to renew the organization every day on behalf of its customers. Hence, all four initiatives for building the organization and the software around the customer must start outside the technology with the changing demands and expectations of the customer.

Given the intention to utilize the organizing principle, all interactions necessarily change. People have virtually unlimited access to an enormous and constantly growing body of information about the organization and its market. Unless there is some common idea about the strategic direction of the organization— some encompassing guidelines on what data are important and to what end the information should be used—brainware will lead to more, not less, confusion, contradictions, and waste. The danger of people working at cross-purposes would be enhanced, not diminished. The technology does not relieve the leader of the responsibility to promote a vision and purpose but instead underlines it and demands that new roles be enacted.

Increasingly, the leader's role will be to help mediate the relationship between strategic concerns and the organization's knowledge base. It is not just that a leader will be a coach or coordinator; he or she will be a coach or coordinator concerned with how information is used, how it becomes expertise.

Information technology allows people to be part of many different work groups simultaneously. Group dynamics will become more complicated as a result. The leader will have to help others sort through which group might have a claim at the moment, which deserves loyalty, and whose priorities go first. Skill in aiding others in ambiguous, dynamic situations becomes more important when information is the fundamental resource around which the company operates. Increasingly, the definition of what activities add value will be defined in terms of what activities the customer perceives as valuable.

To say that an organization gets smart is really to say that a market gets smart. Disintermediation—when a buyer and seller conduct business without the traditional middleman or broker—is evidence of the process. In earlier chapters, we cited examples such as Sedgwick James and the Charles Schwab Corporation. Indeed, the current restructuring of such industries as banking and retail (for example, Home Shopping Network) is in part a function of the disintermediation process. It is facilitated with smart technology.

The picture of business stretching its intelligence around the globe presents a heartening image, too. Electronic exchange encourages collaboration without regard to geography. The organization's knowledge base is what telecommunicators around the world make it. As interactions and connections increase among all organizations, the knowledge base becomes a global intelligence. The possibility of billions of people dipping into a commonly developed and growing warehouse of experience and information leads us from smart products and organizations to a *smart world*. Official doctrines will be challenged, of course, but the opportunity to bring the collective intelligence of people all around the planet to bear on humanity's most pressing problems is unprecedented.

All of these considerations point to the fluid nature of the environment and the need for organizations to be adaptable. A decision to treat the organization as a brain, to build the business around the importance of information and process, is to commit the organization to transformation. Yesterday's view reinforced mediocrity and apathy by stunting thought and initiative. The new environment promotes entrepreneurialism, as it becomes easier to spot initiative. Access to a shared data environment feeds a desire for more information and, ultimately, change. Accountability prospers when people can assert themselves in opportunities they help create.

In summary, customer expectations are constantly changing. The organization needs a way to accommodate these changes effectively in order to do well. By organizing work around software, a way of coordinating a fluid and dynamic set of work processes, the enterprise creates flexibility and order simultaneously. If it builds the software around the customer, the firm organizes itself so that the market, and not out-of-date bureaucratic requirements, determines strategies, priorities, and goals. Each of the initiatives we have discussed for undertaking the changes necessary to build the organization and the software around the customer and to view the organization as brain reflects the centrality of knowledge in creating structures and processes. Nevertheless, the promise that information technology has for creating a world of extraordinary prosperity begins with resolving age-old concerns about human relationships and personal responsibility.

CHAPTER
8

The Coherence Imperative

> *To a creature that lives by reason, nothing is more*
> *terrible than what is formless and meaningless*
> *. . . and it is the fight against chaos that*
> *has produced our most profound*
> *and indispensable images.*
> **—Suzanne K. Langer**

> *All force, no vector.*
> **A retail executive describing**
> **an ineffectual manager on her staff.**

The two organizing principles presented thus far—look a customer ahead, and build the organization and the software around the customer—are revolutionary steps and can seem unsettling. As much as they are crucial for the organization's capacity to jump the curve, they can also magnify whatever fear and disorientation managers already experience as they confront a momentous shift in social and economic patterns. There are also other disquieting organizational realities.

DESTABILIZATION
IN THE EMERGING ERA

In the world of business, two corollary forces further accelerate the trends of destabilization we have described in prior chapters.

These forces, which we consider next, are the explosive increase in diversity and the rapid emergence of unstructured organizational designs. We propose one organizing principle, explained in this chapter and the next, to lend stability and surety of purpose. That principle, briefly put, is to ensure differential employee experiences.

Employment Diversity as a Strategic Necessity

The term *diversity* describes the complexity and variety of people, ideas, technologies, markets, and sources of information that managers must deal with every day. Employment and human resource diversity is an important subset. Unfortunately, diversity in employment is often viewed not as a strategic issue but as a legal or public relations concern revolving around affirmative action goals. This perspective is reactive, defensive, and limited in possibilities. Instead, an increasing number of managers are concluding that for strategic reasons, and regardless of legal personnel mandates, the pluralism of society at large must be reflected in the employee profile of the entire organization.

In today's brain-based global economy, the ability to attract and retain talented people becomes the most important competitive edge a company can have.[1] But where will these talented people come from? Demographic data suggest that only 15 percent of the net additions to the American work force between 1993 and the year 2000 will be native-born white males. Therefore, it seems obvious that leaders concerned about prudent, forward-looking management should waste no time in actively pursuing top talent from among women, minorities, and immigrants.[2] Obviously, no company can realistically expect to corner the labor market of the best and the brightest, especially when other astute and aggressive organizations are following the same strategy. Indeed, one of the rationales for developing expert systems is to give everyone access to the wisdom of those with the greatest talents and best performance. Even so, the quest for top human resources will continue as a critical business priority, and as a result of demographic realities, will inevitably result in a greater diversity.

From a marketing perspective, the call for employment diversity is just as urgent. Data suggest that the fastest growing demographic sectors in the United States are non–English-speaking, non-European groups. If an organization wishes to sell products and services to these groups, commonsense management would seek to incorporate the cultural insights of group members into decision making—as employees, subcontractors, joint-venture partners, and consultants.

There are broad process concerns, too. The academic research literature indicates that on one hand, individuals in problem-solving situations are usually most comfortable when they interact with people who are like themselves. On the other hand, the best solutions to ambiguous, complex, nonroutine problems—the norm in today's business world—are generated by groups with heterogeneous membership. Thus, once again it would make sense to create an organization where people with diverse skills and backgrounds can understand and work well with one another.

Globalization pushes this demand still further. Sergio Autrey, CEO of the Mexican distributor Grupo Casa Autrey made the following observations:

> In reality, domestic business no longer exists.... I must deal with the Chinese to purchase toys and with the Americans for candy.... Our world has shrunk to a set of multicultural environments which must work effectively with other equally diverse markets. We can play in this field, or we can die—at least economically.... Being successful means that we have to think in a totally different way. One key difference is that we must be willing to abandon our devotion to our single environments, and, instead, focus on and take advantage of the diversity in our world.[3]

When Swissair moves five thousand corporate accounting jobs from Zurich to Delhi, it is obvious that the airline would be wise to gain an awareness of and appreciation for Indian cultures. In trying to break Coca-Cola's market-share stranglehold in Israel, Pepsi Cola must be well-versed not only about Israel but also about the terribly complex world of the Mideast; its marketing strategy and recruiting practices for employees and partners should reflect that knowledge. When Swedish software company Scala commits to selling business software to seventy-two countries in twenty-two different languages while employing thirty foreign joint-venture partners, it is clear that for Scala executives diversity is not an affirmative action issue; it is the source of their business success.

And yet, diversity, for all the platitudes surrounding it, often evokes feelings of disorientation and anxiety among practicing managers. One group of middle-aged white male trade representatives in the electronics business confessed that some of the more disheartening and insecure feelings they had experienced occurred when they began dealing with a new, unfamiliar set of purchasing and procurement people. In working with the razor-sharp young women with MBAs and PCs (rather than the "old-boy, golfing-buddy" mix they had grown accustomed to over the years) they often found themselves uncomfortable, even intimidated. The chief operating officer (COO) of a small Sun Belt manufacturing firm told us that over the previous year his most difficult and most essential project had two requirements: first, getting his brilliant, thirty-year-old female Iranian plant manager to be able to communicate and work with her direct reports who were high school–educated white males in their fifties and Chicano males in their thirties, and then in turn getting all of these people "integrated" into the total labor force, which was a mix of Vietnamese immigrants, Hispanics, and whites. He had never before spent as much time on basic cultural and interpersonal issues as he had over the previous couple of years. He discovered that as much as diversity is inevitable and desirable, it is not automatically a harmonious and integrating force.

Unstructured, "Shapeless" Organizational Design

Another major destabilizing force is the emergence of new organizational structures, with intriguing descriptors like "flat," "virtual," "spiderweb," "spaghetti," and "jungle gym." Each structure attempts to minimize the pernicious effects of information restriction and slow, rigid bureaucracy. Each has drawbacks if not well executed. The flat or horizontal organization can end up in bottlenecks if people have to wait for guidance or approval from overworked senior executives. The temporary basis of the virtual organization can cause problems of continuity or customer confidence. The spiderweb, spaghetti, or jungle gym form, with an emphasis on cross-functional coordination, ad hoc task forces, and a network of relatively independent units, can lead to confusion in accountability.

Nevertheless, the advantages of the new organizational forms far outweigh the negatives. Today's business realities demand collaborative brain-based systems and real-time "intimate" information. In the emerging epoch, secrecy, protectionism, arm's-length relationships, closed-door meetings, "need-to-know" data, and not-invented-here parochial thinking are on the wane. They are being replaced by open sharing of knowledge with as many internal and external stakeholders as possible. The organization's ability to apply this flow of diverse knowledge is the key to maximizing its speed, mobility, market responsiveness, and innovation.[4] By necessity, organizational designs are becoming inclusive, permeable—even unstructured and shapeless.

The clues are everywhere. Groupware, cross-functional project teams, self-management, and blurred departmental boundaries are just a few examples. Competence and career mobility are defined differently, as each member of a team is asked to play a range of roles: technical expert one day, quality assurance officer or marketing strategist the next day, leader of one team, member of another—all the while operating with minimal hierarchical authority and with minimal guidance from procedure manuals. Traditional distinctions between "employee," "manager," and "staff" diminish as people begin to be perceived as "businesspeople." Former "employees" and "managers" work collaboratively with full control (and accountability) over the processes, budgets, and resources necessary to complete key projects successfully. And, as businesspeople, their primary concern and allegiance is with the fate of the organization, not simply their "job," department, or "boss."[5]

As the organization becomes more permeable, insiders flow out and outsiders flow in with ease. Suppliers, strategic partners, customers, and "experts" (think-tank specialists, professors, researchers) become involved in open management meetings relating to planning, product design, capital budgeting, personnel systems, and operations.[6] Lead users join product planning and design teams. Customer representatives work directly with in-house personnel on improving delivery systems and service. Meanwhile, everyone on the payroll gets involved with "listening strategies," and starts problem solving with constituencies in order to understand market realities better. The description of the organization's strength is shifted from a list of tangible assets to a tangled web of skills, talents, and networks. The "organization chart" becomes a series of overlapping circles representing cross-disciplinary projects, alliances, and stakeholding relationships, many of which cut across national borders.[7]

And all of that is quite temporal. Project teams accomplish their goals and disperse. "Virtual" alliances like the Apple-Sony Powerbook venture pool their core competencies in the form of temporary affiliations bound by little more than trust and common objectives, and then disband. Just as quantum physics was never able to explain the "virtual particles" that emerged out of nowhere and then simply disappeared, traditional managerialism has difficulty explaining or supporting the concept of highly focused virtual alliances that come and go.[8]

THE NEED FOR COHERENCE

The organization that chooses to jump the curve needs an organizing principle that provides internal unity, integration, and coherence. The challenge for the leader is how to maintain control in the organization and congruence in decision making while taking full advantage of today's historical and organizational realities. How does a leader funnel the vast wealth of diversity (of people, ideas, information, technologies, and markets) into the so-called tent of the organization, and simultaneously create team unity out of that diversity—in the spirit of "e pluribus unum" ("out of many, one")? An organization intending to jump the curve needs a mechanism to keep it together, thereby avoiding being pulled apart by centrifugal forces and shattering in midair. It needs an organizing principle to foster internal integration, so that it remains fully focused and purposeful.

The Center: High Purpose

The importance of the "center," or as the University of Southern California's James O'Toole describes it, "the high purpose," is being alluded to with greater frequency in the business world. For coherence to emerge, members of the organization must own, feel, and live a common philosophy and a common purpose. People in the organization must share a "center" of core values and priorities around which diversity circles like planets around a fixed star. Levi Strauss CEO Robert Haas provides emphasis by saying that in today's environment, the controls an organization uses must be conceptual. He talks about the importance of Levi's values and "aspirations" in shaping his company's management decisions. Ex-Apple CEO John Sculley cites the importance of "compelling purpose." Peter Drucker alludes to the importance of an organization's having a clear "business theory." MIT's Peter Senge and Stanford's James Collins and his colleagues stress the importance of core beliefs, guiding philosophies, and an inspiring, overarching, shared vision.[9]

The specific content of the center or core depends on the organization. In whatever way the center is fashioned, it must engender a sense of ownership, agreement, and commitment throughout the organization—and generate a deep mindfulness of the organization's purpose.

When diverse groups and individuals within an organization hold a commitment to shared vision and values, coherence and control emerge, and diversity of people and ideas becomes a powerful competitive weapon. When Intel CEO Andrew Grove emphasizes that "we are in the business of immediacy," or when Nellcor's "Core Priority" emphasizes the development of customer-responsive new products, or when the Ritz Carlton credo is "we are ladies and gentlemen serving ladies and gentlemen," the "right" courses of action become more clarified and people become more likely to make the "right" decisions. Of course, catchy phrases on their own do not suffice. Executives at Intel, Nellcor, and Ritz Carlton know that people must *share* the core vision and values. This, in turn, means that they understand and embrace their roles in carrying out the vision and values, and that they believe the organization's systems and leadership fully support their efforts.

An organizationwide commitment to a core philosophy and purpose provides people with a solid frame of reference. Within that context, diversity of ideas provokes creative conflict and innovative decision making—both aimed at fulfilling a common goal. A universal commitment to a "core" also provides a safety net for people who are taking risks and advancing unorthodox viewpoints, even tradition-breaking ones.

Without such a shared foundation of direction and ideals, diversity can fragment the organization. When organizations consist of people with fundamentally different philosophies, conflicting agendas and inimical central values, diversity can lead to divisiveness. People become confused about the organization's purpose and priorities; the result is often cynicism, paralysis, and inefficiency. Additional by-products may include scattered unfocused energy, turf-riddled decision making, and destructive win-lose conflict. Organization charts and policy manuals will have minimal impact in such circumstances. Glowing mission statements may adorn walls, inspiring values may be articulated in management retreats, brilliant strategic priorities may be identified in company meetings and publications—but unless they are lived and owned by everyone within the organization, they are not useful tools for enhancing coherence and unity.

THE ORGANIZING PRINCIPLE: REWARDS AND SATISFACTION

Other authors have addressed the importance of creating a common purpose. Our concern is more practical, and for the leader, more difficult. The questions we ask are these:

- How does a leader channel diversity into solidarity, creating a team dedicated to *fulfilling* that common purpose?

- How does a leader help ensure that the organization will live the purpose, that people will own it?

The answers lie in an organizing principle that is simple to understand but that requires great courage to implement:

Ensure that those who live the values and ideals of the organization are the most rewarded and the most satisfied. This is how leaders can enhance coherence and unity while enhancing corporate performance, integrity, and esprit d'corp. Although they can't guarantee who will be satisfied, leaders can increase the probability by making certain that different experiences accrue to individuals based on the degree to which their performance and behavior give expression to the "high purpose." This principle is especially important when an organization is in transition; then the leader should make certain that those on the payroll who best embody the *new* directions, priorities, and philosophy are the ones who feel the most secure and experience the most rewards. Ultimately, ensuring differential employee experiences helps the organization to utilize and focus its diverse resources in an effective and productive manner.

Value in Creating Dissatisfaction

Every manager knows it is virtually impossible to ensure that all employees are equally rewarded and satisfied. Our point of view is that not everyone *should* be equally rewarded and satisfied. The organizing principle insists on nothing less than the strategic management of job satisfaction and dissatisfaction. For the individual manager, a key responsibility is thus quite literally to shape an environment where the "right" people (those committed to the desired culture and vision) are satisfied, successful, and secure, and where the "wrong" people (wrong for your organization—those who oppose the culture and vision) are not.

Before we go further, it is important to make two definitional points. First, by using words like *right* and *wrong*, we are not making judgments about anyone's intrinsic worth and virtue. We are talking about the fit between a person's goals and values and those of the organization.[10] Second, by calling for some people to be more rewarded than others, we do not suggest that the only important rewards are external ones, like pay, praise, and promotion. Research shows that attempting to influence people only with pay, praise, and promotion (carrots) or punishment (stick) is shortsighted. The mass of findings in organizational psychology is quite clear: motivation is primarily intrinsic. That is, individuals' motivation to work hard, feel conscientious, and be creative on the job is primarily dependent on such factors as how challenging and interesting their work is, how much control and autonomy they have on the job, and how much opportunity they believe they have to learn and develop on the job.[11]

To ensure differential employee experiences, leaders must provide opportunities for intrinsic rewards (growth and self-directed work) and extrinsic outcomes (pay, praise, constructive feedback, promotion). The idea is to draw on whatever factors it takes to create differential experiences among those who are committed to the desired culture, vision, and performance expectations, and those who are not. Again, the intention is to create an environment in which the former are more rewarded and satisfied than the latter.

Managers cannot have it both ways. Those who try to make everyone satisfied, unconditionally, simply ensure that their best people are most likely to be dissatisfied. Consider the scenario in which performance is measured in terms of initiative, quality, innovation, teamwork, contribution to the bottom line, and adherence to organizational values. Suppose that under these criteria Manager A is productive and Manager B is not. Manager A must *feel* more rewarded and appreciated than Manager B in order to experience a sense of psychological "equity," or fairness. Without this sense of equity, Manager A will not be satisfied. From the organization's perspective, Manager A's dissatisfaction is an undesirable outcome. The organization's failure to discriminate between the performance of the two managers not only diminishes Manager A but also reinforces the complacency of Manager B and the lowest common denominator of performance standards.

Differential performance demands differentials in compensation, recognition, visibility, career opportunities, job assignments, and growth responsibilities. All too often, by failing to support these outcomes, organizations have created environments where the best contributors are the ones who become the most upset at inequities. They are the ones who become the most frustrated and cynical about the organization. The consequences often include high employee turnover among the most talented people.

This is true even when the organization hopes for voluntary attrition. One division of a large multinational corporation was facing significant earnings woes and offered a voluntary retirement package in the hopes that at least 2,500 people would terminate their employment. In fact, over 4,500 people did, but many of them were precisely those the organization should have kept: superb engineers and scientists, creative marketing people, aggressive product managers. They left, according to one, "because we'd had it. We were fed up." What she then described was an overly bureaucratic and stagnant environment where rewards were administered indiscriminately.

When a company finds that its good people leave and that those who stay are either less marketable or comfortably ensconced in their routines, the organization faces a *strategic* crisis, not merely a personnel one. The same holds true with recruitment. Chairman James Morgan of Applied Materials argues that though his semiconductor equipment company operates in the ferociously competitive Silicon Valley arena, his greatest source of anxiety comes not from other firms' products but from their abilities to recruit the most talented and creative people—from his company or from a finite talent pool of excellence. These sentiments are especially important for companies in the service and information sectors because there the talent *is* the asset.

Taking the issue a step further, one implication of the organizing principle is that people who insist on *not* sharing the core values and priorities of the organization should be excluded from the organization. A participant in one of our seminars put it this way: "If I'm coaching a basketball team, I want everyone thinking basketball. I don't want good baseball players, not even future Hall-of-Famers. The team can figure out how to best get from one end of the court to the other, but I sure as heck can define what game we're going to play."

The late Bill Gore, founder of W. L. Gore and Associates, used a comparable metaphor. The company consists of forty-four plants worldwide and more than 5,300 "associates." There are few job titles and virtually no hierarchy.[12] Although associates have an extraordinary sense of freedom, creativity, and power in their work lives, they must adhere to certain inviolable, nonnegotiable values—values that Bill Gore insisted on.[13] He would ask his people to imagine the organization as a boat in the middle of the ocean. Below the waterline, he said, are the company's core values, philosophy, and vision. They could not touch anything below the waterline if they wanted to stay on the boat. Manipulating or lying to other associates, failing to collaborate, and being unwilling to take personal responsibility for commitments meant that one was unlikely to remain at Gore. Below the waterline was sacred, but anything above the waterline—routines, habits, policies, decisions, processes—was open to inquiry and change. The charge for everyone on the deck was, and is, to challenge the system to improve it in any way, incrementally or radically.

To quote researchers Frank Shipper and Charles Manz, within this context Gore associates can work "without structure and management." Their freedom and accountability are supported by numerous opportunities for in-house and university training. In addition, one associate makes this observation about the company: "It's not for everybody. Yes, we do have turnover. If you can't handle it, you gotta go. Probably by your own choice, because you're going to be so frustrated."[14]

Making the Break

Ensuring differential employee experiences becomes doubly painful when a leader has to acknowledge that some of the "best" people in yesterday's world are no longer the "best" in today's realities. Turnaround consultant Eugene Finkin is blunt: "If an employee is no longer useful, he must be terminated or retired early. Carrying dead wood destroys the sense of urgently fighting for the company's survival that you are trying to communicate to employees. The company cannot afford unproductive employees, either financially or psychologically. It must also guard against transferring these employees to other departments that don't really need them."[15]

Bob Stempel of GM, John Akers of IBM, and Kay Whitmore of Eastman Kodak were all competent, decent individuals who spoke grand visions of decentralization, accountability pushed down, delayering, and market sensitivity. Nevertheless, they were unable to "shake things up" and hence failed in their efforts to implement their visions. Shaking things up entails managing in such a way that those who have been successful in the old system will have to change their priorities and behaviors to be successful in the new system. Turnarounds demand that those who will not or cannot change will be less comfortable and less rewarded (dare we say, less compensated) in the new system. For leaders, this is a difficult state of affairs because they are faced with numerous interpersonal and emotional obstacles, such as discomfort in confronting the below-par performance of people they have worked with for years or difficulty in disengaging from a program or strategy they have identified with for a long time. Thus, it is no surprise that many turnaround efforts fail, and many successful efforts occur when incumbent CEOs and division general managers are supplanted by someone brought in from outside.[16]

Effective leaders open up possibilities of the new ball game to anyone who wishes to play, but the underlying message is that the new ball game is non-negotiable. Those who wish to play will work in an environment that will make them feel satisfied and successful. Those who don't wish to play will ultimately choose to seek other pastures, or the organization will help them find a venue that is a better fit.

Whither Justice?

Is ensuring differential employee experiences just? Is it fair?[17] Unequivocally, yes. First, one can ask whether current alternatives are just. Does justice exist when those who do live the values and ideals become frustrated, disillusioned, or cynical as a result of how the organization treats them? Does justice exist when expediency predominates, as when performance reviews are padded or inappropriate behavior is ignored in the interest of avoiding conflict, or when exceptional behavior consistent with organizational ideals is not acknowledged because it is taken for granted?

These problems and inconsistencies are evident not only in practice, but also in principle. University of Texas philosophy professor Robert Solomon observes that the standards we label "just" or "unjust" in business organizations differ across situations. "Justice is contextual," he argues, "and it virtually always involves conflicting considerations . . . [and] there is no possible formula . . . that will tell us how to judge such cases."[18] He notes that the standards used by organizations as benchmarks for "fair" decisions are often contradictory: equality (ignore all differences in performance), results (performance outcome and meritocracy), effort (those who work harder get more), ability (competence and potential), need, market value (pay what it takes to keep them from leaving), rights (the "right" to an annual bonus), the public good (what has the best effects for the whole organization?), risk and uncertainty (greater rewards go to jobs requiring risk and people who take risks), seniority, and loyalty. Each of these standards has validity, and since it is not unusual for many of them to have the same priority within the organization, unity, clarity, and coherence—as well as perceptions of justice—often suffer.[19]

By this point, it should be no surprise that there are a variety of approaches to justice. Justice and fairness are usually divided into three categories, each with its own set of tenets. Compensatory justice deals with how those who have been wronged or have suffered are compensated. Retributive justice deals with the fair imposition of punishment and penalties on those who have done wrong. These two perspectives are not as germane for our discussion as is the third category, distributive justice. Distributive justice deals with the fair distribution of society's (or the organization's) benefits and burdens. Fair distribution is especially important when different people put forth conflicting claims, and the society or organization does not have sufficient resources to satisfy all of them.[20]

One can take any of a variety of approaches in confronting the challenge of distributive justice.[21] Under egalitarianism there are no relevant differences among people that can justify unequal treatment. The difficulty with this viewpoint, according to Santa Clara University's Manuel Velasquez, is that "if everyone is given exactly the same [rewards], then individuals will have no incentives to exert greater efforts in their work; as a result, society's productivity and efficiency will decline."[22] We suggest that many organizations are currently operating under this principle without even being aware of it.

Another approach is socialism, or justice based on need. Here, responsibilities are distributed according to abilities, and benefits are distributed according to needs. The historical failure of this approach is now an empirical fact, but many people in organizations still feel that these are the circumstances under which they operate when it comes to annual budget allocation, work responsibilities, and rewards for contribution. As one manager remarked: "The most inefficient departments are the ones who max out on their budget. I'd be dumb to be efficient; I'd get less next year." Another manager said: "Management won't do anything about the dead weight, and the good people have to carry the bad. That causes lots of unhappiness."

The third approach to distributive justice is libertarianism, a viewpoint most elegantly proposed by philosopher Robert Nozick: "From each according to what he chooses to do, to each according to what he makes for himself."[23] Nozick advocates a minimalist environment that protects any and all free exchanges among consenting adults. The emphasis on freedom from coercion and a stress on individual rights are paramount values in Nozick's argument. To be sure, doing one's own thing and reaping the rewards is one way to stimulate entrepreneurship and personal accountability. Unfortunately, for work organizations, the strict application of libertarianism can result in a divisive, Darwinian culture that can tear apart any collaborative or team efforts.

We now come to the two views of distributive justice that form the primary rationale for the organizing principle: justice based on contribution and justice based on fairness. Briefly, the former—sometimes referred to as capitalist justice—advocates the distribution of benefits and rewards according to the contribution each individual makes to achieving the aims of the group.[24] This viewpoint emphasizes effort and productivity as the basis for reward distribution. But as a theory of justice applied to a social organization, it needs to be complemented by other ideas that more directly address the "fair" distribution of inputs and outcomes in a cooperative effort. John Rawls's theory of justice provides a comprehensive view that is appropriate but beyond the scope of this book. In brief, however, it posits several fundamental axioms:

1.   Each person has equal rights and equal liberties consistent with equal rights and liberties for others.

2.   The distribution of wealth and power should include fair and equal opportunity for everyone to qualify for more privileged positions.

3.   Society will take steps to improve the position of the most needy members of society.

4.   Assuming the above conditions hold, those who contribute the most have the claim to unequal portions of the output.

Consistent with Rawls's propositions, the organizing principle invites everyone to participate with equal access and rights, insists that everyone has a fair and equal opportunity to succeed, proposes that the organization provide support and training to help people through the learning curve, and states that those who contribute the most to the organization's values and performance have a claim to the greatest rewards.

Ensuring differential employee experiences is also consistent with Velasquez's conclusion: "The fundamental principle of distributive justice is that equals should be treated equally and unequals, unequally."[25] Once again, those who live the ideals of the organization should be treated unequally from those who do not.

The Importance of Consistency

Simply pronouncing the existence of new values and priorities does not mean that they will be executed, even if there seems to be genuine collective enthusiasm for them when they are introduced. In the real work world, bureaucracies tenaciously resist and compromise change, and without courage and fortitude on the part of the leader, bureaucracies emerge as the victors.

When leaders do not face up to these realities with the clarity and precision required by the organizing principle, any opportunity for coherence is smothered by confusion and cynicism within the ranks. People remember who was terminated, who was not; who was hired, who was not; who was promoted, who was not; who was applauded, who was not; who was confronted, who was not. They remember who got the strokes and attention, who got the plum assignment, which questions were asked or avoided at the meeting, what performance outcomes were commended or criticized, what criteria were emphasized in performance reviews. In doing so, they may observe a distinct lack of consistency in the direction and tone of management decisions. Hence they conclude that the organization either has no priorities, is unsure of its priorities, or is hypocritical about its priorities. In any case, organizational integrity, coherence, and performance suffer.

A leader's willingness to define purpose and act consistently often generates feelings of great relief among all hands, not merely the top performers. That is because people find the lack of consistency between stated purpose and actual practice truly debilitating. The feeling is even worse when the purpose itself is unclear, as is often the case. Research suggests that middle management in many organizations has only partial or no understanding of corporate objectives, and the situation worsens as one goes down the corporate ladder.[26]

We have found that *lack* of clarity and consistency causes confusion, anxiety, cynicism—and, for that matter, perceptions of injustice. Our observations are consistent with the research results of Northwestern University's Denise Rousseau, who found that when the stated ideals are not followed up by consistency in action, people have feelings of betrayal and distress akin to "moral outrage."[27]

This discussion has important implications for leader integrity and reputation. Marshall Shashkin and Richard Williams report research that lists trust and consistency as the first elements of "fairness."[28] According to researchers James Kouzes and Barry Posner, trust and consistency are crucial variables in creating credibility, a key attribute in leadership effectiveness. Kouzes and Posner note that the etymological root of the word *credibility* is *credo*, meaning "I trust, I believe." Their research leads them to conclude that "credibility is mostly about consistency between words and deeds. People listen to the words and look at the deeds. Then they measure the congruence. A judgment of 'credible' is handed down when the two are consonant."[29] Trust emerges from credibility. Credible leaders are consistent, and thereby earn their colleagues' trust.

Two things become crucial: the core purpose—the central values and ideals of the organization—must be defined explicitly; and the subsequent behavior of people in the organization must be consistent with those values and ideals (even when that means challenging existing traditions that run counter to the stated ideals). Ensuring differential employee experiences does not imply anything extreme, short of integrity.

Unifying the Vision

The Tokyo-based SANNO research report mentioned earlier states that a new principle—one that unifies worksites that have diverse work groups, a variety of jobs, and managers who have disparate methods and ideas—is needed in business today. The report says, "In order to unify diversified work and workers, it is essential to have a common vision. . . . Promoting a common vision has become even more essential for managing worksites during a period of innovation."[30]

Ensuring differential employee experiences takes the SANNO charge a step further. The greatest vision in the world will not have impact unless it is executed with consistency and integrity. The idea is to have people live it, own it, and use it as a frame of reference as they adapt to changing circumstances. Thus, learning, collaboration, and work in the shapeless organization have a common foundation, and a common direction. In the next chapter, we look at how a leader takes on the role of creating alignment with organizational purpose.

9

Linking Success to Values and Ideals

*I hope you will remember that he who sets two strings to
one bow may shoot strong but never straight.*
—Queen Elizabeth I

*The best performing companies are the ones where
people are filled with pride. In every case—and I have
seen the same pattern repeatedly—there is
accountability, equity, and common
understanding of a vision.*
—Dede Barsotti
Vice president and corporate controller, Raychem

Chapter Eight argued that the organization's ability to cope with
epochal transitions and jump the curve is greatly enhanced when
people adhere to the same vision and values, the same underlying
business philosophy and ideals, and the same strategic priorities.
This alignment enhances unity, leadership credibility, and organizational performance.

ALIGNING VALUES
AND IDEALS WITH
BEHAVIOR AND PERFORMANCE

The organizing principle of ensuring differential employee experiences is a vital tool for the manager who wishes to create this
kind of environment. To help the leader in this quest, we pro-

pose four initiatives. These initiatives—take charge of redefining and living the organizational agenda, be inclusive, use human resources strategically rather than as a function, and discriminate according to individual differences in responsiveness—are outlined in Table 9.1.

Initiative 1: Take Charge of Redefining and Living the Organizational Agenda.

The first job of the leader is to begin a revolution of minds by clarifying the core purpose, underlying philosophy, and overarching perspective of the organization. A well-defined organizational agenda provides the foundation for coherence. It also provides the stimulus for trust. Without this first step, the organizing principle cannot be applied.

Thirty years ago Peter Drucker advised executives to ask the question: What business are we in? Today we can up the ante by challenging leaders and organizations to choose what they *stand for*. To say that an organization "stands for" profits says

---

Table 9.1. Ensure Differential Employee Experiences.

Initiative 1: Take charge of redefining and living the organizational agenda.

- Ask the "deep" questions.
- Use and reference the new agenda every day.

Initiative 2: Be inclusive.

- Be clear in communicating that there is no prejudgment.
- Don't run away from continuity with the past.
- Commit to organizationwide business literacy.

Initiative 3: Use human resources as a strategic activity, not as a function.

- Ensure that the measurements reflect your core purpose.
- Reinforce the new measurements with rewards and positive feedback.
- Ensure that hiring, firing, and promotion policies are in alignment with your core purpose, and that they are stringently followed.

Initiative 4: Recognize individual differences in responsiveness, and discriminate accordingly.

- Systematically discriminate on the basis of commitment and results.

nothing at all. Yes, every organization needs profit just like every body needs food. (Even nonprofits have to declare a surplus over expenses.) But it is just as absurd to say that the purpose of an organization is to make money as it is to say that the purpose of a human being is to eat or breathe.[1]

For the leader who is committed to taking charge of the new organizational agenda, we offer the following suggestions:

■ *Ask the "deep" questions.* The specific content of the organizational agenda depends on the organization, of course. But to have impact, it will address questions like these: What is our business? What do we stand for? What is our business philosophy? What are the values we wish to live by? What are we striving for? Whom do we serve? How will we define success? How will we behave toward one another and toward our customers and partners in the process? What do we need to do to ensure that we can all rally around a common purpose? How do our roles and behaviors change as a result of this process?

Confronting these issues is imperative during organizational transition. This theme was echoed in an interview with Taro Okabe while he was executive vice president and chief operating officer of Fujitsu Microelectronics. He said that most deliberations among American management take about fifteen minutes for philosophy and about ten weeks for techniques and formulas. "That is the reverse of what it should be. We should know what our philosophies are and where they came from. . . . And the most important part is that everyone in the company is responsible for making the philosophy real."

Even those most noted for techniques and measurements—W. Edwards Deming, Philip Crosby, Joseph Juran, and others in the quality movement, for example—all place a strong emphasis on organizational purpose and philosophy. We have been surprised that many TQM devotees are unaware of the first of Deming's fourteen principles: Create constancy of purpose toward improvement of product and service. The failure of many quality programs, and change interventions in general, is that the emphasis is too often on tactics and measurement and not on the ideals and business perspective that must underlie them.

■ *Use and reference the new agenda every day.* Defining the agenda is not a one-time event. It is not represented in one speech or memo. The "product" objective is not a mission statement, though that might be one among many outcomes of the process. Defining the agenda is an ongoing, evolving affair, requiring continuing dialogues, feedback and coaching sessions, mutual exploration of the implications of the new vision and culture, and joint development of action plans.

However, though the process is collaborative, leaders must lead. They articulate the mandate, they take the first steps, they initiate the process, they champion it, they demonstrate it in their daily actions. Most important, they do not shirk from defining the new game as non-negotiable. Under conventional thinking, management is advised to make its mandates and expectations clear, and then step back to allow people to meet those challenges. As broad general advice, this is accurate but insufficient. Ensuring differential employee experiences demands a richer, deeper involvement of the leader. As McKinsey partner Jon Katzenbach notes: "The common assertion that a team cannot 'own' its purpose unless management keeps at arm's length is wrong."[2]

In March 1987, CEO George Lynn kicked off the new organizational agenda for Atlantic City Medical Center with a management retreat that was as much educational as problem solving. The organizational agenda—and the title of the meeting agenda—was PACE, or Patients Are the Center of Everything. Lynn made it clear that PACE, and the idea of revolving all operations around the needs of patients, was to be "the" purpose at ACMC, a two-hospital system. With that premise as a background, for four days Lynn and two consultants led the one hundred members of his management group in grappling with questions such as, Where is health care going? Why do we need radical changes in management? How can PACE help us? What does PACE imply for us? What will we do, what can we change, how will we behave, so as to make it happen?

Back at work in the hospitals, Lynn continued to define the new agenda relentlessly, every day, in every meeting and forum, like a broken record. It was at the top of his meeting agendas. It dominated his informal "speakeasy" discussions with groups of employees throughout the hospital. He related operational problems and issues to it—from capital budgeting and project assignments to choices of vendors and outside partners. He publicly linked management decisions to it. In one meeting we attended, Lynn told his directors to "treat PACE with the same emotion with which you would budget variance or cost overruns." He encouraged people at all organizational levels and functions to prudently link their own decisions to it. He also promised that he would personally protect anyone from unfair retaliation, even from their own bosses—and he kept his promise. By his repeated words and actions Lynn made it clear that PACE was not a program of the month, but something that defined how everyone in the hospitals would conduct their business. The fact that patient satisfaction scores, physician referrals, and operating margins improved over the next two years simply added fuel to his commitment.

As noted in Chapter Five, Atlantic City Medical Center has recently become part of a larger health network pioneered by Lynn. But seven years after the initial kickoff, Lynn says that "PACE is still the philosophy of managing the hospitals. It is because of PACE that we hit all of our performance targets—financials, patient satisfaction scores—as a matter of routine." Most compelling, PACE is no longer even a visible slogan; it is simply the deeply ingrained driver of how people in the hospital conduct their business. The change was evidenced by the most recent Joint Commission accreditation site visit, where one of the commission members—who was unaware of the PACE initiative—concluded her visit by saying: "After five days here, it is clear that the patient is the center of everything this hospital does."

This state of affairs did not come about by serendipity. It developed because Lynn envisioned a new "organizational movement" and defined his own *daily* role as a change agent toward the realization of that transition. This is a responsibility that leaders cannot avoid or delegate if they want to galvanize their organizations for jumping the curve. It demands significant calendar time and personal involvement. It must be visibly demonstrated to others as a top business priority.

Initiative 2: Be Inclusive.

In many ways, this initiative is self-explanatory. Leaders must be prepared to spend time and effort in demonstrating their commitment to an inclusivity that is both genuine and results-based. There are a couple ways that this can be done.

■ *Be clear in communicating that there is no prejudgment.* There are two required elements for being inclusive. First, it is crucial to convey the message that everyone can participate in this new game. Nobody will be automatically excluded; everyone can join and everyone can win. This is a non–zero sum game, where the successes of one person do not come at the expense of another. The effective leader communicates that everyone will be treated as a potential ally and winner, as someone who can add value if he or she tries. Everyone is worthy of achieving fulfillment on the job; everyone is worthy of concern, compassion, training, help, and patience. Second, make it very clear to people that while everyone gets an honest chance to change and play the new game, those who will not change or cannot play the new game will, regrettably, find themselves increasingly unhappy in the new environment. Change is expected; differential magnitudes of change by individuals will lead to differential rewards and experiences. The leader must take responsibility for helping to prepare people so they will have a decent chance to attain those rewards. Part of the preparation is psychological. Repeated assurances of inclusion and support from the leader are vital.

■ *Don't run away from continuity with the past.* It is important to recognize that many people have sincerely worked hard in the old "game," even when they may have been frustrated by the contradictions and the ambiguities of the rules. Disregarding that past will demoralize your staff. So in your rush onto a new playing field, do not be stingy in lauding prior achievements of the company and the efforts of the individuals who helped it succeed. Deliberately choose positive highlights of the past and praise them. When CEO Ray Larkin of Nellcor launched his Core Priority revolution, after which all hands were expected to disregard hitherto sacred functional barriers and job descriptions in order to contribute directly to new product development, he made it a point to laud repeatedly the entrepreneurial highlights of Nellcor's brief history. He talked about past acts of heroism, and highlighted the current managers and engineers who were part of those efforts. He did this not only to boost morale but also to educate. He wanted to illustrate and reinforce the kind of entrepreneurial culture that Nellcor once had, and needed again.

What Larkin did is an especially important step during the early stages of the change process. To create transformation, the leader must engender a dissatisfaction with the present and a sense of urgency in moving to the future. People can more easily move on into tomorrow's new ball game if they feel pride in the good things they did yesterday, and if they know you understand and empathize with the realities they have faced and overcome. Don't dwell on the past or let people live in the past, but don't ignore or belittle previous achievements, either.

■ *Commit to organizationwide business literacy.* Preparing people for change demands more than psychological support. As Harvard's Michael Beer and colleagues noted, "Once an organization has defined new roles and responsibilities, people need to develop the competencies to make the new setup work."[3] To ensure that these competencies are developed is why successful companies as diverse as Motorola, Quad/Graphics (printing), Johnsonville Foods (sausage), Worthington Industries (specialty steel), Chaparral (steel), Chesapeake Packaging (freight transportation), Manco (industrial tape, weatherstripping), and Southwest Air (the only profitable major U.S. airline in 1992 and 1993) make business literacy a key success factor.

Business literacy begins with knowledge. Full disclosure and discussions about company strategy, sales, financials, and delivery cycles are de rigueur. Information—whether about customers, inventories, budgets, costs, quality problems, competitors, work methods, engineering, or design alternatives—permeates the organization and is accessible to individuals and teams without the need for any sign-off.

This openness is supplemented with regular education and development opportunities. Making sure that everyone is taught to understand income statements, computers, market research, statistical process control, and how to run a meeting becomes a key success factor, not just a training task. At Chesapeake Packaging, in-house staff people such as controllers and analysts regularly teach employees (some of whom have less than a high school education) about the business fundamentals of cost accounting and systems applications. At Chaparrall Steel, managers and employees are encouraged to take developmental sabbaticals—enrolling in a university or working on a customer site, for example. At Manco, employees can enroll in any outside course and be fully reimbursed as long as they pass. Augmenting business literacy is an obvious outcome of Manco's policy, but CEO Jack Kahl's rationale is intriguing: "It lets people know . . . that one of the highest values in Manco is to be curious and allow curiosity to take place."[4] Whatever the organization's purpose and vision, its people must have the skills and knowledge necessary to move it toward that end. Success requires a mindset nicely encapsulated by one of Quad/Graphics' credos: "Learn, Know, Improve, Teach." At Quad, it is not unusual for people at all levels and functions to be in classrooms—either as students or teachers—for up to four hours per week. Apart from the culture of innovation this fosters, employees with high school degrees are able to take over multimillion-dollar presses, client relationships, and profit and loss responsibilities.

Initiative 3: Use Human Resources as a Strategic Activity, Not as a Function.

Steven Floyd of the University of Connecticut and Bill Wooldridge of the University of Massachusetts offer managers the following suggestion: "Realign rewards, systems, and structures so that they embody the intended strategy. These [elements] communicate strategy to managers more than any words."[5] To put these words into practice, we recommend particular care in several key personnel processes: measurements, hiring, firing, and rewarding. Let us examine each of these elements in turn.

■ *Ensure that the measurements reflect your core purpose.* In times of transition, organizations committed to jumping the curve will find it necessary to adopt new measures of organizational success. Harvard's Robert Eccles predicts that over the next few years, "every company will have to redesign how it measures its business performance."[6] Eccles notes that current methods for measuring financial performance are sophisticated and entrenched (for example, double-entry bookkeeping has been in use for five centuries). Nonetheless, we expect that over the next few years, as a consequence of the processes we have been advocating, there will be greater emphasis on measures that reflect market penetration, innovation, speed, knowledge acquisition, teamwork, alliance building, quality, customer service, and customer satisfaction. These measures will be reported organizationwide and will take on an equal if not greater footing than traditional financial data. Senior managers will work closely with general managers, human resource professionals, and controllers in developing measures that tap into these kinds of organizational priorities.

Harvard's Robert Kaplan and consultant David Norton foresee that tomorrow's managers will require a "balanced scorecard" linking financial perspectives with those of the internal business (At what must we excel?), innovation and learning (How can we continue to improve and create value?), and customer perspective (How do customers see us?).[7] Key success measures such as lead time, defect level as perceived by customer, on-time delivery, turnaround time, percentage of revenue and earnings from third party relations, percentage of revenue and earnings from products introduced over the past three years—or six months—will not be uncommon. They may well be elevated to the status of current financial ratios. Tom Peters also makes a strong case for "unconventional measures," including number of "differentiators" added to each product every ninety days, customer evaluations of "intangibles" (service, responsiveness, empathy, reactions of "delight"), and percentage of people in team configurations.[8]

Consistent with its core priorities, Manco, Inc. already focuses on four key measures: number of new customers this year, number of quality improvements, number of new products introduced, and number of million-dollar ideas. At Norstan Communications, the six "key measures" are quality of work life, customer satisfaction, market share, bookings, revenue, and profit. At Xerox, a monthly questionnaire sent to forty thousand customers worldwide asks questions like the following: How satisfied are you with Xerox overall? Would you buy another product? Would you recommend Xerox to an associate? The data are carefully analyzed as key indicators of organizational effectiveness. These corporate examples show that the specific measures used will depend on the organizational agenda. In all cases, however, there is an interest in using measures that are more obviously connected to the mission and values of the company.

New standards should also be applied to individual performance evaluations. The examples cited above might be used to assess the performance of senior managers directly, as is the case at Manco and Xerox. But with any position, even at so-called lower levels, you will want to include unconventional performance evaluation standards. During performance reviews, ask people questions such as: How, specifically, are you adding value vis-à-vis our new agenda? To what extent did you take the initiative to change your job over the last year to better realize our core objectives? How many new project teams or pilot tests did you champion? How many new products, customers, or cost-saving ideas can we attribute to your efforts? How many counterproductive old policies, regulations, and traditions did you change last year? What did you do to upgrade your own skills, the skills of others, or the knowledge base in this organization?

There is a caveat: do not let the measurements and control systems be developed solely by consultants or functional specialists. Involve all employees and managers in defining and implementing measures for the new values and directions of the organization. Encourage the formation of cross-disciplinary task forces that will address these issues and come up with concrete, high standards of evaluation. However you do it, make sure that involvement is the byword. The leader's role is to drive the process visibly and to insist that people develop high standards aligned with the agenda. Let technical specialists act as in-house consultants and team members, not as so-called gurus who create a system behind closed doors and unfurl it (read: impose it) on the rest of the organization.[9]

■ *Reinforce the new measurements with rewards and positive feedback.* Ensuring differential employee experiences means that those who meet the challenge of the new measurements receive the highest rewards. Those who show genuine effort in trying to meet the new standards are also worthy of accolade. Selective reward and corrective feedback become driven by the new measurements. It is especially important for organizations that are in a transformation process to reward people who take these challenges seriously. Too many managers spend an inordinate amount of time trying to change the opinions of career skeptics rather than supporting and reinforcing the efforts of the people who are excited by the change. Don't ignore your allies. Be visibly effusive in acknowledging their behavior and efforts, even when their actions lead to temporary setbacks. Make sure the plum projects and assignments, exciting growth opportunities, praise, perks, and awards go to them, and tell everyone why. Be seen "hanging out" with them; attention is a powerful motivator.[10] Concentrate on making participation a positive experience rather than on making reluctance a negative experience.

While these steps are important in validating and legitimizing the new measurements, the most important step is to insist that financial compensation reflect the new measurements. Pay may not be the most important motivator, but it is certainly one to which people are exceedingly sensitive. Measurements that are aligned with compensation have "teeth." At $100 million in revenues, Spectra-Physics Scanning Systems, a manufacturer of supermarket checkout scanners, the core priority revolved around increasing flexibility, brainpower, and creative teamwork. Accordingly, manufacturing manager Abe Kosol recounts that "we asked how to structure things so people would be paid for their knowledge, be flexible, and not be out only for themselves."[11] One of the results was the development of a customized, comprehensive pay-for-knowledge compensation plan.

Smaller companies like $28 million Chesapeake Packaging have found that meaningful profit sharing makes a particularly visible impact in reinforcing the priorities of the organizational culture. Larger companies such as Xerox have found that tying the bonuses of individual operating units to the accomplishment of team standards on the monthly customer satisfaction questionnaire has significant impact on getting functions like sales, accounting, and purchasing to focus on a common goal.

Unfortunately, in too many firms, measurement and reward systems of the old curve are left intact as the organization attempts the transition to a new curve. The result is a brake on the power of the transition. This is true even for small interventions. One of the key reasons that the results of quality interventions are mixed and often disappointing is that compensation for managers in most companies is based more on financial returns than on quality.[12] An Ernst & Young study found that in the automobile, computer, banking, and health care industries, quality performance indices like defect rates or customer satisfaction scores play a key role in determining senior management pay in fewer than 20 percent of organizations.[13] Short-term profitability still counts the most, meaning that creative accounting and financial sleight-of-hand too often take precedence over commitments to quality. Companies like Motorola, Federal Express, Xerox, and Milliken are exceptions to this trend, and their reputations related to quality and subsequent returns shine accordingly.

Certainly managers must have flexibility in determining their people's pay. But if coherence is to occur, they must ensure that total compensation coincides with the new values. It is not enough to develop new measures that are aligned with a new agenda; the measures must be adhered to scrupulously with differential rewards, both financial and nonfinancial. This step will create differentials in satisfaction and dissatisfaction throughout the work force, which is the whole point of the organizing principle.

■ *Ensure that hiring, firing, and promotion policies are in alignment with your core purpose, and that they are stringently followed.* Especially because the sensitive personnel decisions of hiring, firing, and promotion are so public, they tell people a lot about what is really important in the organization. Many managers argue that a fit between the values of the company and the values of the employee should be the most important criterion for hiring and promotion.[14] By recruiting, hiring, and promoting only those whose values mesh with the organization's new direction and priorities, leaders do several things: One, they help

mobilize a team of individuals who have a compatible set of visions and core philosophies. Two, for the sake of the individual's
well-being, they reduce the probability that he or she will enter
a work environment that will be frustrating and dissatisfying.
Three, they provide the "good" people on the payroll with additional allies. Four, they provide the "problem" people with a
sobering reality check. As an aggregate result, the "right" people
become more satisfied.

Managers in companies as diverse as Hewlett-Packard, 3M,
Nellcor, and Pan-Pacific Hotels have told us that in recruiting
and promoting talent, they consider a prospect's values and ability to "fit into" the corporate culture as important as, and often
more important than, the length and breadth of the person's resume. As one example, an accountant at Hewlett-Packard described his experience during the recruitment process:

> I was in interviews for twelve hours! Many of my inter-
> viewers were people outside of accounting. Some of my in-
> terviewers were people who would report to me. It was
> amazing how seriously they took this process, especially
> since it wasn't for a high-level position.
>
> But what really amazed me was that not once did any-
> one ask me an accounting question. I learned later that
> once they reviewed my resume, they assumed I knew ac-
> counting. What they really wanted to know was how I
> worked on teams, how fast would I take on responsibilities
> without being told, how cooperative was I, how did I feel
> about risk, and how easy was I to work with.

Paul Quinn, vice chairman of software developer Park City
Group, reports that in his company, someone who is not enthu-
siastic about cross-disciplinary collaboration has no serious hope
of being hired or promoted, regardless of technical background
or tenure. In her analysis of the available empirical research,
Northwestern University's Jennifer Chapman concludes that requiring a fit between the organization's values and those of the
individual is of benefit to the latter as well as the former. Yes,
people can and sometimes do change their values, but why
handicap them up front? Why put them in a situation where
they will be unhappy? She cites evidence that "entry level audi-

tors whose values matched those of the public accounting firms they joined adjusted more quickly, were more satisfied and tended to stay with their firms longer."[15] Better to forgo someone with the glowing resume if her adherence to the organizational values and norms is suspect. Better to continue a search than to hire the first "reasonable" candidate simply for expedience. Speaking to this very issue, Chesapeake Packaging human resources director Tim Parkent says: "You don't have to worry about what's going on in the plant if you've hired the right people."[16] It is worth the patience and extra effort to ensure alignment in values and ideals up front at the recruitment stage.

The same emphasis on "fit" applies to termination. Increasingly, managers are coming to understand that humanely releasing those who continue to resist change—even when they are technically competent—is necessary if successful transformation and growth are to take place in the organization. At the end of 1991, Andre Dippenaar, senior manager of Power Plants at South African Airways (SAA), launched a cultural change aimed, among other things, at enhancing teamwork, promoting self-management, and eliminating a "command and control" mentality. Dippenaar's division of 210 people is responsible for the vital tasks of aircraft maintenance and engine repair. In 1992, over a three-month period, thirty individuals—including seven supervisors—were released with an early retirement package. All were highly experienced and technically superb, but their inability to accept a new culture after two years was sabotaging the changes Dippenaar felt were crucial for future business success. "They were brake pads on our systems," he explains, and despite the highly technical nature of their work, he felt little compunction in letting them go. Now that global economic sanctions against South Africa have been lifted, SAA has become a cost and quality benchmark in the world of turbine engine repair, due in large part to the performance of Power Plants. Airline companies and engine manufacturers around the world are joining forces with SAA in both an outsourcing and strategic alliance capacity. Dippenaar attributes many of these developments to the new organizational systems that he and his team felt so strongly about supporting—even to the point of terminating individuals whose functional skills were exceptional.

The failure to take on a Dippenaar-like challenge can also lead to lower morale among those who do support change. Atlantic City Medical Center's George Lynn learned that there are times when the "wrong" people must be selectively terminated if the "right" people are to remain satisfied. He recalls the time when several of his best frontline people (who by then were serving as leaders of self-managed project teams) asked him why, three years after the initiation of PACE, "we still kept some of the frontline people and middle managers who were clear obstacles to our goal."

> They pointed out that I had been infinitely patient, overly patient in fact. They said it was obvious that those people were not going to leave like their counterparts had, and they were not going to "get it" either, so they were undermining our progress.
>
> I remember having a mixed reaction to their comments. On one hand, I was elated; if front-line people were urging me to get rid of career skeptics, then it was clear that our new PACE culture was really ingrained in the organization. On the other hand, I recognized that they were right; that I had waited too long and by doing so I had frustrated my good people and created an unnecessary drag to the goals we were seeking.

Leaders must be prepared to remove people whose motives continue to sabotage the sense of community and purpose they are trying to build. Delays in doing so sap the organization's strength and undermine any sense of coherence. It is for this reason that Dave Carlson, CIO of K-Mart, observes that "the most expensive decision a manager can make is to procrastinate on letting someone go who is not working out."

Initiative 4: Recognize Individual Differences in Responsiveness, and Discriminate Accordingly.

Whenever a new agenda is introduced, reactions to it may range from hostility to excitement. Effective leaders have always recognized that they must deal with different individuals in different ways: discrimination, in its classical sense, is needed.

Discriminating among individuals who vary on performance and on commitment to the new values is a particularly
important challenge. GE Chairman Jack Welch distinguishes
among four kinds of managers:

> Type 1: those who live the values of the company and who
> meet performance commitments—financial and other-
> wise;
> Type 2: those who neither share values nor meet commit-
> ments;
> Type 3: those who miss commitments but share values; and
> Type 4: those who deliver on commitments but do not
> share the values.[17]

This typology offers the leader an initial step in realizing
the potential of the initiative. Accordingly, we present one major
piece of advice for the manager.

■ *Systematically discriminate on the basis of commitment
and results.* Figure 9.1 represents our own illustration and adaptation of Welch's schema. As shown, the figure presents a 2 x 2
typology, where each quadrant represents one of the four "types"
described above.

Welch argues that Types 1 and 2 generate the easy decisions: T1 managers presumably get generous rewards and recog-
nitions, including promotion and career mobility within GE. T2
managers receive the most painful performance reviews and
ultimately—assuming no improvements are made—are asked
to leave.

In theory, Welch is right. Consistent with the idea of ensuring differential employee experiences, T1 people should be made
to feel distinctly more satisfied than T2s. In reality, however, we
have seen too many organizations where this is not the case:

■   T1 managers get bypassed for budget, authority, and pro-
    motion, sometimes in favor of T2 managers.
■   T1 managers get chewed out for skirting standard operat-
    ing procedures that are inimical to the values to which the
    organization ostensibly adheres.

Figure 9.1.   A Typology of Performance Levels and Congruence in Values.

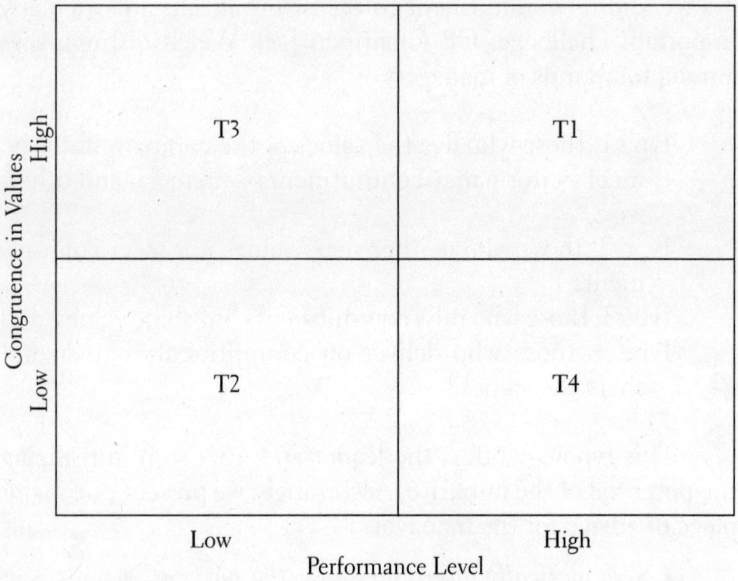

High	T3	T1
Low	T2	T4

Congruence in Values

Low   High

Performance Level

- T2 managers are rarely confronted by their superiors about either their performance or their values; indeed, some of these managers lead long healthy careers in spite of the fact that their staff, direct reports, and colleagues in other departments recognize their precarious standing on both dimensions.

- An ambiguous mix exists, where some T1 and T2 managers get rewarded while some get punished.

Any of these conditions is sure to generate confusion as well as cynicism regarding the values and priorities of the organization. Apparently, even the so-called easy choices are often not easy in practice.

With Types 3 and 4, the dilemmas become even thornier. What does one do with a T3 manager who lives the values but does not meet performance commitments, or with a T4 manager who delivers the numbers but does not share the values? At GE, according to Welch, T3 managers get another chance, perhaps in their current jobs, perhaps in another part of the company. While business realities preclude endless patience, it makes sense that T3 managers be given some room to develop. Assuming that they can grow into their jobs to meet the high financial and productivity standards needed for success in the 1990s, the values of these managers can be the foundation of extraordinary corporate growth. In effect, they can become tomorrow's T1 managers.

T4 managers present the stickiest dilemma. At GE, observes Welch, "this is the individual who typically forces performance out of people rather than inspires it: the autocrat, the big shot, the tyrant . . . [but] in an environment where we must have every good idea from every man and woman in the organization, we cannot afford management styles that suppress and intimidate."[18] When we discussed this typology at insurance broker Sedgwick James, top managers described T4 field managers as people who played a lone wolf–Lone Ranger role, autocratically using office personnel as servants to follow up on the field managers' own sales. They were described as having little interest in some of the emerging Sedgwick values: developing entirely new products based on new technologies, providing customized after-sales service, coaching and developing customer-support staff, and collaborating with other offices in information and resource exchange. Nobody blamed the T4s, mainly because they had never been confronted about their behavior. On the contrary, their low-on-values, high-on-numbers profile had been repeatedly reinforced within the company by career advancement, public accolades, and big bonuses for the sales they delivered.

The problem, as noted in Chapters Four and Five, is that tomorrow's results will be a function of today's decisions and processes. By tolerating T4 managers because they deliver in the short run, Sedgwick President Don Morford points out that the company is allowing them and the people they lead "to ride the same old path, which leads off a cliff." Welch's reasoning is similar: using their old styles and decisions, T4 managers will not deliver in the long term, because their ways will collide with the new values and directions of the organization. A manager who delivers today's numbers with an intimidating style, an egocentric personality, a disgruntled work force, a myopic capital-budgeting policy, or a control system that destroys solidarity is not likely to deliver the numbers tomorrow. Further, the T4 style has a corrosive effect on others' performance and morale. It may inhibit those who want to align with the new organizational priorities. It may undermine the credibility of the organization, since people will ask or wonder why a manager who stands for everything the organization supposedly does not is being applauded.

It is not merely that value congruence leads to desired results. National Semiconductor vice president Dennis Samaritoni observes that "if the business is driven only by results, you have no values." Accordingly, at National Semiconductor, President Gil Amelio has initiated a variation of the 2 x 2 typology. It is used as a tool with the intention of helping people become process sensitive as well as results oriented, and specifically, moving people closer to the core values of cross-functionality and teamwork. An increasing number of senior managers are coming to appreciate the perspective of people like Welch, Morford, and Amelio in emphasizing the synergistic relationship between values and performance.

Using the 2 x 2 matrix in Figure 9.1 as a framework for productive discrimination, we now suggest the following actions.

■ *Ensure that T1 managers are the most satisfied in your organization, T2 managers the least.* Dissatisfaction leads to turnover, and you want T2 managers to leave, not T1 managers.

Provide regular feedback to your T2 managers; explain to them why the rewards are not coming their way. Encourage them to change so that they and the organization will benefit. If there is no quick sincere movement on their part, either toward change or toward the door, you would be well advised to terminate them.

■ *Provide T3 managers with regular, concrete performance feedback, including your expectations for improvement.* Simultaneously, provide these managers with time for development and make sure you also provide them with resources, education, encouragement, and coaching to help them succeed in their performance. It is in your best interest that they do succeed, because they already hold the values that will be crucial to your organization's success in the future. Give them more slack than you would a T2 manager, but if it becomes clear that they cannot raise their performance to meet your high standards, then encourage them to consider another job within your organization, perhaps at a different function or level, where they can be successful and satisfied. Help them in this search. You want to keep them if possible, but only if they can find a spot where they will add real value and feel good about themselves in the process. Otherwise, you must let them go.

■ *Accept that conversations with T4 managers will require the most effort.* Acknowledge and commend their numbers, but explain that the new values are part of management performance criteria because they are the precursors of long-term corporate success. A T4 manager is likely to be surprised and upset: suddenly the numbers are not given unequivocal applause, and you are changing the rules. There is no gainsaying this. It's true, and you must explain why: the business environment has compelled a change in the rules of the game—if not the game itself.

T4 situations are particularly tricky. If a T3 manager doesn't show signs of change, letting him go seems readily defensible—after all, the numbers weren't up to par. But how can you justify not promoting or—even worse—letting go of someone whose tangible numbers are exceptional but whose intangible, unseen values are problematic? You can give the T4 manager time and support to develop, but understand that too much patience can be destructive. If time has run out, you must be able to justify your decision without qualms. Chairman Roger Milliken of successful textile manufacturer Milliken & Company did this in 1983 when he promoted a young T1 Tom Malone to the presidency over a number of veteran T4 types. Milliken was prepared to have the latter leave the company of their own volition, but he did not want to lose Malone.

In each instance, you must talk about your decisions in terms of preparing for the future, and in terms of the positive or negative impact each manager can have in influencing the course of an organization. Throughout, it is extremely important that you be clear, firm, supportive, and fair.

THE ORGANIZING
PRINCIPLE IN ACTION

These four initiatives help create coherence in strategy, unity in direction, credibility in leadership, and integrity in organization. They help the leader harness the diversity of talents, skills, decisions, and daily actions within an organization into a powerful force for corporate success. They help the organization stay clear and focused as it jumps the curve.

Understanding the Principle

Since we have spent considerable time outlining what the organizing principle is, let us briefly note what it is *not*. First, ensuring differential employee experiences most definitely is not an endorsement of exclusion (such as favoritism or discrimination) on the basis of any criteria other than representing the values and performance expectations of the organization. Nor is it a call for a simplistic "love it or leave it" philosophy, a Darwinian zero-sum game, or a Machiavellian divide and conquer strategy.

Exclusion solely on the basis of race, gender, or age is counterproductive and, rightfully so, illegal. Exclusion on the basis of more subtle factors like past friendships or old-boy networks is also a liability. On the other hand, the discrimination generated by the organizing principle is both necessary and unambiguous: all other things being equal, for example, a recent hire who fervently embodies the organization's perspective *should* feel more rewarded and satisfied in the organization than an employee with twenty years' tenure who persistently sabotages its direction. Legal constraints notwithstanding, no manager concerned about fulfilling fiduciary responsibilities should feel defensive about providing differential treatment on the basis of who is and isn't "walking the talk."

Further, the organizing principle is anything but an excuse for bland conformity and groupthink. Indeed, it separates those who merely mouth platitudes from those who actually help to build a culture driven by shared vision and values. Thus, the organizing principle creates space for higher levels of innovation, individual self-expression, diverse thinking, and constructive conflict within the organization. (Dennis Samaritoni notes that at National Semiconductor, for instance, the company's value commitment to cross-functional teams *ensures* diversity of opinions.) The goal of ensuring differential employee experiences is nothing less than the maximization of organizational and individual performance.

Ensuring differential employee experiences is not an autocratic set of barking orders, either. It is true that people who are not committed to the values and purposes of the organization may ultimately be encouraged to leave; but, as we have noted, it is more likely they will find themselves so unhappy with the new environment that they will choose to depart on their own.

To summarize, everyone is invited to participate. Everyone is given a chance to play the new game and grow into the new environment. As long as there is sincere effort and progress, the rewards and encouragement are available. Those who try hard but stumble may not necessarily receive the same rewards as those who try and succeed, but they will be acknowledged and rewarded for their efforts and progress, and they most certainly will be treated with patience and respect. Those who cannot or will not change will still be treated with compassion and sensitivity—but they will not be as satisfied as those who do change. Ultimately, if they don't leave on their own, they ought to be asked to go.

Ensuring differential employee experiences requires leaders daily to make a stand on behalf of what they say they believe in. Every day, leaders are faced with numerous choices. Each decision they make reflects either expediency (the myopically "easy" or politic way out) or honor (the way consistent with the ideal). People recognize and admire leaders who show honor, who behave in alignment with their values, who have a clear vision for their organization and live accordingly. Ensuring differential employee experiences helps a leader move in this direction. For many leaders, that alone will make the organizing principle attractive.

Extending the Principle to Partners

We also predict that as organizations become increasingly permeable, and as they take on a more interconnected web structure with "outsiders," leaders will extend the organizing principle to constituencies like suppliers, strategic partners, perhaps even customers. Already, companies like Motorola are insisting that their suppliers apply for the Baldrige Quality Award, indicating that a shared commitment to the value of quality is paramount in "hiring" partners.

But we think the trend will grow even further. Vice president and general manager Ken Olevson of Connecticut-based Quantum, a small, 140-person subsidiary of Chromalloy Compressor Technologies, is representative of the new breed.[19] He argues that a compatibility of vision and values is a primary determinant (more important than price) of who gets to be and remain his supplier. Quantum repairs specialized parts of jet turbine engines. According to Olevson, the only way Quantum can effectively compete in a brutally competitive industry is to offer the airlines something that no other vendor, including the airlines' own in-house machinists, can.[20] For Quantum, the key is turnaround time. A fast turnaround time in engine repair significantly reduces investment expenses and inventory costs for the airline, and also allows the airline to boost its revenues by getting the plane back in operation quickly. In an industry that suffered losses in excess of $4 billion in 1992, these are important considerations.

While maintaining a superb quality record, Quantum has managed steadily to reduce turnaround cycle time for its clients to the point that speed is now the company's chief competitive advantage. The results are due partially to the self-managed problem-solving teams operating within a flat Quantum organization. But just as important, argues Olevson, is Quantum's special relationships with suppliers.

Quantum subcontracts a number of services, including welding, machining, plating, cleaning, and surface finishing. As Olevson explains: "We don't pick our suppliers on the basis of price. We insist on a fair price, not the lowest. Since we must be able to depend on the performance of our partner/supplier as much as we do our own departments, what is most important to us is someone who does fast, high quality work, and shares our values about speed, service, and collaboration." In line with the organizing principle, these are the kinds of suppliers that Quantum wants to keep satisfied and successful.

Accordingly, the spirit of win-win mutual benefit is pervasive: "We always approach the problem collaboratively; how can we both make money while reducing turntime? It's amazing the kinds of creative solutions that both parties can come up with." Quantum's commitment to its supplier/partners is so strong that on occasion it actually buys the capital equipment for them. Certain machinery and tools are too expensive for smaller suppliers to afford. Quantum's philosophy is that superb trustworthy partners (those who share Quantum's values and ideals) are worth strengthening; by doing so, Quantum becomes stronger as well. Olevson explains how this process worked with his plating supplier:

> We purchased the additional tanks, heaters, power supplies and other accessories required to allow the plater to dedicate the equipment to our use. We also agreed, in the spirit of mutual benefit, that the plater could use the equipment for other customers when it was not required for our parts. We also agreed to help the plater become qualified according to OEM requirements, to give him the opportunity for additional new business. The dollars Quantum expended were relatively small to us but significant to our partner. In return, the plater agreed to give us first priority whenever he received our parts.
>
> Our plater is now approved by the FAA and for OEM work. Our plater has shared the benefit of the additional workload with us by lowering his price to us 53 percent to help make both of us more profitable. In addition, joint meetings between our shop floor people and his shop floor people have resulted in the turntime for his operations being reduced from twelve days to one to two days.

Quantum's approach to suppliers has allowed it to reduce typical turntime to its airline customers from between twenty-five and thirty days to ten days. The value of this quick cycle time is so great to the airlines that Quantum has grown in sales every year since it entered the engine repair business, even though the company charges 50 to 100 percent more than its chief competitor. This record is remarkable when one considers that the airline industry worldwide is obsessively cost-conscious, and turbine engine maintenance is one of the higher costs of airline operation. Olevson concludes: "Our response to providing what the customer wants is directly supported by the partnerships we have and are developing."

Contrast the mind-set at Quantum with the more typical exclusionary ("we can't involve them in *that*"), distrustful ("we can't be *that* open with them"), and even adversarial ("let's see if we can squeeze some more out of them by scaring them a little") relationships that many "partnerships" have. What Olevson understands is that a supplier, or strategic partner whose core agenda is fully compatible with yours, and whose values augment your trust, is worthy of being made satisfied and successful. Such a partner will provide a much more valuable support and synergy to your business than someone who looks good on paper. Plastics supplier Nypro, for another example, deliberately and selectively chooses its customers (Johnson & Johnson, Gillette, and others) based less on the customer's size or prestige than on the compatibility of both companies' goals and workstyles. Nypro has chosen this route to support its focus, which is to create a long-term, value-adding working relationship with a select cadre of customers.

In conclusion, jumping the curve is facilitated by an all-hands purposeful dedication to a common cause. Ensuring differential employee experiences is a way to make that happen. The leader who uses this organizing principle with integrity, consistency, and fairness will find it to be a valuable tool.

Former Sony Chairman Akio Morita argued that an organization is "a community bound together by a common destiny."[21] In effect, then, the aim of ensuring differential employee experiences is to build community. Whether construed as one organization or as a partnership among the organization, its suppliers, and customers, the challenge is the same: to promote behavior and business decisions consistent with shared values. What is at stake is not only productivity and profits, but also an effort to build enterprises that are focused, harmonious, and just.

10

The Responsibility Imperative

Life has no meaning except in terms of responsibility.
—Reinhold Niebuhr

If we don't reinforce a sense of responsibility
at the same time we build a culture of empowerment,
we are headed to social chaos.
—Rita Ricardo-Campbell
Senior Fellow, Hoover Institution

The principal social and business problem in the United States today is the absence of responsibility. The pervasive "me first" and litigious "sue, sue, sue" mentalities, the reckless excesses in personal and public spending, the escape from ethical conduct, the failure to respond to severe social ills—these impulses all reflect a philosophy that diminishes obligation, accountability, and duty. The distress is everywhere. Citizens demand ethical, responsive government; politicians complain they can get reelected only by pandering to voters with special interests. Teachers demand that families take on the roles that schools should not and cannot fulfill; parents insist that teachers become less concerned with their own interests and more concerned with the welfare of students. Parents go to seminars to learn how to instill a sense of responsibility in their children; children accuse parents of not living the codes of conduct they espouse. Executives call on the rank and file to step up to the challenges that confront the organization, while employees begrudge management for having the security and parachutes that employees can only dream about.

Sometimes there seems to be no limit to what can push through the responsibility screen. In the summer of 1990 Salomon Brothers acknowledged that it was under investigation for violation of certain rules connected with its role in Treasury auctions, the buying and selling of government bonds. The regulations were clear that no single one of the forty "primary dealers," who make money by buying the issues from the government and then reselling them to investor clients such as mutual funds and pension plans, could hold more than a 35 percent share of the government securities sold at one time. Salomon was accused of buying additional securities in the names of its customers and then, as prearranged, buying back the securities from its customers, at cost, for its own account. In this way it would be able to corner the market and have a control on prices that could reliably yield handsome profits.

The argument was made that public criticism of Salomon's behavior was unjustified because the strategy may have saved taxpayers money by reducing the costs of funding the federal deficit. Presumably, inefficiencies in the market were circumvented by the trading house's collusion with others. Another argument was that collusive behavior and price-fixing in the $2.3 trillion treasury market had been standard for years, and besides, Salomon's share or control of the total market was far less than 1 percent. Bottom line: the problem wasn't with Salomon; the fault was with the regulators.[1]

It would be a mistake to look at any of these apologies as simple matters of rationalization. Instead, reliance on phrases such as "everyone does it," "it's no big deal," or "the end justifies the means" should more accurately be seen as attacks on the notion of responsibility. The community trust was violated. Although the role of the forty dealers included a service provided on the community's behalf, their responsibility for taking this role seriously at Salomon was marginalized in several instances by a combination of greed, self-importance, and personal ambition. The Salomon case was one in a succession of instances of betrayed public confidence, including the savings and loan and BCCI scandals, as well as multiple examples of corporate malfeasance.[2] Yet any tendency to point the finger at Big Bad Business is misleading. As the United Way and university grant scandals have demonstrated, there seems to be no corner of society that is immune from the kind of attitude illustrated here.

Greater interdependencies and fate sharing make responsibility a critical issue in the emerging epoch. They sensitize an increasing number of thoughtful managers to the importance of mutual obligation. In a technologically linked, tightly intertwined global economy, our individual actions have an impact on others more frequently and profoundly than ever before. Hence, the necessity of taking personal responsibility for the effects one's actions have on others and on one's own well becomes more apparent.

RIGHTS VERSUS RESPONSIBILITIES

The idea of responsibilities has often been overshadowed by emphasis on other values. America's founding fathers were greatly influenced by numerous scholars who stressed the importance of individual rights and freedoms as the foundation of a healthy society. French philosopher Jean-Jacques Rousseau argued that human beings are born free and that the only legitimate government is one that protects and maximizes that condition. John Stuart Mill argued that society can legitimately restrain individuals only if their actions harm others. John Locke argued that each individual has the right to life, liberty, health, and property. These and other writers tended to view collective institutions, including government and society, as potentially hostile, repressive forces. Accordingly, their emphasis was on protecting individuals from such institutions and, ultimately, creating a consensual body politic that would protect individual rights, not diminish them.

The application of these social philosophies in the United States has contributed to the most prosperous democracy in history. Yet the promises and perils of an exaggeration of rights are unfolding before us. The Jeffersonian ideal of three basic rights—

life, liberty, and the pursuit of happiness—has become an enormous tangled collection of individual rights: from the right to an organ transplant to the right to carry assault rifles, from the right to walk safely in the streets to the right to live on the streets.

While rights represent a core element of democracy, we have become a rights-happy society, and this condition has led to two pernicious developments in our culture:

1. A *"me-first" excessive individualism.* By this we are not referring to self-reliant behavior that reflects free choices and launches entrepreneurial initiatives. Rather, we are referring to an egotism that is preoccupied with self-interest and psychological "self-realization."

2. A *legalistic emphasis on behavior and relationships.* By this we are referring to the self-protective, self-enhancing preoccupation with the *letter* of agreements rather than with the *spirit* of agreements. As numerous management experts have noted, excessive codification of behavior and relationships reduces trust, flexibility, collaboration, and risk taking.[3]

These two attitudes mirror a set of societal conditions in which rights and entitlements become much more valued than responsibilities and accountability. The consequences for organizations are significant. In addition to "hear no evil, speak no evil" as in the Salomon Brothers case, two other frequent outcomes are indifference to long-term organizational interests and a lack of commitment to organizational goals. These outcomes are correlated with—sometimes caused by—executive decisions that indicate minimal organizational concern toward managers and employees.

Results include an organization's weakened capacity to advance its performance on various scorecards (profits, ROA, patents, market share, customer attitude surveys) through new, fresh ideas that are key to success. Most important, this state of events paralyzes the organization's ability to jump the curve; when employees and managers do not feel a sense of duty and personal obligation toward advancing the fortune of the organization—and vice versa—the organization remains stuck in old patterns of behavior.[4] Responsibility within organizations becomes so diffused that it is devoid of any meaning. Bringing forward ideas that are crystallized in brainstorming discussions takes months in order to ensure the proper cover. Management is conducted by radar: signals are sent out to determine who is thinking what, in order to carve away risks and hand off accountability. Eyes in the company are all set in the same direction: up. Managers hesitate to put their opinions in writing except for going on record with a safe harbor position (to establish their "out") and are reluctant to stake out a position without co-opting their bosses first. They commit "unequivocally" to long-term goals while setting up numerous and resource-demanding escape hatches along the way. They hide behind a myriad of rules and policy manuals when the outcomes of their decisions are questioned. The answer to "who's responsible for what?" becomes obscured. Bureaucracies in particular, as C. Wright Mills wrote in the 1950s, can be thought of as vast systems of organized irresponsibility.[5]

The consequences of organized irresponsibility also extend to constituencies outside the organization. The "me-first" self-protection, self-enhancement attitude can exist when organizations deal with suppliers, customers, partners, and local communities. Suppliers who have been dropped with no prior warning and homeowners who find that their contractors have used cheap, shoddy materials are examples. Organizations that hide behind the technicalities of a legal agreement—even if the customer is unhappy—provide further illustration.

RECONNECTING ORGANIZATIONS AND CUSTOMERS

These attitudes keep organizations in a perpetual state of artificial separateness from outside constituencies—occasionally even a state of combativeness—and once again, they lower the organization's capacity to enhance its own fortunes in the long term.

Quality is a good case in point. Research conducted by consulting firms Arthur D. Little, Ernst & Young, Rath & Strong, McKinsey & Co., and A. T. Kearny suggests that only one-fifth to one-third of TQM interventions have achieved significant or even tangible improvements in quality, productivity, competitiveness, or financial returns.[6] One reason, cited earlier, is the emphasis on technique rather than on underlying values. Another is that most TQM interventions are grounded in a managerialist mind-set focusing on organizational self-interest. Managerialism assumes that the organization's obligation to total quality is attained when technical specifications are met, conformance indices are adhered to, industry standards and government regulations are followed, and the terms of contracts are carried out. More progressive organizations will add "zero defects" reliability to the list. When these requirements are met, the businesses assume that quality is achieved and the customer will be happy. Just as important, they assume that the organization has met its obligation to the customer and will be protected from legal attack.

These assumptions are not without some validity. Failure to perform to standards can result in lawsuits or government retaliation—and can devastate a company's cost structure. A colleague who worked with a major Fortune 500 industrial described an internal study showing that to catch an error when a product was already in the marketplace cost the company more than *three hundred times* the cost of finding and fixing the error early in the manufacturing process.

Even more damaging is the impact on the revenue side of the equation. Research studies have repeatedly demonstrated that relative to new customers, current long-term customers generate lower operating costs, spend more, pay premium prices, and provide valuable personal references.[7] The failure to meet the standards outlined above can destroy customer loyalty and word-of-mouth marketing. When a defective metal washer required Chrysler to recall more than four thousand cars in late 1992, including the new LH sedan billed as the "Car of the Future," the damage to corporate reputation and potential revenues exceeded the not inconsiderable direct costs of the recall itself.

The managerialist assumptions about quality are not wrong, but they are grossly insufficient. That is why the results of quality interventions are so spotty. Managerialist assumptions about quality—meeting specs, attaining zero defects, adhering to contracts—are today simply the price of admission. Nowadays, customers *expect* vendors to keep verbal and written agreements. They *expect* industry standards and government regulations to be followed. They *expect* products and services to be reliable, accurate, precise, and flawless in performance.

Customers take for granted that the product will be delivered as promised, that the newly purchased CD player will play well for years, that the plane will take off on time, that the luggage will be delivered intact with them when they land, that the paperwork on a bank loan will be error free, and that the long-distance line will be clear. We once asked a complaining customer in a hospital to explain what determined a poor quality lab test. His responses included lengthy turnaround time, long waits in queues, frontline people who could not access his file quickly because the system was not computerized, a failure of the hospital to phone back at the time agreed on, and a patronizing and unsympathetic attitude on the part of physicians and hospital employees. We pointed out that he had said nothing about the test's accuracy, reliability, and clinical comprehensiveness. His response: "Hell, that's a given."

Zero defects and contract compliance are a marked improvement over the old "let the buyer beware" philosophy that used to define attitudes toward the customer. But today, an organization that wishes to maintain customer loyalty will find that its responsibility to them needs to go much deeper than strict adherence to a contract alone.

Committing to the Customer

The kind of responsibility that will lead to competitive advantage is described in an organizing principle that focuses everyone's attention on a shared obligation and duty to the customer.[8] A genuine commitment to the customer provides the organization with a meaning and motivation for jumping the curve. If a sense of duty to the customer is shared within the organization, then transformations in the business world and in customer preferences will galvanize the organization to do whatever it takes to fulfill that commitment. A healthy fear of being left behind may motivate some organizations to jump the curve, but a sense of responsibility to customers, given that they change over time, serves as a more positive constructive force for organizational change. Many organizations trumpet the ideology that the customer is king, queen, or center of the universe. The organizing principle that we propose is the means of putting teeth to that position. If the commitment (read: responsibility) to the customer is genuine, then the honorable organization has little choice but to subscribe to this organizing principle: *Make customers the final arbiters by offering an unconditional guarantee of complete satisfaction.*

Without a strong commitment of this kind, all the language and posturing about customer satisfaction, quality, and service are bromides and cheerleading, empty of real consequence. But when taking responsibility through guarantees is the center point for organizational structure and process, the goal is set and all functions—from marketing to finance to personnel—are touched with a common sense of duty and accountability.

With rare exceptions, guarantees in the marketplace today do not meet the spirit of the organizing principle we propose but are instead developed with marquee-value in mind. Life in the 1990s is awash with puffy but unclear "satisfaction guaranteed" promotional pieces, limited warranties with further disclaimers in little print, and irritating hurdles that customers must cross if they wish to invoke the guarantee.

Even the apparently sincere guarantees are laden with conditional subtleties that do little to inspire confidence on the part of the customer. The big bold headline on a promotional brochure for a nationwide hotel chain reads: "100 Percent Satisfaction Guarantee." In much smaller, hard-to-read print are the words: "We guarantee high-quality accommodations, clean, comfortable surroundings, and friendly and efficient service." Underneath, in even smaller print, "If you're not completely satisfied, we don't expect you to pay." What is this "guarantee" other than a promotional piece based on carefully developed, hedge-your-bet, legalistic thinking? Why the unreadable print? Is there a subtle meaning to "we don't *expect* you to pay"? What sort of pseudo-promise is being made here?

In the managerialist mind-set, guarantees are made with marketing as the dominant interest, as a means to effortlessly differentiate the company from competitors and spur sales.

Ironically, this step is self-defeating. Because the guarantee is a promotional tactic, nonmarketing functions and operations are not much affected by it; the organization will no doubt be able to "meet" the guarantee without altering its current operations or culture. The lawyers have already determined that the guarantee is presented in such a way that the organization's exposure to claims is negligible.

But when it's so easy to do, everyone can do it. A multitude of watered-down, meaningless cliches about satisfaction guaranteed result in more "noise" that customers have to sift through in the marketplace. The managerialist-based guarantee is not grounded in an organizationwide, all-hands responsibility to the customer and is thus almost invariably weak and conditional in its impact. It does little to differentiate the organization from the rest of the pack. Even worse, the guarantee easily becomes a simplistic gimmick to ensnare the customer for a quick sale, which too often turns out to be a one-shot deal. The cost of customer acquisition is not adequately matched by a stream of revenue over a sustained period.

In 1991, Doctor's Hospital in Detroit attempted to get out of its deepening financial morass by offering a guarantee that said that if the patient is not seen in the emergency room within twenty minutes after arriving, the treatment is free. Even though "being seen" often just meant a brief dialogue with a nurse, the hospital received a lot of press and many inquiries from other hospitals. But since the guarantee was basically a promotional piece aimed at quickly boosting revenues, it did not require significant change in anyone's habits or behavior (whether doctor, nurse, administrator, or patient). After a few months of minimal results, the guarantee faded from sight, and the hospital filed for bankruptcy in 1993.

In contrast, taking responsibility through guarantees eschews the marquee orientation. Based on the assumption that the business exists to serve a customer, the organizing principle views the guarantee as the primary driver of the entire business. It is a way of engaging *everyone's* attention and eliciting a sense of responsibility to the customer's experience. It means that the customer's complete satisfaction becomes the top business priority. It determines how people get trained, how capital gets allocated, how results are interpreted, how managers get paid. In short, the guarantee influences all management decisions.

Taking responsibility through guarantees raises operational standards. It focuses the organization's attention on meeting the rising expectations of customers and stimulates people to initiate improvements in performance standards based on customer feedback. A university whose students complain about the course registration process will act quickly to discard existing systems and substitute faster, more convenient (and ultimately, more cost-effective) avenues for student registration: electronically, by phone, or by mail. A small business in touch with customer concerns about convenience will start staying open on weekends and evenings. A manufacturer whose customers want a much quicker turnaround time will not flinch from making new investments in technology and developing new relationships with distributors. Such decisions help create a learning organization, affecting *all* internal organizational functions.

In adopting this organizing principle, the organization must interpret "responsibility" with a fresh perspective. It cannot be seen as a necessary evil or as a millstone around the organization's neck, but as an inspiring, exuberant imperative that raises people's motivation and concentrates their behavior. It is illustrated by one executive's description of his corporate culture: "We have a compulsive, obsessive drive to excellence, a burning need to do the best we can for every client."[9]

By raising the standards of operations, organizations that take responsibility through guarantees also build in quality from the front and throughout the process, from first step to after sale. Every employee and manager in the process chain takes personal responsibility for helping to carry out the guarantee. Even more significant, the organizing principle redefines the very term *quality*, be it service or product quality, in ways that are relevant to the customer.[10]

Customer-Defined Satisfaction

Just as the idea of unconditional guarantees is the first component of the organizing principle, the second fundamental element is the goal of *complete satisfaction*. Meeting legal standards may satisfy customers in a limited sense, but that is not the same as serving their needs. Serving their needs extends well beyond meeting specs and written agreements. *Complete* satisfaction is what some vendors refer to as "delighting" customers, or giving them the experience of "Wow!"[11] In today's crowded marketplace, only "delight" and "wow!" ensure customer loyalty and word-of-mouth referral. Complete satisfaction goes well beyond satisfaction, which is the customer's bland acknowledgment that the formal—shall we say, minimal—agreements were met.

Without the capacity to redefine total satisfaction, providers miss out on what customers define as real value and what it takes to satisfy them. In judging the total quality of the products and services they receive, customers look well beyond narrow technical or contractual standards. Customers perceive quality in a much broader, deeper, more personalized context. Managers' ability to do the same will provide them with the information necessary to deliver a guarantee that matters to the customer. In order to do this, the vendor would be wise to absorb a richer, more thorough perspective on quality. This customer-relevant concept of quality has three elements—total experience, ease/convenience/excitement, and the high-value solutions—each of which we describe in turn.

■ *Quality is the total experience that a customer has with the organization*. Customers are starting to apply the standard of "zero-defects" to the vendor organization itself, not merely to the vendor's output. The actual products and services are simply one element embedded in the customer's total experience with the organization. A vendor whose products are impeccable but whose invoicing, after-sale service, or responsiveness to unanticipated requests is poor will not receive high quality marks. This outcome is emerging in all industries. Computer companies have learned that "softer," more intangible customer experiences such as easy integration with existing systems; effective training; friendly manuals, software, and other teaching tools; and outstanding telephone troubleshooting services are essential for customer perceptions of total quality. Similarly, banks and other service providers have learned that fast, timely decisions, short queues, quick turnaround on complaints, individualized caring information and advice, and frontline responsiveness and empathy are as essential (some research studies suggest even more essential) to customer perceptions of total quality as the actual technical properties of the service packages. The bottom line is that the customer no longer separates the "product" from the experience of dealing with the organization that provides it. The total experience defines total quality.

■ *Quality is the ease, convenience, excitement, interest and/or fun that the organization provides to the customer.* Adding ease, convenience, and excitement requires stretching the meaning of quality. It has strategic implications because it requires a change in organizational focus. Professor Sandra van der Merwe of IMD in Lausanne, Switzerland, reports that a division of Du Pont Europe was perplexed because continuous investment in research on and development of high-quality carpet fiber was apparently having little impact in the marketplace. Further probing found that what customers wanted in the product itself was not a two-thousand-year life span, but stain-resistance and other forms of easy aftercare. Moreover, since most customers found the entire experience of buying carpets intimidating and depressing, Du Pont reacted by providing complementary services aimed at increasing customers' ease, convenience, and interest in the carpet-buying process. In addition to developing stain-resistant fiber, the company added services aimed at all customers in the distribution chain—carpet mills, retailers, and final purchasers—and included an array of user-friendly written information, a twenty-four-hour telephone hot line, and a significant boost in after-sale maintenance services.[12]

For total satisfaction, the bottom-line issue for many customers is becoming this: Is it pleasant to do business with this company, and do its products make my life easier? Those vendors who can also add excitement and fun to the equation ratchet up the total satisfaction dimension. See, feel, and use a portable Power Book and you realize that Apple Computer is not only selling convenient computing power but also aesthetics, sensuality, excitement, and fun. With its Create-A-Card Kiosks, Hallmark has made an enormous leap in meeting the expectations of today's more demanding customer. According to our colleague Chip Bell, today's customer is no longer satisfied with a salesperson's statement of "I know you want it fast, good, and cheap; and I can get you two out of three." Now the customer says, "I want it fast, good, cheap, *and my way*."[13] Hallmark's Create-A-Card Kiosks allow customers literally, and conveniently, to make up their own professional greeting cards. For many customers, this personalization process meets the criteria of ease, convenience, excitement, and fun.

More and more communities are enjoying bookstores that have taken quality beyond offering a wide selection of volumes tastefully presented in a comfortable ambience. The stores now offer customers a coffee bar and gourmet delicatessen with complimentary magazines people can read while sitting indoors or out. They might feature frequent visits by local and international writers—sometimes very high-profile authors—to speak about their work. These stores are turning themselves into more than places where books are efficiently ordered and stocked; each is becoming an event, an experience—fun, if you will.

■ *Quality is the ability to provide customers with high-value solutions.* Customers today are no longer buying products or services. The quality value of a company's output to a customer is directly proportional to the extent to which it alleviates or solves the customer's problem. Several years ago, Ingersoll Milling Machine Company was able to stem market share decline and become competitive again by doing the following: The company first reduced the defects in the machine tool products themselves, thus leveling the playing field with its Japanese competitors. It then went further, reconceptualizing the concept of "quality product" in a way the Japanese were less likely to emulate. Ingersoll realized that customers invest in machine tools for, minimally, two simple reasons: to maximize productivity and to enhance profitability. Accordingly, the company began to position itself as a vendor who could help customers do precisely that. Ingersoll people worked directly with operators and engineers of client firms in custom-designing machine tools and sophisticated parts-making *systems* in a manner that would best fit the unique operational needs of each firm. The manufacturing consulting services that were part of the new "product" increased value-added to the client. So did the company's willingness to guarantee the client's productivity gains as part of the partnership. The company now says it sells solutions, not simply machine tools.

Thinking and executing solutions requires both a new mind-set about quality and an organization that is flexible and responsive. Don Bice, a regional president of Norstan Communications, says that the ability to think and execute total solutions is how Norstan can top much larger companies in winning contracts for voice information processing and videoconferencing systems. "We are very serious when we tell organizations that we will work with them in order to help them create solutions for their problems, *and* for their customer's problems."

Solution-based outcomes occur when vendors stop thinking in terms of the official product/service mix as defined by the annual report. It takes a major breakthrough in strategic thinking and execution to be willing to wrap an organization's resources around each client's particular needs and thus develop an appropriate "product" in response.

The organizing principle helps people understand that only the customer can define the experience of total satisfaction. Taking responsibility through guarantees spurs the organization on to approach quality in terms of the three elements—the total experience, the ease/convenience/excitement, and high-value solutions—that create the experience of complete satisfaction in the customer. The idea is to help people in the organization redefine the goal of "quality" in a way that acknowledges that the customer is the final and most important arbiter, the only one who can determine whether complete satisfaction exists and whether the guarantee has been met.

Taking responsibility through guarantees encourages the organization to adopt a new perspective in relationship building. To tap into customers' changing needs and to redefine quality in terms of the above three elements, the organization has no choice but to work in partnership with the customer and all other external constituencies who have an impact on the customer, like suppliers and distributors. Inventing ways to do this is the challenge. Strong, trusting, interactive partnership relationships provide the vendor with clarity about the ever-changing problems that individual customers experience and what it would take to "knock their socks off." Such relationships stimulate all parties (vendor, customer, supplier) to generate jointly an ongoing, dynamic stream of creative solutions to solve customers' problems and address specific needs. The organizing principle helps create a personal and professional bond among the parties. Apart from the innovative customized "delightful" solutions this perspective generates, the relationship bond in and of itself contributes to the customer's experience of complete satisfaction. And when the bond exists, the status of the vendor is less susceptible to attempts by competitors to undermine the relationship by offering cutthroat prices or flashy promotions.

A Bigger Picture

In an interdependent world economy, our self-interest is dependent on others. By taking care of others, I take care of myself. By making others stronger, I make myself stronger. That is the essence of enlightened self-interest, and the underlying premise of taking responsibility through guarantees.

Unfortunately, amid the excesses of individualism and legalism, many managers adopt a dualistic Either/Or perspective when they consider responsibility to others. Robert Solomon observes that "the standard contrasts between 'self and others' and 'duty versus self-interest' . . . introduce vicious dichotomies that lock us into destructive 'either/or' modes of thought."[14] Managers tend to think in terms of attention to profits *or* attention to people; concern with shareholders *or* concern with customers; my group's priorities *or* their priorities. What prevails is "us versus them" thinking: management versus labor, department versus department, colleague versus colleague, organization versus customer/supplier/regulator/partner. The environment of "every man for himself" grows and festers.

In contrast to typical Either/Or thinking, Jonas Salk's proposal that the emerging epoch will yield a Both/And perspective involves a simultaneous acceptance and integration of points of view that are often presumed to be in conflict. It is the idea that companies help profits grow by nourishing people's efforts and talents, that shareholder value is enhanced when customers experience complete satisfaction. It is the idea that my group gains new strength from working with your group for mutual gain. In discussing his PBS special "Challenge to America," Pulitzer Prize winning journalist Hedrick Smith observes that in contrast to Japanese and Germans, Americans "tend to see the individual *opposed* to the group. And I think it's going to take us some insight into discovering that is not the case."[15]

On a broader scale, George Washington University sociologist Amitai Etzioni notes that the "individual and the community make each other and require each other. . . . Individuals and community are both completely essential, and hence have the same fundamental standing."[16] Thus, cooperation and concern for others are seen as natural needs—needs that drive human behavior as effectively as self-indulgent goals. Individual achievement and group collaboration are not mutually exclusive. The attitude is that self-interest *includes* a sense of social obligation and a feeling of responsibility regarding one's impact on others. There is, in short, the quest for *both* self-satisfaction *and*, in no less equal measure, the desire to serve others. From the perspective of Both/And thinking, these are the same path.

Taking responsibility through guarantees enhances a personal commitment to real human beings, not legal abstractions. Minimally, this means that the organization sharply reduces, even eliminates, the steps and hassles that a customer typically faces in making a complaint or invoking any official warranty (like writing letters, filling forms, repackaging the product with original boxing, or waiting at length for official responses to queries). But much more significant is the overall spirit in which the organization deals with the customer; in particular, whether it provides customization, careful attention to details, solutions to idiosyncratic problems, demonstrations of empathy and caring, exceptional after-sale care, and immediate overresponsiveness to complaints. These all reflect the sense of duty and obligation to a constituency that supersedes short-term, self-protective compliance with formalized agreements. Finally, and most important of all, the readiness to take responsibility and to engage in corrective action in the face of customer dissatisfaction—*even if that action is not stipulated in any formal agreement*—reflects the approach to customer relationships inherent in the organizing principle.

MEANING,
MOTIVATION, AND MYTHS

The self-enhancement philosophy common in management and the majority of motivational prescriptions over the past thirty years have been derived, directly or indirectly, from Abraham Maslow's theory of motivation. Maslow assumed that after satisfying some minimum requirement of other needs (like food, shelter, and affiliation), people work toward becoming everything they can possibly be. His original theory, focusing on the pursuit of self-actualization and self-realization, has for years served as an intellectual foundation for compensation schemes, rewards, career pathing, and job design. Again and again, the focus has been on self. And indeed, Maslow's earlier writings are filled with discussions of self-actualization, self-fulfillment, self-awareness, and self-confidence. These are important concepts, for there is considerable research that shows that work conditions that enhance self-actualization lead to higher motivation and productivity.[17] The issue is to determine exactly what self-actualization is.

Maslow found that his research samples of self-actualized individuals—he called them "good human beings," or "GHBs"—were not "looking out for number one" at the expense of others. They were neither egotistic nor narcissistic. Though their actions in life put them on the path to achieving their full potential, they didn't seem consciously obsessed by a need to "self-realize." The more Maslow considered the emerging evidence, the more he began to believe that his original orientation toward the need satisfaction of the individual was incomplete. In an appendix to one of his last published works, Maslow reached conclusions that were at odds with his original premises:

> I now consider that my [earlier work] was too imbalanced toward the individualistic and too hard on groups, organizations and communities. . . . I can say much more firmly than I ever did, for many empirical reasons, that basic human needs can be fulfilled *only* by and through other human beings, i.e. society. The need for community . . . is

itself a basic need. Loneliness, isolation, ostracism, rejection by the group—these are not only painful but also pathogenic as well. . . .

The empirical fact is that self-actualizing people, our best experiencers, are also our most compassionate, our great improvers and reformers of society, our most *effective* fighters against injustice, inequality, slavery, cruelty, exploitation [and also our best fighters *for* excellence, effectiveness, competence]. And it also becomes clearer and clearer that the best "helpers" are the most fully human persons.[18]

These are important admissions. Before he died, Maslow made it a point to revise his original writings with appendices and prefaces that reflected his new thinking. Moreover, his one book that deals directly with business management is full of anecdotes of cooperation, cross-disciplinary collaboration, team decision making, and participatory management that he documented at Non-Linear Systems in San Diego.[19] His observations there led Maslow to elaborate on the values of "synergy," a concept that his friend and colleague Ruth Benedict had used to describe foreign cultures in which cooperation is valued as morally as well as socially and economically advantageous to all.

Recent data suggest that Westerners, Americans in particular, may be more responsive to the newer interpretation of self-actualization than pundits and executives give them credit for. Sociologist and theologian Andrew Greeley has cited data from a large international study to argue that Americans, reputed individualists, are often motivated at work by a desire to help others. The International Social Survey Program questioned large samples of workers in eleven countries, including the United States, Europe, and Israel. The results indicated that the Americans scored as high as Italians, Dutch, Austrians, and Irish on questions that dealt with the motivation to help others. They scored significantly higher than Germans, English, Hungarians, Norwegians, and Israelis. In regard to whether people worked primarily to earn money, the Italians, Norwegians, Dutch, and Americans scored the *lowest*, with no statistical difference among them. Other data are cited by Greeley as well, the upshot being that on a comparative basis at least, it appears that

Americans have moved into a social period in which self-indulgent, consumerist, and "I"-centered motivations might be less strong than the popular mythmaking would suggest.[20]

The work of philosopher Paul Tillich offers some practical perspectives that are in alignment with Maslow's final conclusions. In attempting to balance the tension between the self and others, Tillich suggests that each individual has three options in life: individualization, participation, or self-realization through interdependence.[21]

In individualization, the primary focus is to reach one's potential and improve one's personal lot in life, be it financial, emotional, familial, or social. The positive outcomes of this strategy range from personal heroism to successful entrepreneurship. However, potential by-products include loneliness, alienation, frustration, and a wariness of others. Other outcomes include a constant restless desire for "more," a quasi-permanent feeling that one has to prove oneself to others, a feeling that one always has to win in order to maintain self-respect, and an incessant, driven belief that even greater self-realization is just around the corner.

The second alternative is participation. Here, the person submerges the self into the social group. The positive by-products of this strategy are a sense of personal security and social comfort. The danger is a dissolution of one's own sense of self, an overdependence on others, an overconformance to norms and fads, a mental rigidity, a constant desire for "more" (this time for "keeping up with the Joneses"), and a weakening of one's belief that one can have an impact in the world.

The third approach, self-realization through interdependence, is consistent with Maslow's later conception of self-actualization and is the one Tillich considers the best and the most courageous. Tillich proposed that in true integration, the essence and spirit of the individual is not only maintained but *enhanced* by freely integrating the self into the world that exists beyond the self. This is a difficult concept because traditional Western thinking tends to be mechanistic rather than holistic; but note that it is also consistent with quantum physicist Niels Bohr's conclusion that the properties of any particles can only be defined as they interact with other systems.

Today, a shift is under way that places attention on others not just alongside attention to self but as part of it. The open, collaborative, win-win approach to responsibility is as much about watching out for one's self-interests as it is about duty to others. Responsibility to others becomes a responsibility to self. It is in that spirit that the organizing principle of taking responsibility through guarantees is presented. An unconditional guarantee of total satisfaction as the customer sees it is not a legal millstone or an advertising ploy. Rather, it is a sign of an organization's deep, enduring responsibility to the customer as a valued human being. Fulfilling that responsibility leads, in turn, to the organization's economic and psychological success.

As a demonstration of that responsibility in practice, we look to the philosophy expressed by Jonathan Perdue, executive vice president of fast-growing, $50 million Conifer Crent Company. In mid 1993, he reminded his fifty regional salespeople that "we are no longer just selling industrial and retail packaging, nor are we just selling protection and transportation of the product. Our mission is bigger: we are selling our desire to enter into a close relationship with people who are very valuable to us—our customers. Their willingness to enter a permanent relationship with us depends on how well we serve their needs. Making the first sale is easy. It's the second, third, fourth and so on sales that are hard. We don't want to go back to square one and struggle to make the next sale every time we meet the customer. Our challenge is to create a climate in which the customer *wants* to be involved with us—not just for today, but for years and years. If we do that, the sales will follow."

Customers (and for that matter, suppliers and employees) will turn to organizations who take on the responsibility of providing them with something valuable that will help them survive and thrive in the chaos they face daily. In the next chapter, we describe specific initiatives, based on unconditional guarantees, that organizations can use to help create value for customers and develop long-term relationships with them. Each initiative not only helps the organization jump the curve, but also reminds all constituencies why the organization is in business.

11

Guaranteeing
That the Customer
Is the Final Arbiter

New occasions teach new duties.
—James Russell Lowell

Our guarantee is the cheapest investment we can make.
—Timothy Firnstahl
CEO, Satisfaction Guaranteed Eateries

Customers will experience complete satisfaction only when they believe that the organization is genuinely on their side. Taking responsibility through guarantees is a tool by which organizations can orient everything they do to ensure that experience. The idea of making the customer the final arbiter by unconditionally guaranteeing the customer's complete satisfaction—as defined by the customer—significantly raises the standard with respect to the organization's responsibility.

RESPONSIBILITY
FOR THE GUARANTEE

Genuine, nongimmicky guarantees are still enough of an anomaly in the marketplace that those companies offering even modest ones have found that they reap financial and marketing benefits. In 1988, New Jersey industrial gas distributor JWS Technologies offered the guarantee that if it were late with a delivery for any reason, the customer would get the ordered gas free. That guarantee, coupled with the small bonuses set aside for workers for each no-late-delivery day, improved delivery rate, efficiency, customer satisfaction, and employee morale.[1] Around the same time, banks such as Wells Fargo, Maryland National, and Key Bank of Wyoming achieved similar benefits when they began to offer customers small cash payments (usually $5–$10) if the bank made any mistake on the customer's account.[2]

More recently, Tor Dahl, CEO of Manpower Scandinavia, told us that the strength of his business in the face of a Scandinavian recession is in large part due to a guarantee that goes beyond providing a temporary office worker with the requisite skills. The company guarantees that if the client determines the temporary employee is technically competent but does not fit in with the client company's team or corporate culture, Manpower Scandinavia will provide another temp free of charge. Guarantees such as these are certainly valuable. However, they are not sufficiently deep or comprehensive to define the kind of new responsibilities that will have an impact on customers in the way that organizations want.

Delta Dental Plan (DDP) of Massachusetts represents a movement in the right direction.[3] Delta is an insurance company that caters primarily to managers of employee benefits who buy group dental coverage for their companies. The company's Guarantee of Service Excellence (GOSE) has seven points:

1. *Minimum 10 percent savings over the course of each policy year.* If the client doesn't realize these savings, Delta refunds the difference.

2. *No-hassle customer relations.* DDP will either resolve the customer's question immediately over the phone or they guarantee an initial update within one business day and continuous follow-up to resolution. Otherwise, the client group is paid $50 per unanswered question.

3. *Quick processing of claims.* Over the course of a policy year, 90 percent of the client group's claims will be processed accurately within fifteen calendar days upon receipt of completed claim forms, or Delta credits the group the administrative fee charged for the group's last month of service.[4] This credit can go as high as $12,000.

4. *Smooth conversion as defined by the group.* The criteria for each group's successful conversion to DDP is based on a checklist mutually determined by the group and DDP. If the customer determines that the conversion was "not smooth," Delta credits the group the administrative fee charged for the group's second month of service—again, as much as $12,000.

5. *No balance-billing of patients by participating dentists.* Individual patients will not be billed for the difference between their dentists' usual fees and Delta's discounted fees. If they are, Delta pays $50 for the error and takes the responsibility for educating the dentist.

6. *Accurate and quick turnaround of ID cards.* A complete and accurate identification card for each subscriber will be mailed to the client group within fifteen calendar days, or $25 for each missing or inaccurate ID card will be paid to the group. (The potential payoff for error is significant in a one-thousand-person group, for example.)

7. *(Timely) management reports.* At the group's request, several standard reports (on claims, cost containment, utilization) will be mailed to the group within ten calendar days following the end of each month, or else $50 per late package will be paid to the group.

According to senior vice president Thomas Raffio, the real power of the guarantee's seven points is their capacity to operationalize Delta's overall commitment to providing service the customer will define as outstanding. Point 4 is a good example. The customer determines what is hassle-free conversion. Initially the customer works with Delta to develop a customized checklist that identifies what he or she needs in order to experience a smooth, hassle-free conversion from the existing plan to Delta's. The idea is to gain a clear agreement as to what is important to the customer and what Delta needs to concentrate on in order to provide the service. If for any reason the customer does not believe that the conversion was smooth, regardless of whether he or she had specifically discussed the potential problem in the initial dialogue, Delta still pays out.

Each of the other points reflects the same spirit. In point 2, Delta shows a respect for the customer's time with a promise to do whatever is necessary to resolve problems fast. Throughout, the financial penalties are large enough to be significant for both parties, showing that Delta is serious about its obligations.

Raffio summed up the positive payoffs of the guarantee for the company: "We have attributed 20 percent of our new subscriber growth to our GOSE program[5]—each subscriber represents approximately $350 in revenue. We have grown from 240,000 subscribers since GOSE's inception [in 1989] to 360,000 by the end of 1993. At 20 percent, or 24,000, of 120,000 subscribers, this represents $8,400,000. During this period we have also maintained 95–99 percent of our existing business (which is annually renewed), which favorably compares to the 80 percent industry average. Further, Delta Dental Plan of Massachusetts has achieved the position as the lowest cost Delta Plan of plans over $20 million in revenue."

Other figures attest to the power of the Delta guarantee. Within the first year of offering it, sales leads increased by 50 percent. The close ratio improved 66 percent—a level of performance that has been sustained since then. Profitability increases directly attributable to the guarantee have been estimated at close to $8 million from 1991 through 1993.

The seven points of Delta's guarantee can be copied by anyone; the commitment and spirit of Delta's sense of duty to the customer cannot. Raffio points out that "the seven points represent what we have learned are the services that corporate customers want from their insurance companies. But our philosophy, and the spirit of how our people operate, is embodied in the paragraph [of the guarantee] that precedes the seven points." That paragraph includes the following:

Delta Dental Plan of Massachusetts is committed to providing the highest level of service to all its customers. . . . It
is our belief that when our people are inspired to seek excellence in servicing our customers, all those who share in
Delta Dental Plan of Massachusetts will benefit. To underscore our commitment, we are guaranteeing major areas
of service as outlined below and backed by our comprehensive refund policy.

Note the suggestion of responsibility throughout, but most
important, note the words "to underscore our commitment."
The words support Raffio's comment about philosophy. *The
guarantee is not the seven points*; they simply reinforce the underlying code of duty that the company holds toward its customers. The guarantee is the spirit of responsibility.

Delta's guarantee is neither perfect nor complete. Nor can
it remain static over time. But when compared to conventional
guarantees, it merits attention as an illustration of taking responsibility through guarantees.

It is not an easy task to move from a mind-set that sees a
guarantee as marquee material to one that interprets a guarantee
as genuine, deep, enduring responsibility to each customer. As
mentioned earlier, embracing the latter viewpoint requires a different way of approaching business. For those who plan to incorporate this viewpoint into their own organizations, we offer four
initiatives. These initiatives, outlined in Table 11.1, are: ground-
ing the guarantee in strategy and operations, not marketing and
public relations; preparing everyone to go 100 percent; raising the
ante on strategic listening; and preventing conventional financial
and legal caution from inhibiting the power of the guarantee.

Initiative 1: Ensure That the Guarantee Is Grounded in Strategy and Operations, Not Marketing and Public Relations.

If it is to be more than a gimmick and to have more than short-
lived, marginal utility, a guarantee must drive the business.[6]
Operational decisions around each management function must
be grounded in the guarantee. The answers to the questions
"How do they apply to the guarantee?" and "How do they en-

Table 11.1.   Take Responsibility Through Guarantees.

Initiative 1: Ensure that the guarantee is grounded in strategy and operations, not marketing and public relations.

- Define the guarantee, and then work backwards to define the organization and business processes.
- Insist that the spirit of the guarantee shape how people think and behave toward one another inside the organization.

Initiative 2: Prepare everyone to go 100 percent.

- Be obsessive about conducting preliminary dialogue with customers, planning for customization, and tracking results.
- Allow anyone on staff to invoke the guarantee on the spot.

Initiative 3: Up the ante on strategic listening.

- Think multiple methods, multiple groups.

Initiative 4: Don't allow conventional financial and legal caution to inhibit the power of the guarantee.

- Base the guarantee on simplicity and trust.
- Be willing to invest dollars to get the returns.
- Realize that customers who invoke the guarantee are boosting your organization's fortunes.
- Think twice about accepting business from customers who don't fit with the spirit of your guarantee.

hance the guarantee and our ability to deliver on it?" help shape decisions about where resources must be allocated, what needs to be improved, and what paths should be followed. In effect, everything that occurs in the organization "backs into" the guarantee.

At Federal Express, where the "absolutely, positively" overnight guarantee is taken seriously, management attention and resources are affected accordingly. Because of the guarantee, the company is on a perpetual and obsessive quest for better package handling, shorter lead times, more efficient package tracking and transportation, and so on. Timothy Firnstahl, CEO of a small Seattle-based chain of restaurants operating under the corporate name of Satisfaction Guaranteed Eateries, adheres to the same philosophy: "Honoring the guarantee has led to new training procedures, recipe and menu changes, restaurant redesign, equipment purchases and whatever else it took to put things right and keep them right."[7]

Guarantees obviously have marketing advantages, but that should not be their primary goal. When guarantees are designed to drive quality improvement, and when they serve as feedback loops from customers to improve business processes, marketing benefits become the *consequence* of organizational action. Robert Gregory of microfilm vendor First Image was being only semifacetious when he told us: "Don't even tell your marketing people about it until you have to."

For the manager who wants to use unconditional guarantees as a strategic and operational tool, research and experience suggest the following:

■ *Define the guarantee, and then work backwards to define the organization and business processes.* The idea is that the guarantee defines the shape and character of the organization. Nobody exemplified this concept more than Alvin "Bugs" Burger, who launched the legendary pest-control Bugs Burger Bug Killer (BBBK) in August 1960. The company's phenomenal reputation and growth, even while charging literally five to ten times the fees of its competitors, was due primarily to its truly extraordinary guarantees, which included the following:

> You don't owe one penny until all pests are eradicated.
> If you are ever dissatisfied with BBBK's service, you will receive a refund of up to twelve months of the company's service, plus fees for another exterminator of your choice for the next year.
> If a guest spots a pest on your premises, BBBK will pay for the guest's meal or hotel stay, pay for a future meal or stay, and send a letter of apology.
> If your facility is closed down due to the presence of roaches or rodents, BBBK will pay all fines, all lost profits, plus $5000.[8]

Announcing this kind of guarantee simply as a marketing tactic would have ensured the quick bankruptcy of the company because delivering on the promise would have been impossible.

(This is why so many companies try to have it both ways by offering a weak conditional guarantee that is legally acceptable and easy to deliver, but uninspiring or irrelevant from the perspective of the customer.) In contrast, to quote Christopher Hart, "Burger began with the concept of the unconditional guarantee and *worked backward, designing his entire organization to support the no-pests guarantee*" (our emphasis).[9] The recruiting, training, planning, capital budgeting decisions, and after-sale service at BBBK were driven by the guarantee.

One restaurant manager who was a BBBK customer described the BBBK pest control men who would show up at his facility every month: "[They] are fantastic. I never did business with anybody like them. They stand by what they say, they're men of their word. Like with the guarantees. I have a friend, there was a roach that came into his restaurant on a delivery, it came in on a box, and they honored the guarantee. They said that it shouldn't have lived."[10] This restaurant manager also mentioned that BBBK would send three men each month, staying five hours each time and using the best materials. In contrast, he said the companies he had used before typically would send one man, who stayed for twenty minutes and would use cheaper, diluted chemicals.

For Burger, the four points of his guarantee were less important than the underlying values of service excellence they represented. He told us that as a strategic and operational tool, the guarantee demanded constant attention. This attention was vital for creating a guarantee-driven business environment at BBBK.

■ *Insist that the spirit of the guarantee shape how people think and behave toward one another inside the organization.* For most organizations, a movement toward a BBBK environment demands a major cultural shift—especially in terms of how people think and work together. Cultural shifts require, minimally, considerable training and education. Everyone must understand the assumptions underlying responsibility, unconditional guarantees, complete satisfaction, and customer as final arbiter. All employees must understand how their responsibilities on the job might be redefined to support the delivery of the guarantee.

Cultural shifts include changes in job expectations and support systems. In order to fulfill the promise of total quality and complete satisfaction, managers must see their roles as agents of change. Employees who cannot access relevant information or middle managers who need sign-offs from two layers above them will not be able to deliver quickly and adequately on an unconditional guarantee of complete satisfaction. Hiring and rewarding people whose skills and interests are inconsistent with fulfilling the guarantee makes no sense. Neither does a training process that does not revolve around the guarantee. The organization must embrace an extensive amount of collaborative planning and overhauling of existing systems. All this needs to occur prior to, during, and after the launch of the guarantee. Shaping the organization culture around the promise to the customer is a continuous process.

In a culture where colleagues do not respect agreements among themselves, it is unlikely that they will respect agreements with customers, either. At the successful Preston Trucking Company in Maryland, each employee signs a Commitment to Excellence statement which reads, in part: "Once I make a commitment to a customer or another associate, I promise to fulfill it on time. I will do what I say when I say I will do it."[11] This sort of cultural practice is a necessary precursor for the successful implementation of the organizing principle. As Delta's Tom Raffio explains, "You can't have an external guarantee if people don't honor internal guarantees. The only way to keep the commitment to the customer is if everyone helps each other and keeps their commitments to each other."

This commitment is relevant not just for formal agreements that people within an organization make to each other. It is also relevant for the myriad of small, informal agreements (such as "I'll get back to you tomorrow," "I'll have the information on your desk next week," or "I'll support you on that") that people regularly make—and often thoughtlessly break. Integrity means keeping promises, or at least, letting the other person know right away when any change to a promise needs to be made.

Leaders have an important obligation to push for an inhouse culture where promises are sacred, for three reasons.

1.   They help create a culture of responsibility.

2.   They help develop a culture where "collaboration" and "teamwork" are real, not just words.

3.   They help others understand the importance of honoring one another in pursuit of service to the customer.

The idea is to get people to reduce their traditional dependence on rigid arrangements, where the primary behavioral skills are knowing how to maneuver one's work within the narrow, inflexible constraints of organizational rules and procedures. In a culture of responsibility and teamwork, people understand that delivering on the guarantee requires everyone in the organization to commit to going beyond legalistic, me-first thinking. Notions like "going through channels," "blaming the other guy," and "not my job" make no sense if one is serious about implementing an unconditional guarantee of complete satisfaction.

Initiative 1 calls for organizations to significantly raise the bar in terms of their own standards and their customers' expectations. But no organization should promise what it can't deliver. Thus, the initiative calls for total integrity among all hands and across all organizational activities. The organization and those affiliated with it are committed to keeping the promise inherent in the guarantee, and thus walking the talk.

Initiative 2: Prepare Everyone to Go 100 Percent.

This initiative means 100 percent commitment to complete satisfaction as the customer defines it. There are no hiding places, no pseudo-guarantees, no weasel language. With it, the organization is committed to doing whatever is necessary to create the complete satisfaction experience for the customer, or else be prepared to suffer a significant penalty.

At First Image, an independent division of First Financial Management Corporation, the guarantee is 100 percent and the customer is 100 percent the final arbiter. First Image has sixty-two locations that provide computer-output microfilm and microfiche to diverse organizations around the United States. First Image's guarantee is about as straightforward and unconditional as one can get: total satisfaction, period. If a client is unhappy with *any* aspect of the service, he or she can deduct any portion of the fee, *up to 100 percent.*

Robert Gregory, vice president of production, ticks off the benefits of a 100 percent guarantee: "The guarantee keeps us focused and on our toes. We get great feedback from customers who invoke the guarantee. The feedback allows us to continually improve and realign our operations so that the problem never occurs again. We win the business of quality-driven companies like GTE and Motorola; without the guarantee, we would have never gotten through their front door. Several accounts who each provide us with several hundred thousand dollars of business per month have told us that the guarantee is why we have their business. And what's also especially important to us is that the guarantee is an important consideration in maintaining a strong relationship between us and our customers."

How does First Image manage to survive, much less thrive, on such a powerful guarantee? As per Initiative 1, all sixty-two locations orient their operations and management attention toward meeting the 100 percent guarantee. But the leader who is prepared to go 100 percent can take some additional steps:

■ *Be obsessive about conducting preliminary dialogue with customers, planning for customization, and tracking results.* First Image takes three actions in the delivery of the 100 percent guarantee:

1. All service is necessarily customized, which means a great deal of dialogue goes on up front between First Image and the customer as to the latter's needs and expectations. Surprises or ambiguities about what the customer needs are kept to a minimum.

2. The company has developed an industry-leading formal system to document exactly what the customer wants and when, from the kind of distribution system to the ways of setting up machines. The protocols that comprise the system are not perceived as legal documents but are a way for First Image people to track their progress on service delivery for each customer.

3. Foul-ups and complaints are tracked obsessively and thrown into a Pareto analysis to generate trends and ideas. The company responds quickly to these and sets general guidelines, such as those for turnaround cycle time and frontline courtesy.

As a result of these actions, First Image gets about 250 claims on its guarantee every month, which translates to about $10,000 in penalties monthly. Gregory tracks the annual cost of the guarantee at under 1 percent of revenues, a minuscule figure relative to its payoffs in financial gain and industry reputation. The bottom line is one of integrity: "Basically," he says, "we put our money where our mouth is."

■ *Allow anyone on staff to invoke the guarantee on the spot.* Satisfaction Guaranteed Eateries, mentioned earlier in this chapter, has a "no-hassle" guarantee that revolves around an obligation that 100 percent of each diner's experience will be positive. Technically, one element of the guarantee actually exceeds 100 percent, and is summarized by CEO Timothy Firnstahl as "replace plus one." The idea is to reduce the customer's inconvenience as well as dissatisfaction with the meal or service. Firnstahl explains: "If a guest doesn't like her salad, don't charge her for it. But what about the Hassle Factor? Replace plus one. By all means, give her the salad free of charge. But buy her a drink or dessert as well—or whatever else it takes to make her happy."[12]
What Firnstahl is conveying is that for a 100 percent standard to exist, everyone—managers and employees—must have the power to invoke the guarantee on the spot, and to take actions they deem necessary in order to honor it. This is true whether the employee is a waiter, a warehouseperson, a truck driver, or a receptionist.
Firnstahl, Delta's Tom Raffio, and First Image's Robert Gregory literally *encourage* their people to invoke the guarantee on their own when such action is warranted, *even when the customer doesn't request it.* Gregory, for example, encourages First Image people to coach customers that they should deduct some money from the fee if they have voiced a dissatisfaction. Raffio notes that Delta employees periodically make payout on their

own even if it's not explicitly one of the seven GOSE points. Actions like these give substance to the guarantee and provide a valuable shot of corrective feedback, but most important, they illustrate a culture that strives toward integrity and honor. The organization shows its genuine commitment to both the employee and the customer.

Unfortunately, these viewpoints are exceptions. As noted, most guarantees are anything but unconditionally 100 percent. Moreover, for all the talk of "empowerment," employees and field people in most organizations don't have the kinds of power needed to make the decisions described above. Constituencies other than customers seem to carry more decision-making weight in many organizations when it comes to defining an organization's priorities and obligations to customers. To say that the customer is the final arbiter of total quality takes courage because by definition, others—the "boss," the lawyers, the marketers, the MBAs and Ph.D.s, the quality and guarantee staff experts, the consultants, and the trainers—are not. The conformance indices, the technical specs, the contracts, and the regulatory requirements also are not the final arbiters. All these sources and constituencies are relevant, but they should not be the ultimate source of decisions. It takes real courage and integrity to wrap the organization around a 100 percent commitment that will be judged by the constituency for whom the guarantee is created. Not coincidentally, that constituency is the same group that the entire organization ostensibly exists to serve.

Initiative 3: Up the Ante on Strategic Listening.

In Chapter Five, we discussed strategic listening in terms of looking a customer ahead. We now revisit listening, this time in the context of discovering and addressing what the customer values for complete satisfaction.

If the organizing principle is to be implemented properly, active strategic listening must be built into new relationships between vendor and customer. The relationships must be close, trusting, mutually problem solving, and permeable. Without such relationships, the vendor cannot keep a finger on the pulse of the customer, nor can the vendor effectively collaborate with the customer in developing the right responses in an efficient way.

Every organization we studied that had a strong unconditional guarantee also had a strong listening process. For an organization to be successful—indeed, to survive—delivering on an
unconditional guarantee of complete satisfaction requires listening. One cannot simply guess at what different customers define
as complete satisfaction. One cannot guess at how a customer's
perceptions of total quality change over time. One cannot assume, or hope, that a standardized product or service will on its
own be reacted to in the same way by every customer.

The payoff to listening emerged when we discussed the
idea of taking responsibility through guarantees with managers
from Columbus, Ohio-based Nationwide Communications,
Inc. (NCI), a group of television, cable, and radio stations located throughout the United States. One participant argued
that "our customers are advertisers, not just viewers. We can't
guarantee advertisers that their sales will go up if they buy time
from us." Others in the group, however, quickly responded that
those sorts of guarantees would probably not even be expected
by advertisers. "We don't know what would delight them in a
business relationship," said one. "We don't even know what's *really* important to them when they deal with us," echoed another.
The consensus quickly emerged that if NCI managers could
begin to establish close, candid, problem-solving relationships
with advertisers—not just contractual relationships—they
would come up with mutually beneficial agreements that would
serve as guarantees and as potential sources of entirely new revenue possibilities—for both sides.

In regard to strategic listening in the context of managing
unconditional guarantees, one recommendation stands out:

■ *Think multiple methods, multiple groups.* At Delta, a
rotating twenty-person customer partnership committee, with
members like Polaroid, Gillette, and unions, helped devise the
original guarantee and is actively involved in monitoring its value.
The company regularly surveys three groups of customers—the
client companies, their employees, and the dentists in the plan.
Companies are contacted by phone or mail four times a year, dentists are asked to participate in annual surveys and small focus
groups, and employees are surveyed randomly. Survey data are

taken so seriously that they are analyzed in-house rather than farmed out, in order to ensure intimacy with the findings and to maintain an organizationwide sensitivity to the program.

Listening is also vital to Intuit's guarantee and, according to CEO Scott Cook, its extraordinary growth rate. Intuit is a California-based company that has amassed a 70 percent share of the personal finance software market. With its recent acquisition of ChipSoft, the company now has a 60 percent share of the tax-preparation program market as well. Its flagship products are Quicken, a program that allows individuals and small businesses to write checks and keep track of financial transactions on PCs, and QuickBooks, a small-business bookkeeping software package. Intuit's guarantees reflect its promise of fast, easy-to-use products, even for computer-illiterates: order Quicken by mail, pay $8 for shipping and handling, and if you're not doing useful work within a few minutes (Intuit suggests six), don't pay for the $69 product and don't return it: keep it, free. Manager Sheryl Ross told us that the message Intuit sends to its customers is best expressed as "Try our product, and if you're not *in love* with it, don't pay."

In order to make such an extraordinary commitment, Intuit must understand what the customer considers to be a fast, easy-to-use product. Listening is the vehicle. Employees at all functions and levels, including senior managers, are required to put in several hours a month on the technical support lines to familiarize themselves with the hands-on difficulties that customers are experiencing, and then to take follow-up action accordingly. Follow-up is focused not only on helping the customer who has the problem but also on shaping the delivery of the guarantee. That is, customer feedback is crucial for new product development and product refinement, as well as ancillary features, such as written instructions, packaging, and support services.

Intuit takes the notion of listening a step further. During test marketing, at the onset of a product life cycle, the "Follow Me Home" program literally has engineers and developers go home with willing customers who have purchased the program at a retail outlet. Intuit people silently watch customers unwrap the package at home, read the instructions, and try it out. Watching customers' body language and frowns, noting their frustrations and "aha's," conversing with them afterward, sometimes for several hours—all provide data that are analyzed back at headquarters. Throughout the product life cycle, engineers and senior managers host monthly and quarterly socials (lunch, cocktails) with customers to talk about the product.

Listening allows organizations to understand the unique needs of their customers and to respond accordingly. Listening also allows the organization to establish collaborative working relationships with customers so that both partners take on the responsibility for creating customized solutions and experiences. The organizing principle, therefore, forces the organization into the discipline of listening to customers so closely that a collaborative problem-solving bond is established with them.

Initiative 4: Don't Allow Conventional Financial and Legal Caution to Inhibit the Power of the Guarantee.

As we noted in the last chapter, most guarantees today are prisoners to so many financial and legal restraints that they have little impact on either the organization's management processes or its customers. In order for an organization to reap the rewards of a genuine guarantee, it is imperative that excessive legalism and financial caution be rejected. For the prudent manager who is willing to try some unconventional thinking, we offer several brief pieces of advice.

■ *Base the guarantee on simplicity and trust.* The more complicated and conditional the guarantee, the less useful it is. Instead, it is necessary to adopt a twofold premise: one, customers are trustworthy; two, the overwhelming number of customers will not only *not* take advantage of you, but they will help make your business a success. In pushing for meaningful unconditional guarantees, Delta's Tom Raffio and First Image's Robert Gregory both said they had to overcome the prevailing paranoia that customers would take unethical advantage of the guarantee. Raffio notes that in 1988, the conventional wisdom was that no other insurance company was offering an unconditional guarantee because people would cheat. That meant if Delta were to embark on this foolish path, it would have to aggressively protect itself with a myriad of legal loopholes. "They wanted a fifty-page document," laughs Raffio. "You've got to replace that type of thinking with trust in your customers and in your employees."

Both companies found that the fears about genuine unconditional guarantees were unfounded. As a number of customer-sensitive retailers such as L.L. Bean and Nordstrom have discovered, the overwhelming majority of customers are quite honest and decent. The ones who aren't trustworthy can be isolated and weeded out, but as one successful manager told a colleague of ours: "If 2 percent of our customers are jerks, why would I want to create a system that tells the 98 good people 'we don't trust you because we think you're jerks, too'?" Customers are remarkably tolerant and forgiving when they believe that the organization—even when it messes up—sincerely cares about doing right by them.

The idea is that customers are trustworthy until they explicitly demonstrate otherwise. Michelle Harper, co-owner of the small, Phoenix-based Harper Nurseries chain, attributes the growth and success of her business less to the official Florists' Transworld Delivery (FTD) customer guarantee (with its concomitant requirements of letter-writing, time-deadlines, and proof of purchase) than to Harper's own philosophy, "If you're not happy, we'll make you happy." Period. Conceivably, some customers could take unfair advantage of this promise, in the process receiving larger plants than they might be able to afford, or replacing plants that they have not taken care of. But Harper does not run her business with the suspicion that her customers are crooks. On the contrary, she believes that the guarantee is largely responsible for a steady increase in revenues and profits.

Similarly, as it turns out, the cost-benefit ratio of implementing the guarantee at Delta and First Image was overwhelmingly in the direction of benefit—despite the fact that customers were *encouraged* to invoke the guarantee if their satisfaction was not complete. Even in the first year of Delta's guarantee, while it was working out the bugs, the apprehension was groundless: the company estimated that it would have to pay out $75,000 and wound up paying only $15,000; meanwhile, in that

same year it signed up seven major new accounts as a direct result of the guarantee, thereby increasing revenues by 15 percent
over plan. At Hampton Inn, where the unconditional guarantee
awards a free night's stay, CEO Ray Schultz noted that the first
six months saw a penalty payout of "less than 0.1 percent of
our total room nights, far below our original projections"; the
potential payoff was higher quality standards, less employee
turnover, 2 percent of total room nights due specifically
to the attraction of the guarantee, and 86 percent customer
retention.[13]

The moral of the story is this: a meaningful guarantee cannot be shackled by the straitjacket of legalistic requirements.
The more complicated and lengthy the guarantee is, the less its
validity or impact. The greater the number of conditional constraints placed around it, however well-meaning the intent, the
more watered down and meaningless it becomes. The organizing principle is unequivocal: either the guarantee is unconditional or it isn't, either the guarantee promises complete satisfaction or it doesn't, either customers are the final arbiters or
they are not. There are no gray areas to hide behind.

■ *Be willing to invest dollars to get the returns.* This ought
to be obvious, but it is worth reiterating briefly. Because the
guarantees drive the business when the organizing principle is
followed, capital outlays that support the spirit of the guarantees
cannot be scrimped. Delta invested an additional $100,000 in
new systems and customer service training while preparing for
its guarantee. Technical support for simple personal finance
software is often a lucrative in-house profit center, yet software
vendor Intuit invests up to 10 percent of its revenues in technical support and provides the service free of charge as part of its
total service package.[14]

The bottom line, frankly, is that if the guarantee is driving
the business, it must be constantly replenished with prudent
capital investments, just like any other key business factor.
Leaders who call for strong unconditional guarantees but are not
prepared to make continual investments in that effort are in effect slowly relegating the guarantee to the status of a low-impact
advertising technique. Moreover, they are signaling to the rest of

the organization that they are not prepared to "walk the talk" when it comes to taking responsibility on behalf of the customer.

■ *Realize that customers who invoke the guarantee are boosting your organization's fortunes.* For many managers, the hardest realization is that customers who exercise the guarantee are not draining the company's finances but enriching them. By its quick, visible bubbling of customer dissatisfaction with the organization's processes or service offerings, the guarantee benefits the company. As Hampton Inn's Ray Schultz points out: "A single customer complaint in one location can contribute to improved service nationwide."[15] A dissatisfied customer invoking the guarantee sounds an alarm, signifying a fire somewhere in the organization, a fire that can devastate the organization's financial health. The messages sent by each complaining customer are critical to the company's well-being. At Delta, the term "payout" has been changed to "investment" for this very reason. Raffio explains that "we changed the nomenclature because they [payouts] really are true investments in the future of our company." First Image's Robert Gregory also recognizes the investment payoff of guarantees and makes listening to customers an obsession. He is adamant that people document the reasons that customers invoke the guarantee and that they share that information throughout the organization.

Firnstahl believes that his unconditional guarantee is an excellent investment because, "In our experience, it costs five times more to rectify a guest's problem later than it does to take care of it on the spot." As we have written elsewhere, the expense involved in keeping customers is well worth it, for the revenue impact of lost business and negative word-of-mouth advertising, coupled with the costs necessary to develop prospective new customers, are an extraordinary drain on organizations.[16] Harvard's James Heskett and his colleagues summarize research to make a compelling case that "customers often become more profitable over time. And loyal customers account for an unusually high proportion of the sales and profit growth of successful service providers." They go on to note that several companies have found that their most loyal customers—usually the top 20 percent of the customer base—not only provide all the profit but also cover losses incurred in dealing with less loyal customers."[17] The research of Frederick Reichheld and Earl Sasser indicates that if a company is able to reduce its customer defections by only 5 percent, it can positively impact its bottom line by 25 to 85 percent, after factoring in prospecting costs, operating costs, pricing, word-of-mouth reports, and account balances.[18]

■ *Think twice about accepting business from customers who don't fit with the spirit of your guarantee.* Whereas conventional financial wisdom says "beef up the top line by selling to whomever will buy," those who implement the organizing principle are beginning to use the guarantee to determine selectively whom they even want as customers—which may mean turning away customers who don't "fit."

We have seen that the movement toward customer collaboration and partnerships is leading an increasing number of vendors to be selective in terms of whose business they want and whose business they don't want. The organizing principle supports this trend. An organization that guarantees complete satisfaction can choose to whom the guarantee will be applied. In other words, an organization does not need to set itself up for failure. Whenever possible, the organization would be wise to seek the kinds of customers who have the same values (including honesty and trustworthiness) and who wish to work collaboratively. Those are the customers who will be most responsive to the spirit behind the guarantee.

Al Burger of the old BBBK reminisced that he had no compunctions about refusing work from certain institutions, or even in dropping certain institutions from his customer list. BBBK expected customers to maintain certain cleanliness standards and maintenance schedules when BBBK people weren't on site, and to shut down the facility for a few hours if a problem demanded intense intervention. Those who would not do that were not pursued as customers, or dropped if they already were.

In short, the organizing principle encourages the organization to determine the "good" business to pursue and the "bad" business to let go. It recognizes that in a true collaborative relationship, expectations between vendor and customer are mutual.

GUARANTEES
AND RESPONSIBILITY
IN THE NEW EPOCH

In late October 1993, the Extraordinary Guarantees Conference was held in New Orleans. It featured presentations from companies as diverse as Delta Dental Plan of Massachusetts, First Image, Marriott, Corning, L.L. Bean, GTE Telephone Operations, AT&T 800 Service, and AT&T Universal Card. Clearly, the interest in guarantees is growing, as is the recognition that if guarantees are to mean anything, they must be extraordinary.

It appears to us that for any guarantee to be extraordinary in impact, it must be grounded in the spirit of responsibility and duty. Only then does one realize the scope of the behaviors and actions that bring life to the intent. As the world continues to shrink and become more interdependent, organizations that jump the curve will find this perspective increasingly important.

The roots of the organizing principle rest in organizations taking responsibilities seriously. As we look forward, we note that the power of taking responsibility through guarantees reflects broader social trends that are unfolding. In 1947, Robert Wood Johnson, chairman of Johnson and Johnson, expressed the following: "The day has passed when business is a private matter—if it ever really was. In a business society, every act of business has social consequences and may arouse public interest. Every time business hires, builds, sells, or buys, it is acting for the . . . people as well as for itself, and it must be prepared to accept full responsibility for its act."[19]

More recently, these sentiments were echoed by Walter Haas, honorary chairman and director of Levi Strauss, who suggested that the modern manager is faced with several charges: "Take personal responsibility for your own conduct, follow the spirit as well as the letter of the law, recognize the opportunity you also have to affect the behavior of others in your company, and start to think about how you can influence others in the business community."[20]

The last statement is particularly important. University of California sociologist Robert Bellah and his colleagues have argued that taking responsibility today means taking responsibility in and through institutions.[21] The challenges and opportunities for managers in this arena are growing. The whole notion of an organization's fulfilling its civic responsibilities reflects a wider movement in society to redress the imbalance between rights and responsibilities. This movement has sometimes been called "communitarianism."[22]

The communitarian idea is based on a growing consensus that goes beyond egocentric thinking to the desire to strengthen families, schools, work groups, and other social networks in the pursuit of meeting obligations to one another. Communitarianism alludes to a Bill of Responsibilities as well as a Bill of Rights.[23] In effect, the communitarian perspective suggests that the deterioration in social well-being can be arrested only by a balanced commitment both to individual liberties and to the collective good.[24]

In the early 1990s, a brief article in a news magazine suggested that successful corporations in the coming decade would be "cost wise, creative, and caring." That little phrase has merit. In earlier chapters we have spoken extensively about how the first two elements will shape up in the emerging epoch. The third element, *caring*, is integral to taking responsibility through guarantees. In a broader context, caring extends the spirit of responsibility to all relevant constituencies, like customers and employees. Hence it reflects the sense of communitarianism. The communitarian outlook exists when people inside and outside the organization feel that the organization treats them as valued members of the organization's community—basically, that the organization "cares" about them.

The notions behind caring and communitarianism are important for enlightened self-interest. Remarks by corporate leaders provide ample evidence that the interests of the organization are served by an interest in the welfare of society. While a spirited debate goes on as to whether there is a correlation between profits and "social responsibility" as conventionally defined, there is no doubt that an attitude is emerging that says that even in the absence of immediate profit data, management should "do the right thing." When Levi Strauss refuses to establish facilities in countries with human rights violations, or when furniture manufacturer Herman Miller commits not to use tropical woods from endangered rain forests, we see the results of an ethic of responsibility at work. The same is true when companies like Nike, Reebok, and Wal-Mart develop guidelines on issues like corporal punishment, discrimination, child labor, and forced labor for their global partners (contractors and suppliers). These examples speak to the role organizations can play in the formation of a responsible global ethic.

An increasing number of executives are recognizing that enlightened self-interest is not served by an attitude that is narrow, parochial, "cowboy," exclusionary, or, for that matter, unethical. In a tightly linked, interdependent world, separateness expressed in a perspective that builds protectionist walls in world trade or that views only shareholders as a constituency worthy of special attention is myopic and self-damaging.

In November 1993, economics writer Robert Samuelson encapsulated the issue in an article entitled "The Isolationist Illusion: NAFTA's Foes Think They Can Make the World Go Away."[25] The world will not go away for any manager. It is "closer" to us than ever before. Hence, many executives are finding it difficult to separate a corporation's economic goals from its responsibilities to society. The litany of social problems—crime, education, health care, and environmental quality—is also a list of impediments to corporate prosperity. The world sees more clearly each day that a corporation's success is intertwined with the fate of the society to which it belongs. Arnold Hiatt, chairman of Stride Rite, comments that "you can't run a healthy company in an unhealthy society for long."[26]

Thus, many are concluding that it is in an organization's self-interest—Robert Wood Johnson and Walter Haas would call it responsibility—to help create an environment that enhances its own success. "If we accept this responsibility," writes Haas, "both business and society will flourish, and the lives of every one of us will be better for it. In truth, that's the real bottom line."[27]

In effect, what Haas, Hiatt, and Johnson are saying is that business and society are not separable. There are numerous ways organizations might exemplify this kind of attitude. At the very least, however, taking responsibility through guarantees is an initial step in meeting obligations to a wider community.

Epilogue:
Choosing Our Destiny

You have not lived and suffered in vain.
What has been must go.
What has gone will rise again.
Stop trembling.
Get ready to live.
—Gustav Mahler

Business is moral philosophy with
a dollar and a different name.
—Ray Pacioretty
President, New Canaan Mint

In his novels of the late twenties and early thirties, with revealing titles like *Look Homeward Angel* and *You Can't Go Home Again*, Thomas Wolfe made a point of how ineffective past social and economic norms were in providing a sense of assurance, security, and psychological well-being. In some ways there is a similar message today: one can't look back to the intellectual or strategic "home" of yesterday because it is no longer there. We can do many good things with an informed sense of history, tradition, and abiding institutions, but we can not usefully deny that the past is just that—gone.

This is a particularly piercing realization for those who are in the midst of jumping the curve. They are the ones who have made the conscious choice to leave behind the familiarity and comfort of the past. But those who have yet to jump the curve are by no means safe either. Quite the contrary. As shown throughout history, neither security nor tranquility is guaranteed for anyone during times of epochal transition. In fact, the persistence in old ways becomes increasingly uncomfortable, ineffective, even dangerous.

Leaders in all walks of life are concluding that what may have been premises for successful management in the past are no longer viable. The intellectual foundations of traditional management—scientific management; the industrial model; provincialism; hierarchy; hyperanalysis; the emphasis on stability, order, and predictability; the "business as a jungle" metaphor; the righteousness of bigness; the superiority of mass and scale; the primacy of contracts and "me-ism" over responsibility; the supreme value of tangibles; the categorizing of "domestic versus foreign"; the indifference to ideals—have all been found inadequate and wanting. They cannot shelter managers and organizations from the tumultuous forces buffeting them at this point in history. We are left with the simple but poignant idea that American management is beset with an intellectual homelessness.

INTELLECTUAL HOMELESSNESS

Separated from the traditional intellectual home base, we face the dilemma, Where do we go next? And how do we get there? Developing the basis for future directions cannot be the work of intellectuals only. In our commerce-sensitive culture, where business is arguably our most influential institution, there is a moral imperative for businesspeople to contribute vigorously to the process. As one wag put it, intellectuals get nervous about not having something to say and businesspeople get nervous about not having something to do. They should get to know one another.

The result will make sense only if it reflects the realities faced by businesspeople all over the world. The answer must demonstrate accommodation to today's drivers of transformation, for as Norman Cousins wrote, "Where man can find no answer, he will find fear."[1] And out of fear comes closed-mindedness and resistance to change.

The organizing principles we have reviewed will account, in the main, for the reasons some leaders and organizations will succeed where others will fail. Those who look a customer ahead, build the company around the software and the software around the customer, ensure differential employee experiences, and take responsibility through guarantees are more likely to set a strong foundation for a successful transition than those who do not.

There is an almost infinite number of daily, organization-specific behaviors leaders might adopt in effectively implementing the organizing principles and their corollary initiatives. Motivation, ability, and how-to recipes are not nearly the challenge as much as accuracy of role perception. As we have seen, it will be necessary to enact new roles that include a fundamentally different perception of what a leader is supposed to do. Ultimately, success in using any one of the organizing principles depends primarily on taking on the role of redefining, reinventing, repositioning, rethinking, and ultimately, re-*forming* organizations.

None of these activities takes place in a vacuum. There are technological and social crosscurrents that influence the expectations of the leader and the performance goals of the organization. The winds of change carry ideas from such diverse sources as quantum physics, Jonas Salk and his view of an unfolding universe, John Rawls's ideas on justice, and the communitarian movement. Somehow these need to be accounted for and synthesized into a framework that holds as a center for the individual. "Every age," said Adlai Stevenson, "needs men who will redeem the time by living with a vision of the things that are to be."[2] As a society, we seem to have many of the elements of such a vision, but not the vision itself.

If all this is true, there will be no One Grand Solution nor one Day of Days that will be the way to a new home. The passage will also have to accommodate circumstances that are unique to this age, an age in which outmoded traditions are in question and social institutions are in upheaval. What Susanne K. Langer said toward the end of the Second World War still holds true: we are no longer "in possession of a definite, established culture; we live in an exhausted age . . . and an age still unborn."[3] Human imagination needs to fill the void, to invent new symbols for the world that has begun to stir.

CHOOSING A DESTINY

The root question is what kind of culture, and thus what kind of organizations, are we interested in building? The world can get smaller and smarter, but for what purpose? Social critic Michael Novak is not alone in saying that the twenty-first century will be marked by a "new and deeper economics that takes account of its moral and cultural preconditions."[4] It is our judgment that sustained effort to implement the four organizing principles will lead managers to conclude that effectiveness and prosperity ultimately rest with an orientation that has more transcendental and value-laden foundations than what they have experienced with managerialism.

Each principle we have described is more than a simple technique for jumping the curve. Each reflects a deeper commitment to trust, concern, and meaning. Guarantees, as an illustration, are less about procedures than about the question, How much do you care about your customer? Building the company and the software around the customer is less about high technology than about growing knowledge, sharing credit, acknowledging interdependence, and asking the question, What is our obligation to include and strengthen others? Looking a customer ahead is about courage and optimism. The question it barely disguises is about one's legacy: How do you want to touch the future? Assuring the rewards of those who give expression to the values and vision of the company is about questions such as, How does one create coherence out of tumult? How does one make justice and fairness a centerpiece of work values and organizational ideals? The restlessness that business leaders experience mirrors their sense that a new way of thinking is developing along with their new structures and tools.

These concerns cannot be left as abstractions. Philosopher Christopher Lasch made the larger point precisely. He concluded that abstract respect for the individual cannot replace respect expressed as civility and courtesy in daily life. Nor, as we have seen, can ideals of collaboration and cooperation be allowed to fly on the wings of technology alone. The underlying values that guide the use of the tools are the significant issue.

Values also have a global context. More than ten times as many people have gone to a university since 1945 as before that year. Even so, given the world's population of more than five billion people, only a small percentage have had the opportunities, formally or informally, to take their education beyond the basics needed for survival. Only a relative few have been exposed to the knowledge and information that has accumulated in science, history, literature, and other disciplines of inquiry and accomplishment. For those working in leadership positions in the world of commerce, the issue is pressing and even more personal. Indeed, business leaders today are and will continue to be among the best-informed people and the most educated sector on the planet. The question abides: what will they do with the privilege?

The possibilities are intriguing. Certainly the mood of disgust with current affairs is stronger now than it has been in the past; there is the hope that we are starting to discuss and do the things that make more sense. What is meant by success could change. Success defined as access to material possessions, social advantage, frivolity, and celebrity might come to be treated with skepticism. Achievement by deceit or clever sloth might become less acceptable. Vulgarity and profligate life-styles could be considered inexcusable at any time by anyone. The distortion of self-development into narcissism and self-indulgence could be reversed. We could, instead, come to regard success as infusing a sense of excellence, a sense of virtue, in whatever we do. Self-restraint might come to be viewed as more than a quaint Victorian ideal. We could weigh more heavily the social relevance of what we do. We could engage in what some have referred to as the restoration of a value orientation at work. We could build work environments where people not only get rich salaries and bonuses but where they have the opportunity to be as effective as they possibly can be. We could create an environment where organizations known as honorable and profitable achieve higher market value than those that are only profitable. Choices are upon us.

There are reasons to be optimistic, to believe that we are at the dawn of a tremendous burst in achievement and moral refinement. Foreign investments worldwide reflect the confidence people have in what can be done within other nations. Global interdependence has moved from an interesting idea to an economic given. The world now has the capability to feed and shelter every human being on the planet. The advances toward technological diffusion and demographic pluralism are healthy signs. The resurgence of free-market economics and the renewed support for democratic principles say more about the influence of American ideals than comparisons of military power. Education is prepared for reform. Company policies that are family friendly are more numerous. "Moral talk" is more common now in organizations. Ethics courses and programs are increasing in universities and corporate training centers. Socially sensitive investment funds are growing rapidly. The unavoidable perception is that for all the problems that confront us today, the opportunities to do good for ourselves and for others are equally viable.

The counterpoint is that there is no certainty in the outcome. It was said in 1905 that the world financial markets had become so interconnected that war as a tool of international behavior was outdated. Less than ten years later a member of the British foreign service remarked on the eve of World War I that the lights were going out all over Europe and that they wouldn't be put back on in his lifetime. The catastrophe of the war came; the world survived.

As we close in on the end of the century, we come to the realization that the potential now to catapult civilization to greater levels of productivity and vitality is genuine. The first requirement is to acknowledge the transformative currents at work, to grasp both the continuities and discontinuities with the past, and to go about organizing for the work that, by accident of history and the substance of moral obligation, we are asked to perform.

E N D N O T E S

CHAPTER ONE

1.   Linda Grant, "Firms' Futures Rest on More Worker Involvement," *San Francisco Chronicle*, May 4, 1992, p. B7.

2.   Jane Kramer, "A Letter from Europe: Bad Blood," *The New Yorker*, October 11, 1993, pp. 74–95.

3.   The division of history into special periods was found to be a useful approach to establishing meaning and context long before what we call the Modern Age began. St. Augustine, for example, described six epochs of mankind. Starting with the first, that went from Adam to Noah, and concluding with a sixth, that began with Christ and continued into St. Augustine's time.

4.   The dominant perspective given here—that of Christian Europe, "the West"—should not depreciate the role of other civilizations in shaping the modern world. Many technical processes came from China, such as "mechanical clockwork, segmental-arch bridges, pound-locks on canals, the stern post rudder, and quantitative cartography," as well as printing, gunpowder, and the compass, of which we will have more to say later. See Joseph Needham, *The Grand Titration: Science and Society in East and West* (Toronto: University of Toronto Press, 1969), p. 11.

Indian and Mediterranean cultures first had contact through the Phoenicians, and there is substantial evidence that Indian ideas influenced Greek philosophy. See H. G. Rawlinson, "Early Contacts Between India and Europe," in A. L. Basham, *A Cultural History of India* (Oxford: Oxford University Press, 1975), pp. 425–426.

Islamic contributions are reflected in some of the words absorbed into the English language: algebra, tariff, magazine, sloop, sugar, and mattress. See Will and Ariel Durant, *The History of Civilization*, Vol. 5, *The Age of Faith* (New York: Simon & Schuster, 1954). The list of places, ideas, and events where these three great civilizations interact with the West, affecting its development, is so huge that it is necessarily beyond the scope of this book.

Moreover, Europe's pivotal moments are not the same as the great transition periods of other civilizations around the globe. To focus on Europe can mislead one into thinking that the entire globe surrendered to some kind of economic collapse when in fact that was not the case. Civilization endured outside Europe. But the emphasis on a Eurocentric time line is deserved for one basic reason. Since the termination of the Middle Ages and up to the twentieth century, Europe has been the primary factor, for good or evil, in world history. Its pursuit of empire on a global scale, its domination through conquest and colonization of other cultures, taken as just one element, has been the major dynamic in world events since the fifteenth century. The wealth and power Europe achieved at the beginning of the modern period established its preeminence for centuries to come. Indeed, it is not uncommon for historians to reference the demise of the modern period by describing it as the end of the European Era as well.

5.   Graham Greene's full remark was, "There is always one moment in childhood when the door opens and lets the future in." See Chapter One in *The Power and The Glory* (New York: Viking, 1940). The metaphor has been useful, nonetheless, in describing the change in mind-set that is the essence of epochal change.

6.   Friedrich Nietzsche, *Thus Spoke Zarathustra* (New York: Penguin, 1969).

7.   Arthur M. Schlesinger, *The Cycles of American History* (Boston: Houghton Mifflin, 1986).

8.   Barbara Tuchman discusses this theme in *A Distant Mirror* (New York: Knopf, 1978).

9.   Jaroslav Pelikan, *The Excellent Empire: The Fall of Rome and the Triumph of the Church* (New York: HarperCollins, 1987), p. 80. See also Chapter Twenty-Four in Edward Gibbon, *The Decline and Fall of the Roman Empire* (London: Methuen, 1896).

10.   Paul Kennedy, *Rise and Fall of Great Powers* (New York: Random House, 1987), p. 360.

11.   The parallels to the disintegration that followed the collapse of Soviet communism in Eastern Europe and of European domination in Africa and Asia have been stressed before by other writers.

12.   Richard Tarnas, *Passion of the Western Mind* (New York: Harmony Books, 1992), especially pp. 106–116.

13.   The images we have of the Middle Ages are still valid—the Crusades, knights in armor, and castles—but a new kind of life was beginning. In fact one famous Belgian scholar, Henri Pirenne, has argued that the major break in European history occurred between 650 and 750, a consequence of

Islamic advance in the Mediterranean. He noted in *A History of Europe* (New York: Norton, 1939) that for the first time in history, the axis of European unity and civilization had migrated north from the Mediterranean."

Frequently, the time after the year 1000, about halfway through the epoch, is referred to as the High Middle Ages, as a way of referencing the cultural and intellectual changes that had started.

14.   Will Durant and Ariel Durant, *The Lessons of History* (New York: Simon and Schuster, 1968), p. 12. Also: *The Story of Civilization: The Reformation: History of European Civilization from Wycliff 1300–1564* (New York: Simon and Schuster, 1957), p. viii.

15.   Actually, the Dutch were printing from moveable type several years before. Building on the technologies of China, namely block printing and paper, and European enterprise—for example Flemish expertise in oil paint that found utility as printer's ink—the invention of type and typography had multiple sources. See Eugene F. Rice, *The Foundations of Early Modern Europe, 1460–1559* (New York: Norton, 1970) and J. D. Bernal, *Science in History* (New York: Hawthorn Books, 1957).

16.   Fernand Braudel, *Capitalism and Material Life* (New York: HarperCollins, 1967), p. 298.

17.   Rice, *The Foundations of Early Modern Europe*, p. 6.

18.   As one example, the Telstar satellite has grown into a multibillion dollar business, carrying more than a billion telephone calls between the United States and other countries, excluding Mexico and Canada, before the beginning of the 1990s. Cellular telephone sales alone exceeded $1.2 billion in the United States by the end of 1991. By 1993 subscriptions to Internet, a global hodgepodge of some fifteen thousand on-line services, were growing at a rate of 15 percent *per month*. Even more important, these technologies allow instant communication around the world. It is the immediacy of the communication as much as anything else that has served to knit together global organizations and a global economy. We can share information in real time. In effect, everyone is just around the corner.

19.   Before the advent of the personal computer, there were fewer than a quarter million computers in the United States. By the early 1990s more than fifty million personal computers were in the United States, with another sixty million units outside the country. By 1991, 25 percent of all U.S. homes had computers. As more and more people were expected to do work at home— driven by the demands of telecommuting, the need for supplementary sources of income, or simply to finish the day's work—the personal computer grew in importance.

20.   Larry Ellison, International Data Conference, Napa, California, March 17, 1987. Personal communication from Charles House, senior vice president, VERITAS Software.

21.   Furthermore, printing made its contribution on an international scale. Knowledge became cumulative and transnational. An idea put to print in Leipzig could be assessed or modified in Antwerp and Paris with greater ease. The role of scientists who marked the period is not limited to any one nation:

da Vinci and Galileo of Italy; Copernicus of Poland; Johann Kepler of Germany; Roger and Francis Bacon, William Harvey, and eventually Isaac Newton, of England. It wasn't quite the global village, but certainly it was an improvement on the ideological and geographical parochialism of the feudal period.

22.   Braudel, *Capitalism*.

23.   Personal communication from Elizabeth Gleason, professor of history, University of San Francisco.

24.   Michael Jensen, "The Modern Industrial Revolution, Exit, and the Failure of Internal Control Systems," *Journal of Financial Economics*, 1993, 48(3), p. 842.

25.   Shoshana Zuboff, *In the Age of the Smart Machine: The Future of Work and Power* (New York: Basic Books, 1984).

26.   George Huppert, *After the Black Death* (Bloomington: Indiana University Press, 1986), pp. 10–11.

27.   At the death of Gregory XI in 1378, two men claimed to be the rightful pope, each with his own supporters and administration. The Avignon Pope, supported by the French, and the Roman Pope contested for final authority in the church. In 1409 a third candidate was elected by a council called at Pisa. The controversy, referred to as the Great Schism, ended with the election of Martin V at the Council of Constance in 1417. One result was the assertion by some that a General Council held more authority than the pope.

28.   Hugh Thomas, *A History of the World* (New York: HarperCollins, 1979), p. 60.

29.   Rice, *The Foundations of Early Modern Europe*, p. 12.

30.   Rice, *The Foundations of Early Modern Europe*, pp. 11–12.

31.   Nafis Sadik, "World Population Continues to Rise," *The Futurist*, 1991, 25(2), p. 10.

32.   Lester Brown, Christopher Flavin, and Sandra Postel, *State of the World 1990: A Worldwatch Institute Report on Progress Toward a Sustainable Society* (New York: Norton, 1990); also, Robert D. Kaplan, "The Coming Anarchy," *Atlantic Monthly*, February 1994, pp. 44–76.

33.   Science writer David Quammen has summarized research on little-known but deadly viruses such as Marburg, Ebola, and Sasso, which under the right circumstances could decimate an entire local or national population. Quammen has noted that "modern airline connections put every virus on earth within a day's transit of the United States." See David Quammen, "You Can Run: Emerging Viruses in the Global Village," *Outside*, April 1994, pp. 41–49.

34.   It is tempting to draw parallels between the rise of the nation-state in the sixteenth and seventeenth centuries, to outline the successes of the "new monarchs" Francis I (France), Ferdinand and Isabella (Spain), and Henry VIII (England), and the transformation of the nation-state into something else today. Yet the concepts of nationhood and nationalism have an ambiguity that makes such a comparison highly complex. Even in medieval times, for example, "students at the University of Paris were divided into the Picard, Norman, English and French 'nations.'. . . The Crusaders fought not only as Christians but also as Burgundians, Germans, and Englishmen." The tradition

of unity, particularly military organization, that is associated with the way the concepts are used today, did not materialize in the rest of Europe until the nineteenth century. One could also argue that the rise of nation-states, the centralization of power, and consolidation of authority contributed to a sense of internal order, not chaos, while simultaneously providing another dimension to European, then global rivalry. See Walter Phelps Hall and William Stearns Davis, *The Course of Europe Since Waterloo* (New York: Appleton-Century, 1947), pp. 3–6.

35.   James Westfall Thompson, "The Aftermath of the Black Death and the Aftermath of the Great War," *The American Journal of Sociology*, 1921, 26(5), p. 567.

36.   Massive inward investment is necessary for telecommunications systems, airports, and power plants as well. Exuberant projections exist for expanding markets in all kinds of products and services: airplanes, highways, consumer goods, hospitals, and medical supplies.

37.   Thomas Jefferson, in a letter to Horatio Spafford, March 17, 1814.

38.   David D. Hale, "The Coming Golden Age of Capitalism," *Wall Street Journal*, November 7, 1991, p. A14.

39.   It is estimated that American portfolio investments overseas grew to $125 billion by the end of 1993, essentially tripling in value since 1990. See Thomas L. Friedman, "International Investors Bet Everything on Everything," *The New York Times*, April 17, 1994, p. A1.

40.   Miguel Valero, "A Sleeping Giant Stirs," *Satellite Communications*, 17, no. 6, June 1993, p. 20.

41.   J. D. Bernal, *Science in History* (New York: Hawthorn Books, 1957), p. 253.

42.   Daniel Burrus and Roger Gittnes, *Technotrends: Twenty-four Technologies That Will Revolutionize Our Lives, How to Use Technology to Go Beyond Your Competition* (New York: HarperBusiness, 1993). Burrus and Gittnes provide a discussion of these and related technologies as well as a broader look at technological developments.

43.   Quoted in Edmund L. Andrews, "When We Build It, Will They Come?" *New York Times*, October 17, 1993, p. 5.

44.   The economist Earl Hamilton has shown that an increase in New World bullion and the price level in Europe tended to correlate. In the simplest terms, Spain and then the rest of Europe became flooded with treasure imports, particularly gold and silver brought from Mexico and Peru. Although some of the metals were used for religious ornamentation and items of fashion or luxury (for example, silver cutlery), substantial gold and silver entered the money supply as minted coins. Since productivity did not increase during the same period, more money was available to spend on any particular good. Adam Smith, as quoted by Hamilton, concluded that "the discovery of the abundant mines of America seems to have been the sole cause of this diminution [between 1570 and 1640] in the value of silver in proportion to that of corn. It is accounted for accordingly in the same manner by everybody; and there never has been any dispute either about the fact, or about the cause of it." Once the import of metals declined in

the seventeenth century, prices throughout Europe began to level off. See Earl J. Hamilton, *American Treasure and the Price Revolution in Spain, 1501–1650* (New York: Octagon Books, 1970), p. 297.

In comparison with today's numbers, though, the price spiral that began in the early 1500s was mild. In Spain, for example, the average worker was paying about four times as much for basic commodities in 1600 as he was in 1500. In England, cloth for a school uniform cost 40 shillings in 1500 and 80 shillings in 1580. In Warsaw, the price of beer quadrupled in the one hundred years after 1550. In contrast, some nations today have experienced a doubling in prices in one year, not a century. At 4 percent inflation, about the average rate of inflation during the Reagan years, purchasing power is cut in half every eighteen years.

45.   J. D. Gould, "The Price Revolution Reconsidered," in Peter H. Ramsey (ed.), *The Price Revolution in Sixteenth Century England* (London: Methuen, 1971), pp. 93–95.

46.   Stanislas Hoszkowski, "Central Europe and the Sixteenth and Seventeenth Century Price Revolution," in Peter Burke (ed.), *Economy and Society in Early Modern Europe* (New York: HarperCollins, 1972), pp. 96, 99.

47.   This categorization is adapted from Herman Daly, "Toward Some Optional Principles of Sustainable Development," *Ecological Economics*, 2, 1990, pp. 1–6, as cited in Donella H. Meadows, Dennis L. Meadows, and Jorgen Randers, *Beyond the Limits* (Post Mills, Vermont: Chelsea Green, 1992), p. 46. See also Herman E. Daly and John B. Cobb, *For the Common Good: Redirecting the Economy Toward Community, the Environment and a Sustainable Future* (Boston: Beacon Press, 1989).

Economist Hazel Henderson and others have argued for recalibrating national measures of productivity to include the impacts on life quality, so that processes that damage the environment would diminish performance scores. Others, however, have argued that the cost of environmental policy and regulation is unnecessarily and unfairly prohibitive. See, for example, Dan Cordtz, "Green Hell," *Financial World*, 1994, *163*(2), pp. 38–42.

48.   Inconsistent tax and fiscal policies are also blamed (for example, indexing social expenditures to price increases can accelerate an acceptance and expectation of further increases). Some have claimed that the transition to a service economy, with corresponding lags in productivity, is the major problem. A variety of special circumstances exist as well: in Europe, the integration of West and East Germany raised inflation there. Regarding the United States, economist Milton Friedman has argued that there is about a 2 percent price increase built into the economy. After the expenditures on an information infrastructure, compliance with various federal regulations for the environment, affirmative action and entitlement programs of different kinds, and the increasing need to replace plant and equipment with more modern facilities, there is an unavoidable increase in the cost of doing business.

49.   George P. Brockway, *The End of Economic Man: Principles of Any Future Economics* (New York: Bessie Books, 1991), p. 170.

50.   John J. Accordino, *The United States in the Global Economy: Challenges and Policy Issues* (Chicago: American Library Association, 1992),

pp. 15–25; B. Joseph Pine II, *Mass Customization: The New Frontier in Business Competition* (Cambridge, Mass: Harvard Business School Press, 1993).

51.   Social divisiveness also is inflamed because inflation is seen as unfair. The prices of all goods and services do not rise equally; inflation numbers are averages of a wide range of goods and services. If book costs increase dramatically and I have no need to buy books, the negative side of this inflationary environment does not exist for me. In fact, relative to neighbors who need to buy books and must now spend a larger proportion of their income or wealth on these purchases, I have become richer. I have more money than they do to spend on those things we enjoy in common. Inflation has served to redistribute real income in our community, and I can presume it has done so without my neighbors' assent.

People who have hard assets also benefit. Homeowners outpace renters and gold hoarders do better than holders of currency. As inflation continues, it becomes harder for people without hard assets to accumulate them; the gap between rich and poor grows larger.

52.   Laurence Shames, *The Hunger for More: Searching for Values in an Age of Greed* (New York: Time Books, 1989), p. xi.

53.   John Maynard Keynes, *The Economic Consequences of the Peace* (London: Macmillan), 1919.

CHAPTER TWO

1.   H. G. Wells, *The New World Order* (London: Secker and Warburg, 1940), pp. 160–161.

2.   See E. F. Penrose, *Economic Planning for the Peace* (Princeton, N.J.: Princeton University Press, 1953), for a discussion by a participant in postwar planning activities.

3.   Susanne K. Langer, "Make Your Own World," *Fortune*, March 1945, p. 157.

4.   Cordell Hull, *The Memoirs of Cordell Hull* (New York: Macmillan, 1948), p. 81.

5.   The State Department's policy planning staff described the situation as one in which there was "physical and psychic exhaustion of people everywhere; the feelings of disillusionment, insecurity, and apathy occasioned by the developments of the posthostilities period and particularly by the tendency toward division of the continent between east and west; the destruction and depreciation of physical plant and equipment; the depletion of financial resources, particularly in foreign exchange and external assets; social and economic dislocation, including the breakdown of the prewar institutional patterns and the destruction of the machinery of economic intercourse; the prolonged delay in adjusting the German economy to production for peaceful purposes." See Charles L. Mee, *The Marshall Plan: The Launching of the Pax Americana* (New York: Simon & Schuster, 1989), p. 89.

6.   Peter Duigan and L. H. Gann, *The Rebirth of the West: The Americanization of the Democratic World* (Cambridge, Mass.: Blackwell, 1992), especially pp. 9–55.

7.   Robert J. Donovan, *The Second Victory, The Marshall Plan and the Postwar Revival of Europe* (New York: Madison Books, 1987).

8.   Duigan and Gann, *The Rebirth of the West*, p. 317.

9.   The Marshall Plan, named after the popular secretary of state George C. Marshall to help assure its passage through Congress, actually wasn't a plan at all. It required that Europe decide both as a group and as a single entity on a program that would lead to its recovery. The key feature was that there would be no disbursement of money to an individual nation to do as it pleased. The goal had to be the rehabilitation of all of Europe. America would, with money and people, help Europe help itself, but on the basis of a single Europe.

The reasoning was that the economies of scale and specialization necessary for productivity could only be brought about through some coordinated and collective effort. This seemed to be the only hope in breaking the logjams and bottlenecks that had been thwarting recovery. Proponents recognized, of course, that economic union often prepared the way for political union. (Historian Sidney Fay made reference at the time to the Prussian economic union, Zollverein, that had paved the way for Bismarck's unification of Germany in the previous century.) Europe had to function as a community, said Secretary of State Marshall.

Even with the huge commitment of American resources, there were obstacles to the program. In the United States, the leading Republican, Senator Robert Taft, called it a "global WPA." Other difficulties developed. The French negotiators warned the Americans that no French government could consent to a commitment to German productivity before the French economy had been reconstructed. The British found the whole scheme a repugnant attack on their network of special relations within the commonwealth, the Sterling Area. Also, Britain thought it had a special relationship with America and should therefore be treated differently. And though the program had been offered to all, the Soviets rejected the plan as an effort of American imperialism and compelled Czechoslovakia and Poland to withdraw their earlier agreements to participate. The American policymakers, however, persisted. There is little question today about the impact of the Marshall Plan on the progress of European unity. See Michael J. Hogan, *The Marshall Plan: America, Britain, and the Reconstruction of Western Europe* (New York: Cambridge University Press, 1987); Donovan, *The Second Victory*, and Mee, *The Marshall Plan*.

10.   Hogan, *The Marshall Plan*, p. 427.

11.   The role of Big Business had been subject to some criticism even before the initiation of the Marshall Plan. As early as March 1945, the legendary newspaperman I. F. Stone had questioned the role of bankers and other business leaders involved in the development of postwar policy in Germany. Individuals he listed included Paul Mellon and David K. E. Bruce of the Aluminum Company of America, Alfred du Pont of E. I. du Pont de Nemours, Lester Armour of Armour meat packing interests, and Junius Spencer Morgan of J. P. Morgan & Company, among others. The fear at the time was that busi-

ness leaders would inadvertently assist in the revival of German cartels and ideologies that were antagonistic to a new and prosperous global peace. See I. F. Stone, "American Big Business and the Future of the Reich" in *A Nonconformist History of Our Times: The Truman Era 1945–1952* (New York: Little, Brown, 1988); originally published as a newspaper column, March 19, 1945).

12. Wendell Wilkie, *One World* (Urbana: University of Illinois Press, 1966); originally published in 1943 by Simon & Schuster.

13. Wilkie, *One World*, pp. 202–205.

14. See Richard J. Barnet, *The Alliance: America-Europe-Japan, Makers of the Postwar World* (New York: Simon & Schuster, 1983); Paul Johnson, *Modern Times* (New York: HarperCollins, 1983); and John W. Dower, *Empire and Aftermath: Yoshida Shiguru and the Japanese Experience 1878–1954* (Cambridge, Mass.: Harvard University Press, 1979).

15. George Friedman and Meredith Lebard, *The Coming War with Japan* (New York: St. Martin's Press, 1991).

16. Justin Williams, *Japan's Political Revolution Under MacArthur* (Athens: University of Georgia Press, 1979), p. 102.

17. Charles A. Willoughby and John Chamberlain, *MacArthur 1941–1951* (New York: McGraw-Hill, 1954), p. 348.

18. As one index, by 1950 more than five million acres had been redistributed. See Douglas MacArthur, *Reminiscences* (New York: McGraw-Hill, 1964), p. 313.

19. Willoughby and Chamberlain, *MacArthur 1941–1951*, pp. 344–345. Life expectancy data were reported for men only.

20. Willoughby and Chamberlain, *MacArthur 1941–1951*, p. 347.

21. Walter LaFeber, *The American Age* (New York: Norton, 1989), p. 466.

22. Henry R. Luce, "To the Boards of Directors of American Business," *Fortune*, 1947, 35, pp. 2–4.

23. Duigan and Gann, *The Rebirth of the West*, p. 316.

24. "International News, the Nations," *Time*, July 14, 1947, p. 21.

25. Dan Cordtz, "World War II: The Economic Aftermath," *Financial World*, October 17, 1989, p. 43.

26. For a discussion of these developments and the "new economic game," see Lester Thurow, *Head to Head* (New York: Morrow, 1992), or adaptation of same, "Who Owns the Twenty-First Century," *Sloan Management Review*, Spring 1992, pp. 5–17.

27. John Kenneth Galbraith, *The Affluent Society* (New York: New American Library, 1978).

28. Robert Hayes and William J. Abernathy, "Managing Our Way to Economic Decline," *Harvard Business Review*, July-August 1980, pp. 67–78.

29. Personal communication, Lewis H. Gann, senior fellow, Hoover Institution.

30. John J. Accordino, *The United States in the Global Economy: Challenges and Policy Issues* (Chicago: American Library Association, 1992), pp. 16–18.

31.   Mass production had been an American distinction, if not an innovation. It was instrumental in extending the industrial revolution, started in England around 1760, to the United States. Mechanical manufacture during this period replaced the hand labor of artisans and craftsmen working with simple tools. Mass production replaced production to order or by request. The industrial revolution—notable to historians for its role in population growth, urbanization, technical advance (from the steam engine to the chemical and electrical industries) and liberal economics—was in reality a series of revolutions within the modern era that helped define the age. It extended the scientific discoveries and commercial changes cited earlier, such as the refinement of precision instruments and clocks. Not until the factory system emerged as the main method of work organization, however, did the industrial economic structure, represented by mass production, take its most recognizable form.

32.   Hayes and Abernathy, "Managing Our Way to Economic Decline."

33.   See B. Joseph Pine, *Mass Customization: The New Frontier in Business Competition* (Boston: Harvard Business School Press, 1993). For a thorough examination of business as fashion, see Tom Peters, *Liberation Management* (New York: Knopf, 1992).

34.   Michael Piore and Charles Sabel, *The Second Industrial Divide: Possibilities for Prosperity* (New York: Basic Books, 1984). A similar analysis is made by Peter Drucker in *The New Realities* (New York: HarperCollins, 1989). B. Joseph Pine makes frequent mention of the Piore/Sabel work. Tom Peters has acknowledged the influence of Michael Piore on his own thinking.

35.   John Case, "A Company of Businesspeople," *Inc.*, April, 1993, p. 80.

36.   Sidney Ratner, James Soltow, and Richard Sylla, *Evolution of the American Economy* (New York: Macmillan, 1993); see also, Robert B. Carson and Wade Thomas, *The American Economy: Contemporary Problems and Analyses* (New York: Macmillan, 1993).

37.   Frank Rose, "A New Message for Business?" *Fortune*, October 8, 1990, p. 162.

38.   Max DePree, *Leadership Is an Art* (New York: Dell, 1990).

CHAPTER THREE

1.   Charles M. Savage, *Fifth Generation Management: Integrating Enterprises Through Human Networking* (Bedford, Mass.: Digital Press, 1990), p. 134.

2.   John Case, "Hard to Swallow," *Inc.*, 1987, 9(12), pp. 25–26.

3.   Lewis Mumford, *The Transformations of Man* (London: Allen & Unwin, 1957), p. 192.

4.   See Victor Vroom, *Work and Motivation* (New York: Wiley, 1964), for one of the early, and still stimulating, discussions of the relationship between motivation and ability in the industrial setting.

5.   The consensus is reflected in works such as *Corporate Pathfinders*, by Harold J. Leavitt (New York: Dow Jones-Irwin, 1986), *The Transformational*

Leader, by Noel J. Tichy and Mary Anne Devanna (New York: Wiley, 1986), *The Leadership Challenge: How to Get Extraordinary Things Done in Organizations,* by James M. Kouzes and Barry Z. Posner (San Francisco: Jossey-Bass, 1987), and *The Change Masters: Innovation for Productivity in the American Corporation,* by Rosabeth Moss Kanter (New York: Simon & Schuster, 1983).

6.   This research was conducted in three different firms: a consumer products company, an insurance company, and a financial services company. It was reported in "A New Decade Demands a New Breed of Manager," by Oren Harari and Linda Mukai, *Management Review,* 1990, 79(8), pp. 20–24.

7.   The research was conducted across several divisions of a major computer company, an international food retailer, and an assortment of public service organizations such as police departments and universities, from 1989 to 1993. The distinctions between ineffective and effective managers were evaluated using a combination of questionnaire, private interview, and group discussion formats. Arrangements varied as the series of investigations developed over time. In a study for one company, a survey dealing with how fourteen different environmental factors affected leadership behavior (for example, the rise of small, nimble competitors, or availability of technology) was administered to a group of twenty-five managers. The individual results were immediately scored, collated, and reported to participants. The findings were used as the basis for a focus-group-like discussion on the meaning and implications for management behavior. Patterns of response were summarized and tested against more detailed statistical analyses, including evaluations of correlational patterns across items. Over a six-month period the format was repeated a dozen times with additional groups of twenty to twenty-five managers. An overall assessment of the statistical results and discussions with senior management and administrative staff was combined with a dozen individual interviews to yield the generalizations reported.

8.   In the same spirit, F. Edwards Deming included "driving fear from the workplace" as a key element in his management programs for quality improvement.

9.   In *Driving Fear Out of the Workplace: How to Overcome the Invisible Barriers to Quality, Productivity, and Innovation* (San Francisco: Jossey-Bass, 1991), Kathleen Ryan and Daniel K. Oestreich found that the major fears of employees were loss of credibility or reputation, loss of career or financial advancement, possible damage to relationship with boss, loss of employment, and interpersonal rejection.

10.   Intuitively we recognize the validity of this pattern of behavior. How many times has an executive looked at a banker, a corporate suitor, or a consultant and asked: Do any of them really know my company? The executive is inquiring about more than current profit ratios, inventory figures, and development plans. He or she is asking whether the outsider really grasps the underlying dynamics of the organization, its history and traditions, overarching network of personalities and dilemmas, and the confusing web of data, events, and situations past and present. The executive is asking if any of the outsiders can see beyond some temporal provincialism and get to the forces that have already compelled people to go in one direction or another. In short, the executive is inquiring about continuity.

11.   For more discussion, see William G. Scott and David K. Hart, "The Exhaustion of Managerialism," *Society* (Transaction Social Science and Modern Society), 1991, 28(3), pp. 39–48.

CHAPTER FOUR

1.   Cited by Peter Senge in *The Fifth Discipline: The Art and Practice of the Learning Organization* (New York: Doubleday/Currency, 1990).

2.   Michael Jensen, "The Modern Industrial Revolution, Exit, and the Failure of Internal Control Systems," *Journal of Financial Economics*, 1993, 48(3), p. 831.

3.   Oren Harari, "Don't Let It Go to Your Head," *Small Business Reports*, 1993, 18(10), pp. 59–61.

4.   William McGowan, "Thriving on Chaos, Part II" (Schaumburg, Ill.: Video Publishing House, 1989).

5.   Jensen, "The Modern Industrial Revolution."

6.   We are referring to financials like profits, earnings, and revenues, but the conclusion can also be applied to the activities of bond rating agencies. Kegian Bi and Haim Levy found that a rating agency's downgrading of bonds lags approximately two years behind the market's reaction to the firm's financial distress, the latter itself a delayed reaction as mentioned in the text ("Market Reaction to Bond Downgrading by Chapter 11 Filings," *Financial Management*, 22, no. 3, Autumn 1993, pp. 156–162.)

7.   Peter Drucker, "The Five Deadly Business Sins," *Wall Street Journal*, October 21, 1993, p. A18.

8.   For a more in-depth analysis of this issue, the interested reader is referred to Nicholas Imparato, "Voice Processing, Geothink and the Marketing Challenge in Telecommunications," in Ruby Roy Dholakia (ed.), *Advances in Telecommunications Management*, vol. 4, (Greenwich, Conn.: JAI Press, 1994), pp. 17–28; Oren Harari, "The Secret Competitive Advantage," *Management Review*, January 1994, pp. 45–47; and Oren Harari, "The Thomas Lawson Syndrome," *Management Review*, February 1994, pp. 58–61.

9.   Kashio Uehara, *Vision Management: Translating Strategy into Action* (Cambridge, Mass.: Productivity Press, 1992), pp. 68, 148.

10.   Specifically, ROE can be computed as net income/assets × assets/equity, where the latter is considered the leverage multiplier. Note that algebraically, the equation works out to net income/equity. ROE is crucial to our discussion of business success. William Murray, Barry Doyle, and Daniel Blakely ("A Comprehensive Planning Model for Incorporating Goal Tradeoff," *International Journal of Management*, 1988, 5(1), pp. 88–97) found that the majority of CEOs pursue the goal of maximizing current earnings (EPS, net income, ROE); only a minority pursue the goal of stock price maximization. Of course, one could also argue, as many have, that the former is the most effective precursor of the latter. (See also Gordon Donaldson, "Financial Goals and

Strategic Consequences," *Harvard Business Review*, May-June 1985, pp. 57–66; and Alfred Rappaport, *Creating Shareholder Value* [New York: Free Press, 1986]).

11.   Similarly, Mark McCormack, author of *What They Don't Teach You at the Harvard Business School* and CEO of International Management Group, recalls a plant manager of a Fortune 500 industrial who was frustrated with the same kind of strategyless strategy emanating from corporate head-quarters and growled: "Why don't we shut down every plant we've got? Then we could really save some money around here."

12.   "Hewlett Packard Digs Deep for a Digital Future," *Business Week*, October 18, 1993, pp. 72–75.

13.   Donald G. Reinertson, "Whodunit? The Search for the New-Product Killers," (McKinsey & Co, July 1983), pp. 35–37. See also Reinerston, *Developing Products in Half the Time* (Florence, Ky.: Van Nostrand, 1991).

14.   Thomas J. Burton, "Medtronic Inc. Cardiac Device Cleared by FDA," *Wall Street Journal*, December 10, 1993, p. B3.

15.   Asahi's story is not atypical. The introduction of its Super Dry Beer in 1987 raised its market share 5 percent in Japan, lifting the company from third to second after Kirin. By 1991, Super Dry was accounting for 90 per-cent of Asahi's sales.

16.   See Sharen Kindel, "(Well) grounded," *Financial World*, 1993, 162(20), pp. 90–91; and Nell Margolis, "AMR Revamps IS, Alters CIO's Role: Did Confirm Debacle Influence Moves?" *Computerworld*, 1993, 27(15), pp. 1, 15. One of the recent innovations from the SABRE group is an electronic printer that dispenses airline tickets the same way a bank's automatic teller ma-chine dispenses cash. With this new SABREExpress Ticketing service, cus-tomers are able to pick up their tickets in shopping malls and downtown office buildings. AMR's charge to any travel agency or airline is $3 to $10 per ticket.

17.   In the 1980s, Ford and Toyota decided to challenge the European lock on the U.S. luxury car market. Ford purchased Jaguar for $2.5 billion, even as analysts predicted, correctly, that it would cost Ford a minimum of another $2.5 billion to fix. Toyota developed the Lexus in-house, spending less than $1 billion, in conjunction with key suppliers and partners. Additionally, the learn-ing infrastructure Toyota developed has allowed it to introduce new models and new quality improvements at a regular pace.

18.   Gary Hamel and C. K. Prahalad, "Strategic Intent," *Harvard Business Review*, May-June 1989, pp. 63–75.

19.   Harry Quadracchi, "Thriving on Chaos, Part III" (Schaumburg, Ill.: Video Publishing House, 1989).

20.   "Theories of Technological Innovation as Useful Tools for Corporate Strategy," *Strategic Management Journal*, 1988, 9, p. 18.

21.   Jonas Salk and Jonathan Salk, *World Population and Human Values: A New Reality* (New York: HarperCollins, 1981), p. 3.

22.   Some aspects of Salk's reasoning were criticized by his academic colleagues at the time. About one book in Salk's series of publications on this issue a reviewer remarked that "no library should spend the money for this work" (*Choice*, March 1982, p. 962). It was criticized in part because it "pre-

tends to demonstrate that human values and behavior are changing signifi-cantly." Written under the headline "Man Must Accept the Challenge of the Environment," another review took a later volume to task for laying out an es-sentially teleological argument to explain the manner in which organisms adapt to the environment, that is, that adaptation is driven by causes that have some final meaning or purpose (C. H. Waddington, "Man Unfolding," *New York Times Book Review*). Nonetheless, the body of work is regarded, sometimes by the same critics, as containing "hope for the future" (Joanna Walsh, *Library Journal*, November 1, 1981, p. 2148) as well as "much wisdom" and advice that the world ought to listen to. And to one scientist, the original material *(Man Unfolding)* represented a "closely reasoned work of biological philosophy" (Raymond L. Hough, *Library Journal*, August 1972, p. 2624).

23.   Richard Foster, *Innovation: The Attacker's Advantage* (New York: Simon & Schuster, 1986), p. 102.

24.   John Butler, "Theories of Technological Innovation as Useful Tools for Corporate Strategy," *Strategic Management Journal*, 1988, 9, p. 19.

25.   During some consulting events we have used a series of bell-shaped curves to make a similar point. Along the X-axis is time; along the Y-axis is some measure of contributions to organizational success. Progress for the organization is depicted as a series of bell-shaped curves that move along the time dimension and that enjoy some degree of overlap. This graphic presentation is more com-fortable for some groups; it is easier to recognize that as the upward swing of the first curve begins to level off, there is simultaneously a burst in a second curve that is just beginning. Again, the task is the same: to jump from the old curve to the new one.

Geoffrey A. Moore, *Crossing the Chasm* (New York: Harper Business, 1991) delivers a twist on an older idea about the marketing of technology prod-ucts. He imagines the bell-shaped diffusion of innovation curve cut at various points, but especially between the early adopters and the early majority, the first group of mainstream customers. Moore says that this "chasm" is what companies must cross before they can become enduring competitors.

In the late 1980s, several marketing organizations in IBM followed the lead of IBM Canada and used a similar S-curve to describe the necessity of par-adigm change.

26.   Salk and Salk, *World Population and Human Values*, p. 116.

27.   Salk and Salk, *World Population and Human Values*, p. 163.

28.   Jonas Salk, *Man Unfolding* (New York: HarperCollins, 1972), p. 85.

29.   Michael Hammer and James Champy, *Reengineering the Corpora-tion: A Manifesto for Business Revolution* (New York: HarperBusiness, 1993), p. 17.

CHAPTER FIVE

1.   Arnold Cooper and Clayton Smith, "How Established Firms Respond to Threatening Technologies," *The Academy of Management Executive*, 1992, 6(2), p. 64.

2. See, for example, James Utterback, cited in Tom Peters and Nancy Austin, *A Passion for Excellence* (New York: Random House, 1985), pp. 123–125; and Richard Foster, *Innovation: The Attacker's Advantage* (New York: Simon & Schuster, 1986).

3. Peter Drucker noted that in the mid seventies, "top management practically forbade the PC people to sell to the potential mainframe customers. This did not help the mainframe business—it never does. But it stunted the PC business" (Drucker, "The Five Deadly Business Sins," *Wall Street Journal*, October 21, 1993, p. A18).

4. George Stalk, Jr., and Thomas M. Hout, *Competing Against Time* (New York: Free Press, 1990).

5. Jude Wanniski, "Macroeconomics: The Enemy Within," *Wall Street Journal*, June 27, 1991, p. A14.

6. Northwestern University Professor Steven Toulmin has noted: "People for more than 200 years believed that a Newtonian world was predictable. Chaos shows that this was always a mistaken assumption" (Robert Poole, "Chaos Theory: How Big an Advance?" *Science*, July 7, 1989, pp. 22–24).

7. The booming fax industry is already so chock-full of competitors that just one little segment of the business—the manufacture of PC fax boards, which allow transmission of documents between fax and computer without the need for hard copy—has seen the birth of more than sixty-five competitors worldwide.

8. The 1993 Ernst & Young Entrepreneur of the Year semifinalists included a French bakery, a company specializing in temporary tattoos, an alternative energy retailer, and a wholesale distributor (Lori Stones and Kelly Lynn, "Entrepreneurism and Customer Service = Success," *Management Review*, November 1993, pp. 38–44).

9. "Shooting for the Moon," speech delivered by Ferchat to the Kepner-Tregoe Conference, "Confronting a Volatile Future," April 27, 1989.

10. For further commentary, see Oren Harari, "Ten Reasons Why TQM Doesn't Work, *Management Review*, January 1993; and "The Eleventh Reason Why TQM Doesn't Work," *Management Review*, May 1993.

11. Tamara Erickson, "Beyond TQM: Creating the High-Performance Business," *Management Review*, June 1992, p. 58.

12. Alan Chai, Alta Campbell, and Patrick Spain (eds.), *Hoover's Handbook of American Business* (Austin, Tex.: The Reference Press, 1993), p. 584; "A Dinosaur No More," *Newsweek*, January 4, 1993, pp. 54–55.

13. Woolworth's took another step toward its obsolescence by announcing that it would close 970 of its variety and five-and-dime stores and thus eliminate thirteen thousand jobs in the United States and Canada. The company announced that 250 of the stores would be converted to specialty stores like Foot Locker. An article in the October 14, 1993, issue of the *New York Times*, written by Andrea Adelson, quoted industry expert Alan Millstein: "They've taken the hard decision to give up the core business that gave Woolworth its name." Shares of Woolworth's rose 25 cents after the announcement.

14.   Indeed, his last book was entitled *The Fatal Conceit* (Chicago: University of Chicago Press, 1988).

15.   Frederich Hayek, "The Pretense of Knowledge," *American Economic Review*, December 1989, 79, pp. 3–7.

16.   The very process of analytically detached planning can paralyze a firm from taking any sort of action on behalf of tomorrow's customers. Leadership expert Warren Bennis quotes one of his clients, an executive, who said: "There should be no more prizes for predicting rain, only for building an ark" (proceedings of the Index Forum, October 21-24, 1990, Tucson, Ariz.). We sometimes wonder how Johann Gutenberg would have fared in selling the idea of a printing press to investors using today's planning tools. In Gutenberg's world, marked by mass illiteracy, poverty, and zero distribution systems, any discounted cash flow analyses would have done little but reinforce the notion that global markets for books were but a fantasy. A leader who is committed to looking a customer ahead is more concerned about creating markets than with trying to predict them.

17.   The research of Los Angeles–based author Joel Kotkin (personal communication) and Ronald Takaki (*A Different Mirror: A History of Multicultural America*, Boston: Little, Brown, 1993) makes these points dramatically.

18.   Paul Carroll, *Big Blues: The Unmaking of IBM* (New York: Crown, 1993).

19.   David Cassack, "The Two Cultures of 3M," in *Invivo: The Business and Medicine Report*, Jan. 1991, p. 28.

20.   "Create and Survive," *Economist*, December 1, 1990, p. 77; Peter Senge, *The Fifth Discipline* (New York: Doubleday, 1990).

21.   We strongly recommend Tom Peters's *Liberation Management* (New York: Knopf, 1992) for a thorough discussion of this issue.

22.   Lewis Lehr in Chapter Twelve of *Handbook for Creative and Innovative Managers*, edited by Robert Lawrence Kuhn (New York: McGraw-Hill, 1988), p. 218.

23.   Senge, *The Fifth Discipline*, p. 8.

24.   Senge, *The Fifth Discipline*.

25.   John Huey, "Nothing Is Impossible," *Fortune*, September 23, 1991, p. 136.

26.   Benneton executives do not rely on such research, precisely because it is in the public domain. Instead, they seek data unique to Benneton, which means soliciting quick consumer feedback on merchandise and features that have already been tried in the stores. In our work with radio people, we suggested that a station could usefully employ quick research as a feedback to assess the impact of bold, unique, innovative interventions (programming, on-air personalities, formats, contests) *after* they had been tried, but not as a means of determining which interventions to try. For a more thorough analysis of the limitations of market research see Oren Harari, "The Tarpit of Market Research," *Management Review*, March 1994, pp. 42–44; and "Six Myths of Market Research," *Management Review*, April 1994, pp. 48–51.

27. Eric A. von Hippel, *The Sources of Innovation* (New York: Oxford University Press, 1988).

28. *Pacific Sun*, June 30–July 6, 1993, p. 14.

29. A large U.S. electronics manufacturer did an in-house study that showed that the corporate culture put pressure on payback for every major project investment, while the company's aggressive, more successful Japanese competitor had a culture that expected returns on only one of every five projects attempted.

30. Arnold J. Toynbee, A *Study of History: Abridgement of Volumes I-VI, Part I of II*, edited by D. C. Somervell (New York: Oxford University Press, 1957), p. 199.

31. Clare W. Graves, "Human Nature Prepares for a Momentous Leap," *The Futurist*, April 1974, pp. 72–87.

CHAPTER SIX

1. Steven C. Pepper, *World Hypotheses: A Study in Evidence* (Berkeley: University of California Press, 1961); Max Weber, *From Max Weber: Essays in Sociology*, edited by H. H. Gerth and C. Wright Mills (New York: Oxford University Press, 1946); T. Burns and G. M. Stalker, "Mechanistic and Organic Systems of Management," in *The Management of Innovation* (London: Associated Book Publishers, 1961); and W. G. Bennis, *Changing Organizations* (New York: McGraw-Hill, 1966), are perceptive discussions of the machinelike characteristics of bureaucracy. Paul Lawrence and Jay Lorsch's "Differentiation and Integration in Complex Organizations," *Administrative Science Quarterly*, 12, 1967, pp. 1–47, provides some of the most referenced data on the issue.

2. We are not suggesting that time and motion studies, standardization, and economies of scale per se are not valid. We are criticizing the priority status they attain and the premises that underlie the interventions.

3. Gary Zukov, *The Dancing Wu Li Masters* (New York: Bantam Books, 1979), p. 21. See also Werner Heisenberg, "Planck's Discovery and the Philosophical Problems of Atomic Physics," in Werner Heisenberg, Max Born, Erwin Schrödinger, and Pierre Augur (eds.), *On Modern Physics* (New York: Collier Books, 1961), p. 27.

4. Robert Daniels, "Dun & Bradstreet Closes Sale of Guides, Unveils Additional Restructuring Moves," *Wall Street Journal*, December 23, 1988, p. A7.

5. Roger Lowenstein and Bridget O'Brian, "Trump to Buy Eastern Shuttle for $365 Million," *Wall Street Journal*, October 13, 1988, p. A3.

6. Kathleen Carroll Smyth, "Money and Markets," *Fortune*, January 30, 1989, p. 163.

7. See Tom Peters, *Liberation Management* (New York: Knopf, 1992), p. 659, for a comparison of transaction values and the book values of recently acquired manufacturing and service companies.

8.   Bertrand Russell, *The ABC of Relativity* (New York: Mentor Books, 1959), p. 140.

9.   Rupert Sheldrake, *The Rebirth of Nature: The Greening of Science and God* (New York: Bantam, 1991), p. 111.

10.   Fritjof Capra, *The Turning Point: Science, Society, and the Rising Culture* (New York: Bantam, 1983).

11.   See Margaret J. Wheatley, *Leadership and the New Science: Learning About Organization from an Orderly Universe* (San Francisco: Barrett-Koehler, 1993); George Gilder, *Microcosm: The Quantum Revolution in Economics and Technology* (New York: Simon and Schuster, 1989).

12.   A valuable review of mechanistic, organic, brain, political, and psychic prison metaphors, among others, has been presented by Gareth Morgan, *Images of Business* (Newbury Park, Calif.: Sage, 1986). In his treatment of the brain metaphor, Morgan discusses and draws implications regarding the relevance of cybernetics, decision-making processes, and a holographic approach to organizational design. See also James March and H. A. Simon, *Organizations* (New York: Wiley, 1958), for a landmark discussion of organizations as decision-making systems.

13.   Paul Hawken, *The Next Economy* (New York: Holt, Rinehart, & Winston, 1983).

14.   For an excellent but brief description and categorization of expert systems at work, see "Putting Expert Systems to Work" by Marc H. Meyer and Kathleen Foley Curley, *Sloan Management Review*, Winter 1991, pp. 21–31.

15.   Other developments—from explorations in superconductivity to laser and imaging technology to the discovery of the Giant Magnetoresistive Effect—will accelerate advances. Neural computing, using simulations of the associative reasoning characteristic of a human brain, will permit the expert tool itself to learn through trial and error.

16.   Terry Winograd and Fernando Flores, *Understanding Computers and Corporations* (Reading, Mass.: Addison-Wesley, 1987); personal communication from Thomas White, president, Action Technologies; Stanley Soles, "Work Reengineering and Workflows: Comparative Methods," in *The Workflow Paradigm* (Alameda, Calif.: Future Strategies, 1993), pp. 80–83.

CHAPTER SEVEN

1.   David Sheff, "Mr. Bluejeans," *San Francisco Focus*, October 1993, p. 67.

2.   Nicholas Rudd and Chuck Riley, "New Tools for New Times," proceedings of the Workflow Conference on Business Process Technology," August 12–13, 1993, edited by Layna Fischer (San Mateo, Calif.: Conference Group Publishers, 1993), pp. 269–291; also, personal communication from Nicholas Rudd, C10, Young & Rubicam.

3.   In related research at another organization, a large European division of a major automaker, reports indicated that the primary benefit of the work-

loop approach was the opportunity to create an "intellectual map" about how things were supposed to happen in the company. Ideas had never been a problem there. Execution was the weak spot. Now people from different functions redesigned the system in a way that rectified problems across all departments. "Cross-functional insights," said one employee, "grow when you realize who the customer and performers are and when you see the friendly discipline that can be exerted in keeping commitments." In general, the workloop stratagem was effective because it crafted cross-department solutions for cross-department problems.

4.   Donna Hogarty, "The Future of Middle Managers: an interview with Michael Hammer and James Champy," *Management Review*, September 1993, pp. 51–53.

5.   Erik Brynjolfsson, Thomas W. Malone, Vijay Gurbaxani, and Ajit Kambil, "Does Information Technology Lead to Smaller Firms?" prepublication draft, forthcoming in *Management Science*; personal communication from Erik Brynjolfsson, associate professor of information science, Massachusetts Institute of Technology.

6.   Rosabeth Moss Kanter, "The New Managerial Work," Harvard Business Review, Nov.–Dec. 1989, pp. 85–92.

7.   Peter G. W. Keen, *Shaping the Future: Business Design Through Information Technology* (Cambridge, Mass.: Harvard Business School Press, 1991), p. 3.

8.   Joanne Cummings, "Cost Savings Not a Factor for Firms Moving to EDI," *Network World (NWW)*, 1993, *10*(5), p. 37.

9.   Fred Metzgen, *Killing the Paper Dragon* (Oxford: Heinemann Newnes, 1990).

10.   Judith Kaufman, "The Business Case for Financial EDI—Alcoa's Experience," *Journal of Cash Management*, 1993, *13*(1), pp. 4, 6; David Serko and Barry Kaplan, "Automation on the Border: A Customs Exercise in Irregular Regulation," *Global Trade*, 1989, *109*, pp. 20–21.

11.   Don Pepper and Martha Rogers, *The One-to-One Future: Building Relationships One Customer at a Time* (New York: Doubleday, 1993), p. 15.

12.   The term *mass customization* is generally credited to Stanley M. Davis, *Future Perfect* (Reading, Mass.: Addison-Wesley, 1987).

13.   David G. deRoulet, "Mass Customization: It's Not an Oxymoron," *Transportation and Distribution*, 1993, *34*(2), p. 40.

14.   Susan Moffat, "Japan's New Personalized Production," *Fortune*, October 22, 1990, pp. 132–136; personal communication from Steven Alter, professor of decision sciences, University of San Francisco.

15.   The same point has been made by Andrew C. Boynton and Bart Victor regarding the "dynamically stable organization," in "Beyond Flexibility: Building and Managing the Dynamically Stable Organization," *California Management Review*, 1991, *34*(1), p. 62. See also B. Joseph Pine II, Bart Victor, Andrew C. Boynton, "Making Mass Customization Work," *Harvard Business Review*, 1993, *71*(5), pp. 108–111 +; and B. Joseph Pine II, *Mass Customization: The New Frontier in Business Competition* (Cambridge, Mass.: Harvard Business School Press, 1993).

16. As Peter Keen reports in *Shaping the Future*, p. 247, the associated inefficiencies for organizations are large. An internal report for Exxon indicates that an average of forty copies are made for every corporate document, fifteen of which are destined for the purgatory of filing cabinets. It is estimated that six hundred million documents are produced each day with computers and that over $11 billion are spent on overnight delivery services each year. Most organizations that have bothered to study the issue indicate that about 5 to 15 percent of company information is computerized; the rest is still held on paper. See also Ellen Knapp, "Catalyzing Business Change: The Role of Workflow Technology," *Proceedings of the Workflow Conference on Business Technology*, August 12–13, edited by Layna Fischer (San Mateo, Calif.: Conference Group Publishers, 1993).

17. See James Brian Quinn, *Intelligent Enterprise* (New York: Free Press, 1993), for an integration of concepts, case studies, and methodologies; and N. Dean Meyer and Mary E. Boone, *The Information Edge* (New York: McGraw-Hill, 1987), for a presentation of a specific approach to using information technology that also outlines important considerations.

CHAPTER EIGHT

1. Roy Vagelos, CEO of Merck, and Jim Morgan, chairman of Applied Materials, have made similar statements publicly.

2. Apropos of glass ceilings that keep women from rising in the corporate ladder, we wrote in another forum: "When good creative management is so sorely lacking in so many firms, the failure to promote the best and brightest because they don't fit into the old boy network ought to be grounds for a shareholder lawsuit. No wonder so many women bail out of large somnolent corporations in order to set up their own businesses" (Oren Harari, "What Do Women Want, Anyway?" *Management Review* 1992, *81*(3), pp. 42–43). As of December 1992, the number of Americans employed by organizations started or led by women exceeded the number of Americans employed by the Fortune 500 combined.

3. Sergio Autrey made these sensible, commonsense remarks in a 1993 commencement speech to the graduating class at the University of San Francisco. His remarks have empirical support in the research of the University of Limburg's (Netherlands) Geert Hofstede. For over a decade, Hofstede has presented research indicating that diversity in world cultures is extensive and demands diversity in management approaches (Geert Hofstede, "Do American Theories Apply Abroad?" *Organizational Dynamics*, 1980, and "Cultural Constraints in Management Theories," *Academy of Management Executive*, 1993, 7, pp. 81–94).

4. Richard Normann and Rafael Ramirez make a compatible argument: that the secret of creating value lies in the organization's ability to build a "value-creating system, within which different economic actors—suppliers, business partners, allies, customers—work together to co-produce value" ("From Value Chain to Value Constellation: Designing Interactive Strategy,"

Harvard Business Review, 1993, 71(4), pp. 65–77). For the reader interested in reading more about the "learning organization," the most complete source is Peter Senge's *The Fifth Discipline* (New York: Doubleday, 1990).

5. Xerox vice president Bob Spinrad tells us that "so many companies have been so functionally organized that the business didn't come together until you got to the chairman's office—which meant that the chairman was the first real business person in the chain." Tom Peters's *Liberation Management* (New York: Knopf, 1992) is a thorough review of data and companies that subscribe to the emerging view of employee to businessperson. *Inc.* magazine's John Case has written two outstanding articles illustrating this trend: "The Open-Book Managers" (*Inc.*, 1990, 12(9), pp. 104–113) and "A Company of Businesspeople" (*Inc.*, 1993, 15(4), pp. 79–93).

6. "Relationship investing" is part of this trend. Institutional investors take a long-term, "patient capital" view in return for a more active role in management, possibly even a seat on the board.

7. A look at the Daimler-Benz "organization chart," for example, reveals that the corporation is actually a web of numerous global partnerships, including strategic alliances (Mitsubishi Group, IBM), joint production and research efforts (Thomson, Fiat), and stakeholding relationships (Saab, Banque Nationale de Paris).

8. In one executive seminar, Tom Peters urged his audience to invite people like Stephen Spielberg and Francis Ford Coppola to be speakers. These individuals attract and coordinate a bunch of iconoclastic individuals and companies from around the world to produce one $50–100 million project; the project is then disbanded forever.

9. Robert Howard, "Values Make the Company: An Interview with Robert Haas," *Harvard Business Review*, 1990, 68(5), pp. 132–144; also, interview with *San Francisco Focus*, October 1993, pp. 67–134; James O'Toole, *Vanguard Management* (New York: Doubleday, 1985); Peter Drucker; Peter M. Senge, "The Leader's New Work: Building Learning Organizations," *Sloan Management Review*, 1990, 32(1), pp. 7–23; James C. Collins and Jerry I. Porras, "Organizational Vision and Visionary Organizations," *California Management Review*, 1991, 34(1), pp. 30–52; and James Collins and William C. Lazier, *Beyond Entrepreneurship: Turning Your Business into an Enduring Great Company* (Englewood Cliffs, N.J.: Prentice-Hall, 1992).

10. "Fit" can also be temporary. At Park City Group, a software developer in Utah, leaders accept that people who are "wrong" today might be "right" tomorrow; that is, their proclivity for self-management at work (one of Park City's key values) might not be there today, but in the future it might. Thus, the door for future employment is always open.

11. For a review of the research on the impact of intrinsic and extrinsic factors, both within the United States and abroad, see Oren Harari and David Beaty, *Lessons from South Africa: A New Perspective on Public Policy and Productivity* (New York: HarperCollins, 1989).

12. Comments based on personal discussions with Gore associates and consultants. Also, Frank Shipper and Charles C. Manz, "Employee Self-

Management Without Formally Designated Teams: An Alternative Road to Empowerment," *Organizational Dynamics*, 1992, 20(3), pp. 48–61.

13.   These include creativity, "intrapreneurship," mentoring, commitment to the principles of "unmanagement" and the "lattice" organization structure, and four guiding principles: (1) try to be fair, (2) use your freedom to grow, (3) make your own commitments and keep them, (4) consult with other associates prior to any action that may adversely affect the reputation or financial stability of the company.

14.   Shipper and Manz, "Employee Self-Management," p. 56.

15.   Eugene F. Finkin, "Company Turnarounds—Tough Hiring and Firing Decisions," *Journal of Business Strategy*, 1989, 20(3), p. 52.

16.   In fact, Western Business School's (Canada) Donald H. Thain and Richard L. Goldthorpe summarize their research findings among Canadian companies as follows: "The single most frequent action taken in the twenty-seven successful turnarounds we studied was to replace top management" ("Turnaround Management: How to Do It," *Business Quarterly*, 1990, 54(3), pp. 39–47).

17.   Manuel Velasquez, professor of management at Santa Clara University, notes that "the terms 'justice' and 'fairness' are used almost interchangeably," and that is the approach we will take here. See Manuel Velasquez, *Business Ethics: Concepts and Cases* (Englewood Cliffs, N.J.: Prentice-Hall, 1992).

18.   Throughout this discussion, we are not talking about moral relativism, which implies that there are no absolute standards of virtue or ethics. Rather, we are saying that specific corporate values, priorities, and cultures—and thus perceptions of what is 'fair'—necessarily differ across organizations. See Robert Solomon, *A Passion for Justice: Emotions and the Origins of the Social Contract* (Reading, Mass.: Addison-Wesley, 1990), p. 176.

19.   As leaders ponder choices and consider alternatives, it is important to remember that the prominent theories of justice have generally been developed using society as a whole as the frame of reference. We submit that work organizations have a much narrower charter. Society must legitimately deal with problems like housing, race relations, unemployment, pollution, health care, political rights, military defense, the disadvantaged, and so on. To some extent, any business organization must, and should, do the same. Businesses have a self-interest in helping right society's wrongs—more so than the Milton Friedman/Chicago school of thought would concede—because they live, sell, and draw labor from that society. Nevertheless, a work organization is a much more focused, goal-oriented social body than a society is. Social and economic goals are not mutually exclusive (witness the successes of Ben & Jerry's, the Body Shop, and Levi Strauss), but an organization that focuses on the "social good" to the detriment of its product quality and new product development does none of its stakeholders a service. A weak company that loses customers and lays off employees is not necessarily a virtuous one. This is true even with not-for-profits, who still have to declare a surplus over expenses. One of the senior executives of the Daughters of Charity hospital system emphasized that the effective use of limited resources was of even greater urgency with nonprofits than with for-profits.

20.   Velasquez, *Business Ethics*.

21.   The discussions that follow are from Velasquez, *Business Ethics*; Donald Palmer, *Does the Center Hold?* (Mountain View, Calif.: Mayfield Publishing, 1991); Robert Nozick, *Anarchy, State, and Utopia* (New York: Basic Books, 1974); and John Rawls, *A Theory of Justice* (Cambridge, Mass.: Harvard University Press, 1971).

22.   Velasquez, *Business Ethics*, p. 92.

23.   Nozick, *Anarchy, State, and Utopia*, p. 160.

24.   Velasquez, *Business Ethics*, p. 93.

25.   Velasquez, *Business Ethics*, p. 91.

26.   Authors' personal research; also Steven J. Heyer and Reginald Van Lee, "Rewiring the Corporation," *Business Horizons*, 1992, 35(3), pp. 13–22.

27.   Denise Rousseau, "Psychological and Implied Contracts in Organizations," *Employee Responsibilities and Rights Journal*, June 1989, and "New Hire Perceptions of Their Own and Their Employer's Obligations: A Study of Psychological Contracts," *Journal of Organizational Behavior*, 1990, 11(5), pp. 389–400.

28.   Marshall Shashkin and Richard L. Williams, "Does Fairness Make a Difference?" *Organizational Dynamics*, 1990, 9(2), pp. 56–71.

29.   James Kouzes and Barry Posner, *Credibility: How Leaders Gain It, Why People Demand It* (San Francisco, Jossey-Bass, 1993), p. 47.

30.   Kashio Uehara, *Vision Management: Translating Strategy into Action* (Cambridge, Mass.: Productivity Press, 1992), p. 25.

CHAPTER NINE

1.   None of what we are proposing should be taken to minimize the commonsense idea that in the end, people still need to produce and companies still need to earn profits. The issue is how that might best be done.

The eating-and-profit analogy was recounted in conversation with Robert Solomon. For a related treatment of excellence, virtue, and profit, see Robert Solomon and Nicholas Imparato, "Corporate Roles, Personal Virtues: An Aristotelian Approach to Business Ethics," in Dean Ludwig and Karen Paul, (eds.), *Contemporary Issues in the Business Environment* (New York: Edwin Mellon Press, 1992); also, Robert Solomon, *Ethics and Excellence* (New York: Oxford University Press, 1992).

2.   Jon Katzenbach, "The Right Kind of Teamwork," *Wall Street Journal*, November 9, 1992, p. A10.

3.   Michael Beer, Russell A. Eisenstat, and Bert Spector, "Why Change Programs Don't Produce Change," *Harvard Business Review*, 1990, 68(6), p. 163.

4.   Michael A. Verespej, "Where Ducks and Fun Mean Success," *Industry Week*, 1991, 240(6), p. 29.

5.   Steven W. Floyd and Bill Wooldridge, "Managing Strategic Consensus: The Foundation of Effective Implementation," *Academy of Management Executive*, 1992, 6(4), pp. 27–39.

6.   Robert G. Eccles, "The Performance Measurement Manifesto," *Harvard Business Review*, 1991, 69(1), pp. 131–137.

7.   Robert S. Kaplan and David P. Norton, "The Balanced Scorecard—Measures That Drive Performance," *Harvard Business Review*, 1992, 70(1), pp. 71–79.

8.   Tom Peters, *Thriving on Chaos* (New York: Knopf, 1987), pp. 483–491.

9.   In addition to quantitative measures, one can borrow a page from companies like Hewlett-Packard, GE, Armstrong International, and Pan-Pacific Hotel in San Francisco. In this companies, stories of "best practices"—exemplary actions and heroic achievements—illustrate the kinds of behaviors and results that will be rewarded in the new environment. Do what managers at Armstrong and Pan-Pacific do: print these stories in booklets, float them throughout the organization, praise them in stump speeches, and encourage storytelling in staff meetings.

10.   While not everyone can or should be happy in an organization, implicit in the organizing principle is that *somebody* has to be happy. In his book *Three Blind Mice: How the TV Networks Lost Their Way* (New York: Vintage Books, 1992), journalist Ken Auletta notes that one of the major causes of widespread unhappiness and low morale at both CBS and NBC in the late 1980s was the dearth of praise, acknowledgment, and support, even for singular accomplishment and top performance. With CEO Larry Tisch (CBS), the reason was relatively straightforward: he was the kind of person who didn't relate to the concept and was simply "stingy with praise." As a result, not only did people feel emotionally tense and insecure, but as one CBS executive said: "I don't have the foggiest idea what Larry thinks of me as a manager." With President Bob Wright (NBC), the reason was more complex. Both Wright and Chairman Jack Welch (NBC was a GE subsidiary) correctly observed that complacency often follows success, and both were determined to prevent complacency at NBC even though the network's revenues and market share were greater than those of CBS and ABC. The reason for their concern was the rapidly growing impact of cable television and other sources of media entertainment.

Where Welch and Wright stumbled, Auletta notes, is in believing that any sort of compliment or acknowledgment of NBC's achievements or individual managers' contributions would be a signal for the network to relax and grow complacent. Thus, by ignoring today's good achievements today and continually focusing only on the brutal future challenges of the marketplace, Welch and Wright created an environment where even good performers often felt insecure, unappreciated, and unhappy.

11.   "To Gain a Sharp, Flexible Workforce, Pay for Learning," *On Achieving Excellence*, September 1993, pp. 2–3.

12.   "What gets measured gets done" may be a hackneyed expression, but it is still a valid one.

13. "An International Quality Study," a joint study by Ernst & Young and the American Quality Foundation, 1992.

14. As organizations become increasingly flat and horizontal, the term *promotion* will increasingly include lateral movement, specifically, job assignment. If differential employee experiences are to be ensured, the plum projects, the challenging opportunities, and the enhanced leadership roles should go to those who are committed to the organization's culture and values. Obviously, when promotion is defined as vertical movement, this organizing principle is clear about who should move up.

15. Jennifer Chapman, "Matching People and Organizations," *Administrative Science Quarterly*, 1991, 36, pp. 459–484.

16. "How Employees Take Ownership, Grow Profits by 57 Percent," *OAE*, December 1993, pp. 2–4.

17. The discussion of Welch's reasoning comes from several sources: James C. Hyatt and Amal Kumar Naj, "GE Is No Place for Autocrats, Welch Decrees," *Wall Street Journal*, March 3, 1992, p. B1; N. Tichy and Ram Charan, "Speed, Simplicity, Self-Confidence: An Interview with Jack Welch," *Harvard Business Review*, 1989, 67(5), pp. 112–120; and Stephen W. Quickel, "CEO of the Year: Welch on Welch," *Financial World*, 1990, 159(7), pp. 62–70.

18. Hyatt and Naj, "GE Is No Place for Autocrats."

19. In early 1994, Chromalloy Compressor Technologies promoted Olevson to the position of General Manager and Executive Vice President of the Chromalloy Research & Technology Division.

20. Some airlines (such as British Airways and Scandinavian Air Systems) have divested their engine overhaul operations; others (such as American Airlines and United Airlines) have made major capital investments to build new engine-maintenance centers of their own.

21. Quoted in Jeremiah L. Sullivan, "Japanese Management Philosophies: From the Vacuous to the Brilliant," *California Management Review*, 1992, 34(2), pp. 66–87. To the extent that an organization is a community, Clark Cochran of Texas Tech University observes that "communities are impossible without commitment to shared principles [which] must be made by the members of a community to one another." See Clarke E. Cochran, "The Thin Theory of Community: The Communitarians and their Critics," *Political Studies*, 1989, 37, pp. 422–435.

CHAPTER TEN

1. Jonathan Macey, "Don't Blame Salomon, Blame the Regulators," *Wall Street Journal*, August 19, 1991, A8.

2. After the infamous rigged GM crash video in a 1993 "Dateline NBC" show, *Newsweek*'s Jonathan Alter made this observation: "It's not that [NBC News president Michael] Gartner . . . knew anything about it before the video was broadcast. The problem is that Gartner often neglected to set a tone that would have made such conduct unthinkable in the first place" (*Newsweek*,

March 8, 1993, p. 49). The scandals at Sears auto shops and National Medical Enterprises clinics, where consumers were overbilled for unnecessary work, showed the unwillingness of executives under fire to take responsibility for contributing to a corporate culture where unethical decisions are made.

3.   See Robert Reich, *Tales of a New America* (New York: Time Books, 1987); Tom Peters, *Thriving on Chaos* (New York: Knopf, 1987); Tom Peters and Nancy Austin, *A Passion for Excellence* (New York: Random House, 1985); and James M. Kouzes and Barry Z. Posner, *The Leadership Challenge: How to Get Extraordinary Things Done in Organizations* (San Francisco: Jossey-Bass, 1987).

4.   We are not suggesting that any organization owes its people permanent unconditional employment, nor are we suggesting that people are entitled to that. An organization can demonstrate its sense of responsibility to its people in numerous other ways (for example, outplacement services, reasonable severance).

5.   Mills is cited on page 95 of Robert Jackall's *Moral Mazes: The World of Corporate Managers* (New York: Oxford University Press, 1988).

6.   Each of these studies has been cited by the companies involved and by publications such as the *Economist*, *Wall Street Journal*, and *Business Week*. For more discussion on this point, see Oren Harari, "Ten Reasons Why TQM Doesn't Work," *Management Review*, January 1993, pp. 33–38.

7.   See, for example, Frederick F. Reichheld and W. Earl Sasser, Jr., "Zero Defections: Quality Comes to Services," *Harvard Business Review*, 1990, 68(5), pp. 105–111.

8.   The notion that the organization exists primarily to serve customers—and by doing so will yield greatest long-term returns to investors—has been discussed in one form or another by commentators such as Tom Peters, Peter Drucker, Harvard's Ted Levitt, and by a number of chief executives. See Oren Harari ("You're Not in Business to Make a Profit," *Management Review*, 1992, 81(7), pp. 53–55) for a review of compatible philosophies by CEOs Paul Allair (Xerox), Robert McDermott (United Services Automobile Association), ex-Dow Jones Chairman Warren Phillips, and others. CEO John McConnell of successful specialty steel manufacturer Worthington Industries is most succinct in saying: "Take care of your customers and take care of your people and the market will take care of you" (quoted in Peters and Austin, *A Passion for Excellence*, p. 204).

9.   Cited in Alyse Lynn Booth, "Who Are We?" *Public Relations Journal*, June 1985.

10.   For a more complete discussion of this point, see Oren Harari, *Hotel From Hell and Other Tales of Quality*, a collection of articles published by the American Management Association, New York, 1994.

11.   Paul Sherlock also uses the terms *bedazzle* and *bewitch* in his book *Rethinking Business to Business Marketing* (New York: Free Press, 1991). Our colleague Chip Bell refers to it as a "knock-your-socks-off" experience.

12.   Sandra van der Merwe, "The Market Power Is in the Services Because the Value Is in the Results," in Christopher H. Lovelock (ed.), *Man-*

aging Services: Marketing, Operations and Human Resources (Englewood Cliffs, N.J.: Prentice-Hall, 1992), pp. 298–309.

13. Personal communication. Bell also expounds on these thoughts in Chapter Three of *Customers as Partners: Building Relationships That Cost* (San Francisco: Barrett-Koehler, 1994).

14. Robert Solomon, *Ethics and Excellence* (New York: Oxford University Press, 1992), p. 182.

15. Cited in an interview with senior editor Jeff Posey, "Playing Catch-up," *American Way* magazine, January 1994, pp. 44–48.

16. Amitai Etzioni, *The Moral Dimension: Toward a New Economics* (New York: Free Press, 1988), p. 9.

17. In addition, the focus on self has helped fuel the explosive material and financial success in our capitalist system, which in turn has been far more successful than systems like communism and fascism, both of which devalue the individual.

18. Abraham H. Maslow, *The Farther Reaches of Human Nature* (New York: Viking Press, 1971), pp. 343–350.

19. Abraham H. Maslow, *Eupsychian Management: A Journal* (Homewood, Ill.: Irwin, 1965).

20. See Andrew Greeley, "Habits of the Head," *Transaction: Social Science and Society*, 1992, 29, pp. 74–92. Greeley also anticipates various arguments for why such data should not be considered valid and presents clear retorts. If, for example, one wanted to argue that Americans were lying, the question raised would be, why would one want to think that Americans lie any more than people from the other countries surveyed. On top of that, even if some respondents did lie, they were presumably doing so to look good, that is, to conform to the expectation of what the "good" response was in their culture.

21. See Maslow, *The Farther Reaches* and *Eupsychian Management*; and Paul Tillich, *The Courage to Be* (New Haven, Conn.: Yale University Press, 1952).

CHAPTER ELEVEN

1. Charles Jaffe, "Guaranteed Results," *Nation's Business*, 1990, 78(2), pp. 62–65.

2. Jaffe, "Guaranteed Results"; see also Christopher W. L. Hart, "An Objective Look at Unconditional Service Guarantees," *The Bankers Magazine*, 1990, 173(6), pp. 80–83.

3. Delta's guarantee has been featured in *On Achieving Excellence*, August 1991, and in some depth in an award-winning article by Thomas Raffio, "Quality and Delta Dental Plan of Massachusetts," *Sloan Management Review*, 1992, 34(1), pp. 101–110. The information in this chapter is derived from interviews with Raffio and a number of in-house publications and data he supplied.

4.   The percentage was 85 percent before Delta upped the ante to 90 percent.

5.   If anything, Raffio's estimate of 20 percent is probably a conservative figure. Twenty percent of the newly insured specifically attributed their decision to join DDP to the smooth conversion guarantee. Presumably, other newly insured were attracted by other guarantees.

6.   Implementing Initiative 1 means that strategy, budgeting, administration, and information systems focus as much on the delivery of the guarantee as they do on the prior three organizing principles.

7.   Timothy W. Firnstahl, "My Employees Are My Service Guarantee," *Harvard Business Review*, 1989, *67*(4), pp. 28–34.

8.   Christopher W. L. Hart, "The Power of Unconditional Guarantees," *Harvard Business Review*, July-Aug. 1988, pp. 54–62; also, personal communication with Burger.

9.   Hart, "The Power of Unconditional Guarantees," p. 55.

10.   Joan S. Livingston, "From Pests to Guests: 'Bugs' Burger," *Cornell Hotel & Restaurant Administration Quarterly*, 1987, *27*(4), pp. 22–24.

11.   See Leonard L. Berry, Valarie A. Zeithaml, and A. Parasuraman, "Five Imperatives for Improving Service Quality," *Sloan Management Review*, 1990, *31*(4), pp. 29–38.

12.   Firnstahl, "My Employees Are My Service Guarantee," p. 30.

13.   Ray Schultz, "Satisfaction Guaranteed for Customers and Crew," *Wall Street Journal*, January 28, 1991, p. A10.

14.   Computer Associates, worth $6.1 billion, retaliated against Intuit by literally giving away personal finance programs free, but charging for any technical support. Intuit's customer retention remained high. It appears that its guarantee of after-sale satisfaction is more potent among customers, superseding Computer Associates's promise of free product.

15.   Schultz, "Satisfaction Guaranteed for Customers and Crew."

16.   See Oren Harari, "Thank Heaven for Complainers," *Management Review*, 1992, *81*(1), pp. 59–60; and "Nourishing the Complaint Process," *Management Review*, 1992, *81*(2), pp. 41–42.

17.   James W. Heskett, Thomas O. Jones, Gary W. Lomman, W. Earl Sasser, and Leonard A. Schlesinger, "Putting the Service Profit Chain to Work," *Harvard Business Review*, Mar.–Apr. 1994, p. 170.

18.   In the course of our research, we were struck by how often senior executives stated that the cost of making things right for the customer was more than compensated by the goodwill generated.

19.   Frederick F. Reichheld and W. Earl Sasser, Jr., "Zero Defections: Quality Comes to Services," *Harvard Business Review*, 1990, *68*(5), pp. 105–111.

20.   Quoted in Francis J. Aguilar, *General Managers in Action* (New York: Oxford University Press), p. 536.

21.   Walter A. Haas, Jr., "The True Blue Gospel of Levi's," *Business and Society Review*, 1988, *67*, pp. 45–47.

22.   See Robert Bellah, Richard Madsen, William Sullivan, Ann Swidler, and Steven Tifton, *The Good Society* (New York: Knopf, 1991).

Comments were also taken from an interview (October 2, 1992, National Public Radio) with Robert Bellah and Ann Swidler.

23.   The announcement in early 1992 of the publication of Amitai Etzioni's *The Responsive Community*, a quarterly journal that aimed to fashion a "new way of thinking," may be taken as the formal initiation of the communitarian movement. The journal was favorably reviewed by publications as diverse as *Business Week*, and the *Chronicle of Higher Education*. On the other hand, the journal and Etzioni's subsequent book *The Spirit of Community* have been criticized (see, for example, Charles Derber, "Coming Glued: Communitarianism to the Rescue," *Tikkun*, July–August 1993) for, among other things, imposing a set of moral principles on a highly diverse population. Even so, liberals and conservatives, businesspeople and environmentalists, politicians and students have worked together to foster a communitarian ideal. To the believer, communitarianism is a meaningful alternative to unfettered individualism and interest-group politics.

24.   Among cultures in Asia and Latin America, where sensitivity to social norms is pronounced, it is possible that communitarianism may be more easily integrated into the social fabric. As an example, along with the more familiar concepts of saving face and interpersonal obligation, the notion of personal relationships and networks are critical to understanding how the Chinese manage their everyday affairs (Ambrose Yeo-chi King, "Kuan-hsi and Network Building: A Sociological Interpretation," *Daedalus*, Spring 1991, p. 63). *Kuan-hsi*, or personal relationship, is key not only for companies intending to enter Chinese markets but also for the kind of business environment that is being created worldwide. The network is an invisible web of relationships assuring that the individual is never an isolated, separate identity. It reflects the idea that "the original Confucian intention . . . is the moralization of the person in human relationships." Unlike Western societies the Chinese social system is based neither in the individual nor in the society but in relationships. The focus is not "fixed on any particular individual, but on the particular nature of the relations between individuals who interact with each other. The focus is placed upon the relationship" (Liang Sou-ming, *The Essential Features of Chinese Culture*, Hong Kong, Chi-Cheng T'u-Shu Kung-su, 1974, p. 94, cited by Yeo-chi King, "Kuan-hsi and Network Building," p. 65).

25.   Robert J. Samuelson, "The Isolationist Illusion," *Newsweek*, 1993, 122(21), p. 30.

26.   Nan Stone, "Building Corporate Character: An interview with Stride Rite Chairman Arnold Hiatt," *Harvard Business Review*, 1992, p. 103.

27.   Haas, "The True Blue Gospel of Levi's."

EPILOGUE

1.   Norman Cousins, *Modern Man Is Absolute* (New York: Viking Press, 1945), p. 1.

2.   Gene Smith, *When the Cheering Stopped: The Last Days of Woodrow Wilson* (New York: Morrow, 1964), p. 64.

3.   Susanne K. Langer, "Lord of Creation," *Fortune*, January 1944, p. 152.

4.   Michael Novak, "The Care and Feeding of Human Ingenuity," *Business Ethics*, Jul.-Aug. 1993, p. 26.

I N D E X

The Jossey-Bass Management Series is about people committed to promoting responsible change. With our books, audios, and periodicals, we offer "The Best of the Best" in management thought—the essential tools for charting a clear and thoughtful course to becoming better agents of responsible change in a world that begs each of us for effective and continuous leadership.

Additional Management Insights from Jossey-Bass Publishers

		Price	Qty	=Total
0-7879-0058-3	**Working Wisdom: Timeless Skills and Vanguard Strategies for Learning Organizations** by Robert Aubrey and Paul M. Cohen	$25.00 x	___	= ___
1-55542-707-3	**Leading with Soul: An Uncommon Journey of Spirit** by Lee G. Bolman and Terrence E. Deal	$18.50 x	___	= ___
0-7879-0110-5	**The Leadership Challenge: How to *Keep* Getting Extraordinary Things Done in Organizations— Completely Revised and Updated** by James M. Kouzes and Barry Z. Posner	$27.50 x	___	= ___
0-7879-0114-8	**Visionary Leadership: Creating a Compelling Sense of Direction for Your Organization** by Burt Nanus *(Paperback)*	$18.50 x	___	= ___
1-55542-608-5	**Leading Change: Overcoming the Ideology of Comfort and the Tyranny of Custom** by James O'Toole	$25.00 x	___	= ___
0-7879-0111-3	**Leading Out Loud: The Authentic Speaker, the Credible Leader** by Terry Pearce	$23.00 x	___	= ___

Available at fine bookstores, or order direct:

MAIL

☒ USE THIS ORDER FORM

FAX

800.605.BOOK (2665)
TOLL FREE 24 HOURS A DAY

Please send me the titles I have indicated above. I am enclosing $_____ , including shipping and appropriate state sales tax. (All payments must be prepaid, in U.S. dollars only.)

❑ check/money order   ❑ Visa

❑ Mastercard   ❑ American Express

Card no.: _____

Exp. date_____Day telephone _____

Signature_____

Shipping Charges for Prepaid Orders: $10 and under, add $2.50; $10.01-$20, add $3.50; $20.01-$50, add $4.50; $50.01-$75, add $5.50. CA, NJ, Washington, D.C., and NY residents add sales tax. Canadian residents add GST. Prices and availability subject to change without notice. Valid in the U.S. and Canada only.

Name _____

Address _____

City_____ State _____Zip_____

Jossey-Bass Publishers • 350 Sansome Street • San Francisco, CA 94104